MARATHON TOURISM DOWN UNDER

A Runner's Guide to 25 of the best Marathons in Australia and New Zealand

JIM MANFORD

COPYRIGHT

MARATHON TOURISM DOWN UNDER (A Runner's Guide to 25 of the best Marathons in Australia and New Zealand)
JIM MANFORD
Copyright 2018, JIM MANFORD
Self-Publishing

Jim Manford asserts the moral right to be identified as the author of this work in accordance with the Design and Patents Act 1988

ALL RIGHTS RESERVED. Any unauthorised reprint or use of this material is prohibited. No part of this book may be reproduced or transmitted in any form or by any means either electronic or mechanical, including photocopying, recording, or by any information storage and retrieval system without express written permission from the author/publisher

ISBN: 9798778426153
Imprint: Independently published

"Can't you hear, can't you hear the thunder?
You better run, you better take cover"

'Down Under' Men at Work
Lyrics: Colin James Hay and Ronald Graham Strykert

ABOUT THE AUTHOR

Jim Manford has been travelling the world running marathons since 1985. He has now completed almost 300 of these in more than 55 different countries to date. These days he considers himself to be a dedicated 'Marathon Tourist' – someone who enjoys combining their love of running with their love of travel and visiting new countries. This is the 9th book in his 'Marathon Tourism' series.

By the same author:

Memories of a Marathon Man (Two Years in the Life of a Serial Marathon Runner) 2013
Marathon Tourism (20 Different Marathons in 20 Different Countries in 20 Months) 2014
Marathon Tourism in Spain (A Runner's Guide to 20 Top Spanish Marathons) 2016
Marathon Tourist's Guidebook (For Those Who Enjoy Combining a Love of Running with a Love of Travel) 2016
Marathon Bucket List (A Marathon Tourist's Wish List of 30 international Marathons) 2016
Marathon Tourism USA (A Guide to 20 of the USA's Favourite Marathons)
Marathon Tourism in Europe's Capitals (A Runner's Guide to the Capital Cities of Western Europe)
Marathon Tourism in Eastern Europe (A Runner's Guide to the 21 Countries of Eastern Europe)

Available on www.amazon.co.uk

MARATHON TOURISM

'Marathon Tourists' is the collective term for those marathon runners who enjoy combining a love of running with a love of travel and visiting new countries. Though clubs such as the Marathon Globetrotters and the Marathon Country Club cater for those who enjoy running overseas, Marathon Tourism is more a philosophy and a way of life. It's for those who want to broaden their minds as well as their running horizons. Rather than turning up at the same old UK local events year after year running endless laps round the same old courses, Marathon Tourists prefer to let their running take them further: to new marathons and new countries overseas. There's a whole world of marathons out there waiting to be run, opening the door to a whole range of new adventures. Using the marathon as the focal point of the visit, Marathon Tourists are able to experience new sights and sounds, new cultures, new landmarks, new cuisines, new languages and new people. What better way to see what another country has to offer than to journey 26.2 miles on foot through one of its major cities -supplemented, of course, by a spot of sightseeing and some serious sampling of its food and drink. A kind of 'Marathon Tourism' that's hard to beat.

CONTENTS

Pages

9 Acknowledgements
11 Foreword
13 Hobart Marathon, Australia
25 Canberra Marathon, Australia
37 Rotorua Marathon, New Zealand
47 Hawkes Bay Marathon, New Zealand
57 Great Ocean Road Marathon, Australia
69 Adelaide Marathon, Australia
79 Western Sydney Marathon, Australia
87 Christchurch Marathon, New Zealand
99 Traralgon Marathon, Australia
107 Perth Marathon, Australia
121 Broome Marathon, Australia
131 Wellington Marathon, New Zealand
149 Gold Coast Marathon, Australia
159 Australian Outback Marathon, Australia
171 Brisbane Marathon, Australia
185 Townsville Marathon, Australia
197 Sunshine Coast Marathon, Australia
205 Kangaroo Island Marathon, Australia
215 Dunedin Marathon, New Zealand
225 Sydney Marathon, Australia
243 Melbourne Marathon, Australia
255 Rottnest Island Marathon, Australia
263 Great Barrier Reef Marathon, Australia
271 Auckland Marathon, New Zealand
281 Queenstown Marathon, New Zealand

ACKNOWLEDGEMENTS

Most of what is written in this book is based wherever possible on first-hand experience, if not of the event itself then of the location in which it's held. I wrote to the organisers of all the races I've yet to run, inviting their comments and requesting permission to use photos from their website for illustration purposes. I'm extremely grateful to those who took the time to reply and who provided information for this project. Those who replied have photographs of their events included at the end of each chapter.

In researching further information my initial port of call was to the event's own website. I have also relied heavily on the dedicated tourist information websites of the cities in which the marathon has been held. Where these have failed I've generally fallen-back on my old friend Wikipedia to fill any gaps. The citations that accompany most articles quickly lead to the original source of information. Just because it's free, easily accessible and overused does not make it any less of a valuable resource. I'm also very grateful to those of my Australian running friends whose brains I picked seeking their opinions on the races I've described. Finally, endless hours were spent trawling the internet, looking for articles related to each event and for the hundreds of personal blogs written by those describing their personal experiences of the race. Too numerous to thank by name, I'm appreciative of all those who take the time to put these into writing for the rest of us to read. From looking at their accounts I was able to derive both a flavour of the event itself and a general consensus of how the race organisers had satisfied the expectations of those who'd forked out their hard-earned cash to take part.

Although care has been taken in trying to provide accurate, up-to-date information, marathons frequently change their entry requirements, arrangements at the start and finish, courses, sponsors and Expo locations so always double-check to see if what I've written is still in place. All errors of a factual nature are entirely my responsibility.

FOREWORD

I've travelled a bit further for this selection of outstanding Marathon races, going as the song says to 'A Land Down Under' (I won't continue with the second part of the lyric!) to the countries of Australia and New Zealand. I have a great affection for both of these places, Australia in particular, having lived and worked there for fifteen happy years. During that time I travelled extensively throughout the country and have first-hand experience of most of the locations covered in this book. I wish the same could be said about New Zealand. My one and only visit there being confined to the North Island many years ago. I ran my first marathon in Australia way back in 1985 and, with the benefit of Australian citizenship, have revisited the country numerous times since returning to live in the UK - usually managing to take in a marathon or two while there. I'm fortunate that my son Ross' apartment in the Sydney suburb of Manly continues to provide a place to stay on such occasions. His presence there helps keep me up to date with what's going on between visits, as does my International Membership of the Australian 100 Marathon Club. My ultimate goal is to complete the Club's 'ANZAC Sweep.' This requires finishing a marathon in each of the 6 States and 2 Territories of Australia as well as in both the North and South Islands of New Zealand.

Both Australia and New Zealand have much to offer the Marathon Tourist – those of us who enjoy combining our love of marathon running with a love of travel and visiting new places to experience more than the mere 26.2 miles of tarmac beneath our feet. There's no shortage of marathons to be found in both countries. The Ahotu Marathon Calendar for 2018/2019 lists 52 'road' marathons - 31 in Australia and 21 in New Zealand for the period. There's also a further 31 'trail' marathons shared almost equally between them. Runners have a huge diversity of choice between locations from big city marathons to outback and tropical beach locations, winery runs and exotic island destinations. The biggest problem in writing this book was in choosing which marathons to include and which to leave out of my selection. The 25 events I've written about are those that I've already run and those that I plan on running in the near future. They are arranged in chronological order according to the date on which they normally take place. Apologies to those excellent events that I've omitted on this occasion. Apologies too, to the sponsors of some of the events whose names have been omitted from the chapter headings. Unfortunately, sponsors seem to change on a regular basis (just look at all the different sponsors for the London Marathon since its inception). For consistency's sake I've simply identified the marathons by the locations in which they're held.

As with all my books, I have tried to approach each event from the perspective of the serial Marathon Tourist; someone whose interest lies not only in the event itself but in the historical and geographical context of where it's held, the lives and interests of the people who live there and in the cultural and scenic aspects of its location. Where I've included costs and prices these are always in Australian dollars for Australian events and in New Zealand dollars for all New Zealand events. At the time of writing £1 was worth AUD$1.69 and NZ$1.80.

HOBART MARATHON

TASMANIA

JANUARY

Of all the Australian states only Tasmania could get away with holding a major marathon during the hot summer months. Temperatures on the country's mainland States are generally considered too hot for distance running at that time of year. However, Hobart is so far south the conditions are usually very pleasant on its traditional January date. Given the race's early start, temperatures have historically risen no higher than the low 20s, with the past few years providing generous sunshine throughout the event without being too hot. The Cadbury Marathon came into existence back in 1984. Since then, thousands have participated in Tasmania's largest marathon, with the world-famous chocolate manufacture Cadbury as the major partner every step of the way. This is not one of the bigger Australian marathons but prides itself on providing an enjoyable race experience for the whole family by offering a wide variety of events and, with Cadbury on board, the promise of chocolate treats to look forward to at the finish. Athletics Tasmania the State body for athletics, responsible for the development of athletics in Tasmania is the owner and organiser of the event which is conducted as the State Marathon and Half Marathon Championships.

The Cadbury Marathon on the second Sunday in January each year starts and finishes at the picturesque Cadbury

Estate in the northern suburbs of Hobart right outside the gates of the Cadbury factory. There is a full marathon, a half marathon, 10km, 5km and a 1km event for kids under 12. The current course takes in many of Hobart's scenic delights such as Mt Wellington and the Derwent River and attracts runners from all over Australia as well as a smattering from overseas. Course records for the Full Marathon are 2:23:39 (Men) and 2:46:27 (Women) By far the majority of winners both male and female over the years have been Tasmanian residents. As far as I can determine no overseas athlete has managed to place first in either category. I can only assume from this that the distances involved in travelling to Tasmania deter elite overseas competitors from entering the event.

Tasmania is an isolated island state off Australia's south coast. Even the local tourist website discovertasmania.com website describes it as, 'A curious island at the edge of the world.' It's known primarily for its vast, rugged wilderness areas, largely protected within parks and reserves. Over 45 percent of the state is within national parks featuring spectacular landscapes from highlands carved by glaciers, to quiet solitary beaches, from cool and silent rainforests, to colourful alpine wilderness wildflowers. The rugged terrain lends itself to a wide array of outdoor adventure activities with landmarks such as the Bay of Fires, Cataract Gorge, the Freycinet Peninsula and Wineglass Bay, the Gordon River and Mole Creek Karst attracting outdoor enthusiasts in their hundreds of thousands each year. Despite its overwhelming beauty, Tasmania tends to be known internationally for all the wrong reasons. These include what some have described as the 'genocide' of its original Aboriginal inhabitants, the excessive cruelty towards convicts during its years as a penal settlement and the extinction of the Tasmanian tiger, the largest known carnivorous marsupial of modern times.

Originally called Van Diemen's Land, the island was officially renamed Tasmania in honour of Abel Tasman its first European discoverer on 1 January 1856. Tasmania is located 240 km to the south of the Australian mainland, separated by the Bass Strait. The state encompasses the main island of Tasmania, the 26th-largest island in the world, and the surrounding 334 smaller islands. The state has a population of around 520,000, just over forty percent of which resides in the Greater Hobart precinct, which forms the metropolitan area of the state capital and largest city, Hobart. As Australia's only island state, access to Tasmania is by air and sea only. Hobart city centre is 20 km from Hobart International Airport at Cambridge. The following airlines fly into Hobart: Qantas and QantasLink fly from Melbourne and Sydney, Jetstar flies from Melbourne, Sydney, Brisbane and Adelaide, Virgin Australia flies from Brisbane, Melbourne and Sydney and Tiger Airways flies from Melbourne. A shuttle bus operated by Redline runs between the airport and the Hobart's main transit centre in Liverpool Street, stopping at major hotels and motels surrounding the CBD on the way. The airport shuttle costs $19 one way for an adult or $35 return and takes between 30-40 minutes, meeting every flight arrival and departure. Bookings can be pre-arranged online or made simply when you board the bus. Alternatively, a taxi will cost between $40-50 into the city centre from the airport. Many visitors travel to Tasmania from Melbourne by sea on the Spirit of Tasmania, departing from Melbourne and arriving in Devonport from where it is an approximate 3-hour drive into Hobart. This has the added benefit of letting visitors bring their own car and make the most of Tasmania's touring potential.

Located in the state's south-east on the estuary of the Derwent River, Hobart is the most populous city as well as the state capital of Tasmania. With a population of approximately 225,000 (over 40% of Tasmania's population), it is the second least populated Australian state capital city. Founded in 1804 as a penal colony, Hobart is also Australia's second oldest capital city after Sydney. It grew out of the penal settlement on the island at Risdon Cove, eight kilometres up river, which was founded in 1803 and abandoned five months later for the present site of Hobart. The city's skyline is dominated by the 1,271-metre Mount Wellington with and much of the city's waterfront consisting of reclaimed land. It is the financial and administrative heart of Tasmania, serving as the home port for both Australian and French Antarctic operations and acting as a major tourist hub. In 2016, Hobart received 1.8 million visitors, surpassing both Perth and Canberra and tying equally with Brisbane. The city contains many beautiful historic buildings and precincts, especially in the area around the river. The Tasman Bridge across the Derwent is also a uniquely important feature of the city, connecting the two shores of Hobart and visible from many locations. Hobart is known for its well-preserved historic architecture, much of it dating back to the Georgian and Victorian eras, giving the city a distinctly 'Old World' feel. Salamanca Place, for example, has a terrace of warehouses dating back to the whaling days of the 1830s while nearby Battery Point, the original seamen's quarters of the city and Macquarie and Davey Street offer more than 60 buildings classified by the National Trust.

Entry fees for the 2018 Cadbury Marathon started at $80 with late entries within two weeks of race day rising to $95. Limited to the first 100 purchasers only. Cadbury Marathon and Cadbury Half Marathon entrants could also purchase a 'VIP' entry offering such services as: your name on your bib number, access to the VIP area on race day, complimentary breakfast after the race, complimentary espresso coffee, secure bag drop area, dedicated portaloos and massage therapists and water and stretching areas to use before the race. I believe this extras package cost 'just' $65. I'll leave it for you to decide whether it's worth it. For the 2018 edition the field was capped at: 450 for the Marathon, 900 for the Half Marathon, 500 for the 10k and 500 for the 5km event. It seems that the organisers were being overly optimistic in their expectations. There were 285 finishers in the Marathon, 652 in the Half, 393 in the 10km and 495 in the 5km (almost spot-on with this one) Those who entered online were able to collect their race kit from The Running Edge shop, 73 Murray Street Hobart on the Thursday, Friday and Saturday before the race. Bib collection for paper entries is on Sunday at the race precinct. All races start and finish at the Cadbury Chocolate Factory, Cadbury Estate Claremont. As this is over 13 kilometres from the centre of Hobart those without transport might wish to consider booking into the Best Western Hobart, the official race hotel for the event. Shuttle buses are provided from the hotel both before and after the race at a cost to entrants of $5. These leave the hotel at regular intervals starting from 4:30am and return between 10:00am and 11:00am. There is also a pasta night costing an additional $40 at the Best Western Hobart on the night before race day.

Start times on race day for the four main events on the programme are: Marathon 6:00am, Half Marathon 6:30am, 10K 9:45am and 5K 8:45am. Marathon runners are given 6 hours in which to finish and are helped by the Tasmanian Road Runners who supply pacers at 3:30, 3:45 and 4:00 pace (surprisingly, nothing faster or slower) Marathon runners complete 2 laps of the Half Marathon course. There are 3 drink stations on the course, which are passed twice on each loop. Each drink station has water and electrolyte drink. The course is not one for the Marathon Tourists among us as, by not going anywhere near the city centre, it manages to avoid most of Hobart's visitor attractions. After 2 laps of Cadbury Estate, runners continue West, on Cadbury Road, downhill past the Claremont Primary School where the first drink station is located. They stay on Cadbury Road, until Windemere Primary School, where they enter the school grounds on the first lap and do a circuit of the entrance (on the first lap only). The route continues on Main Road past the second drink station at the 6km mark. Runners stay on Main Road, past MONA, then onto the Brooker Highway. MONA is the acronym for Museum of Old and New Art. Pioneered by Moorilla vineyard owner David Walsh, this recently opened (2011) museum features alternative, and some would say confrontational-style, art intended to get visitors thinking. It also regularly features travelling exhibitions from international artists. For runners wanting to return to the museum after the race, MONA is approximately 20 minutes by road from Hobart's CBD. A standard return ticket on the MR-1 fast ferry costs $22, and will take around 25 minutes from Brooke Street Pier on Hobart's waterfront. Alternatively, Metro Tasmania bus routes 510-522 and X20 service Stop 33 on Main Rd, Berriedale, which is directly outside the museum's picturesque driveway. MONA also features a popular onsite restaurant, beneath which is the cellar door for MONA's Moorilla winery, with wines produced from the vineyards that adjoin the gallery. Be sure to try MONA's Moo Brew beer range while here also – especially the American Dark Ale.

    Runners continue on Brooker Highway until the Derwent Entertainment Centre where they turn left and continue on Llyods Lane until Goodwood Road and the third drink station at the 12km mark. The Derwent Entertainment Centre is the largest indoor arena in Tasmania and the multi-purpose arena is the primary venue in Hobart for large indoor functions and events. It was opened in 1989, having been commissioned as a celebration of the 1988 bicentennial year, and is situated in between the waterfront of the River Derwent, the Brooker Highway and Tattersalls Park. The venue can hold up to 7,500 people for concerts with a seating capacity of 5,400. Its largest concert attendance was for the Foo Fighters 'Sonic Highways' Tour in 2015 when 6,759 attended. Being the largest capacity indoor venue in Tasmania, it often attracts the big name artists that tour the state. It is also the home of the Tasmanian basketball team the Hobart Chargers.

The course next traverses the Bowen Bridge before the turn-around point is reached where Goodwood Road becomes the East Derwent Highway. Participants then head back the same way they came, with the turn point located for the second lap at Claremont Primary School. Marathon runners then repeat the same course, with the exception of the small loop at Windermere Primary School.The Bowen Bridge has an interesting background. It lies on the river about half way between the Tasman Bridge and the Bridgewater Bridge. The Bridge links the East Derwent Highway with the Brooker Highway at Glenorchy some 10 kilometres from Hobart and was built with Federal funds following the disaster that befell the Tasman Bridge in 1975. Living in Australia at the time, I recall the incident well. It made headline news all over the world. In January of that year the Tasman Bridge was struck by the bulk ore carrier Lake Illawarra, bound for the Electrolytic Zinc Company with a cargo of 10,000 tons of zinc concentrate. It caused two pylons and three sections of concrete decking to fall from the bridge and sink the ship. Seven of the ship's crewmen were killed, and five motorists died when four cars drove over the collapsed sections before the traffic was stopped. The iconic press photos of two Holden vehicles perched balancing on the edge of the collapsed bridge still sends shivers down the spine. As a result of the accident all road traffic is now halted whilst large vessels transit beneath the bridge. The depth of the river at this point is such that the wreck of Lake Illawarra still lies on the bottom, with concrete slabs on top of it, without presenting a navigation hazard to smaller vessels. The Bowen Bridge was subsequently built with the intention of assisting the commuters of Hobart, should something again happen to the Tasman Bridge. After crossing the Bowen Bridge for the second time, it's a straight run back to the finish at the Cadbury Chocolate Factory where all finishers receive a Cadbury bag and chocolate at the finish line along with their medal and finisher's T-shirt.

I searched online to see what finishers had to say about this event. There weren't too many comments but those that I found were generally complimentary. On her bibrave.com blog, runner Gillian Light posted the following thoughts, 'I knew Tasmania was picturesque but hadn't really thought much about the course - just knew it was along a highway and in Hobart. In other words, I completely underestimated how gorgeous it was going to be. You're running along the water for most of the course including a bridge at the halfway point which gives you great views to Mount Wellington and the city. Lovely.' Another finisher posted, 'I would also highly recommend the Cadbury Marathon, it was well organised and a good sized, friendly event – not too big. And really, let's be honest, do it for no other reason than the free chocolate at the end!' Similarly, a husband and wife team posting on their website, coupleontherun.com felt that, 'As a destination marathon Hobart offers travellers the opportunity to enjoy a wonderful range of events over a scenic lap course over a period in the calendar year that is usually holiday time for most Australians and a great time for international travellers from the Northern hemisphere to head down under for some warmer weather.'

Having travelled so far for the event, most Marathon Tourists will be keen to see what else Hobart has to offer. The following recommendations are based on my son's recent experience from a holiday there in 2017. His first priority was to climb Mount Wellington almost 1300 metres above the city. Standing sentinel over Hobart, Mt. Wellington is known by locals simply as 'the Mountain.' A visit to the Pinnacle is an essential Hobart experience. You simply can't visit Hobart without taking a trip to the top to see the amazing views over the city. Cloaked in winter snow, Mt Wellington towers over Hobart and, provides a spectacular backdrop to the city. Climbing steadily all the way, it is a challenging and satisfying expedition from the city to the summit. The shelter at the summit provides a great place to look down upon the city and celebrate your achievement. The view from the top of the city and its surrounds is described as exceptional. Salamanca Market, a major Saturday morning attraction for locals and visitors alike, situated in front of large sandstone warehouses converted into more than 300 stalls selling arts, crafts, homewares and produce is another must-do for visitors. The warehouses were mostly built to service 19th century whaling. Battery Point, behind Salamanca Market is another must-go-to part of the city. The area is very old and full of interesting architecture with many of the buildings built in local golden sandstone, giving the older parts of the city a warm golden glow.

Of course, no visit to Tasmania would be complete without touring the site of one of Australia's most infamous prisons, the World Heritage-listed Port Arthur. Separated from

Tasmania by a narrow neck of land, Port Arthur was once known as the 'inescapable prison', housing hardened criminals subject to harsh punishment. Just 90 minutes' drive from Hobart, the historic site is the best preserved convict site in Australia, and among the most significant convict-era sites worldwide. Ruins include the huge penitentiary and the remaining shell of the Convict Church, which was built by inmates. Visitors can take one of the regular coach services from the city for $37 per adult and $17 per child. However, it's possible to find traces of the state's convict past without even leaving the city. In South Hobart, near the Cascade Brewery, is the World Heritage-listed Cascade Female Factory, where thousands of women were imprisoned. Also, in the city centre you take a tour of the Tench prisoner barracks. The Tench, as it was known by its inhabitants, was the convict prisoners' barracks for Hobart Town. It originally spanned over two acres and some 50,000 male convicts passed through the complex. Following the cessation of convict transportation, the site became Hobart Gaol for more than 100 years. Sections of the chapel were converted into two Supreme Courts connected by tunnels to the gaol. An execution yard and gallows were added. The buildings which remain provide a captivating insight into over 175 years of Hobart's shadier past. Now run by the National Trust, access to all areas is by a 90-minute guided tour costing $20.

    Finally, what better way to round up your trip to the marathon than by visiting the famous Cascade Brewery, Australia's oldest continuously operating brewery. Located in the foothills of Mount Wellington, Cascade Brewery was established in 1824 by ex-convict Peter Degraves and is still going strong. You can take a two-hour brewery tour to see all aspects of the beer-making process, from malting and brewing to packaging. Your patience will be rewarded by thirst-quenching free samples at the end. I'm told that the brewery produces a decent 5.8%ABV Cascade Stout from pale malt and dark roasted barley. While there you may as well stay and have something to eat in the brewery's on-site restaurant while taking in the views over majestic Mt Wellington.

CANBERRA MARATHON

AUSTRALIAN CAPITAL TERRITORY

APRIL

The Canberra Marathon, which was established in 1976, is said to be the oldest city marathon in Australia. It takes place early in April each year and these days is prominent among a series of events featured over a Festival Weekend. The 2018 event marks the 43rd consecutive year since the first Canberra Marathon was run. The only year it has been in doubt was in 2010 when the event, being promoted as part of the celebrations for the 2500th anniversary of the Battle of Marathon, was subject to an ongoing dispute between the ACT Cross Country Club who owned the event and Cundy Sport Management who had been running the event on the club's behalf for a number of years. The race, now sponsored by The Canberra Times and Tata Consultancy Services, is part of what is marketed as the Australian Running Festival. The Festival is advertised as celebrating, 'A full weekend of healthy lifestyles, fitness and fun across five scenic courses that showcase the best of the nation's capital.'

The Marathon was given special status in 1984, as a qualifying event for the first women's marathon to be run at the Olympic Games. Lisa Martin (later Ondieki) qualified as the fastest woman in 2 hours 35 minutes before going on to finish fifth at the Olympic Games in Los Angeles and second in Barcelona. Other notable performances have included Colin

Neaves' time of just under 2 hours 17 minutes in 1983 and Garry Hand's Australian record of 2 hours 19 minutes for a male of 40+ years, set in 1987. Runners who complete 10 Canberra marathons are given the honorary title of Griffin, in reference to Lake Burley Griffin, which is at the centre of the marathon and the city of Canberra. The Griffins Programme, operated and officiated by the YMCA of Canberra Runners Club, was founded in 1994. Currently there are 171 runners who have completed ten or more Canberra Marathons. These fall under one of the following categories: 'Griffins' – those who have completed 10 Canberra Marathons, 'Burley Griffins' – those who've finished 20 Canberra Marathons and 'Walter Burley Griffins' – those with 30 Canberra Marathons under their belts.

Over 6,500 runners were expected to converge on Canberra for the 2018 festival weekend. The programme kicks off with 5km and 10km races on the Saturday and the Half Marathon, The Canberra Times Marathon and the 50km Ultra Marathon taking place on the Sunday. The course has changed several times since the 1970s, and the current course has a few hills, twists and turns than previously. Both the starting and finish points are in front of Old Parliament House, and a highlight is the loop around new Parliament House. The courses take runners on a picturesque route following the parliamentary triangle, along the banks of Lake Burley Griffin, and finishing on the East West lawns. 2018 saw yet another a course enhancement for the three main events featuring fewer hills and a more pleasant course for runners. According to the promotional literature runners and their supporters can expect an, 'Immersive event village experience across the whole weekend,' with the West Lawns playing host to an entertainment stage, event expo, elite athlete district, and a little runners' zone. As a one-off experiment the village will have a special live site, broadcasting all the action from that weekend's 2018 Commonwealth Games, live from the Gold Coast. As the Commonwealth Games Marathon is scheduled to take place on the same day as the Canberra Marathon spectators have the opportunity to watch the best marathon runners in the Commonwealth compete live on the big screen.

Canberra, Australia's capital city, is home to some of the country's most iconic pieces of history, and there's plenty of time to check them out before or after the race – perhaps even during the race itself as many of the most important sites are encountered while running around the marathon course. The city is located in the Australian Capital Territory (ACT), an enclave in the south-east of New South Wales. Canberra is a planned city, with national monuments, museums and galleries built next to the large artificial Lake Burley Griffin around which much of the race is run. As a bush capital, Canberra is also a great place to enjoy the outdoors, with excellent cycling, gardens, parks, bush-walking and nature reserves. The city was established in 1913 as the capital for the newly federated Australian nation. The story behind its creation is well known. After Australia became a federation in 1901, Melbourne and Sydney couldn't agree on which of the two would host Australia's new parliament. After years of bickering, a middle way was found - a tiny rural community 300km south-west of Sydney would be the national capital. Following the example of Washington DC, it would be situated in a specially designated capital territory, so no state could hold sway over federal politicians. An international competition was held to choose the best design for the brand new city. Chicago-based husband and wife architects Walter and Marion Griffin won and construction of their unusual geometric pattern featuring circles, triangles and hexagons eventually began in 1913. The ACT was excised from New South Wales and put under the control of the federal government. The creation of the planned city was not without critics who claimed it was a 'waste of a good sheep pasture'.

Canberra's 350,000 residents live in seven distinct districts, each with its own commercial centre. The effect of the Griffins' unusual design is that each district is separated by leafy scrub, allowing Canberra's citizens to have a perpetual feeling of being surrounded by the bush. It also, its detractors say, means inhabitants struggle to get the communal feel that unites a city. Populated at first largely by politicians and public servants, it took time to develop its own identity and culture. Extensive building of national facilities and a concerted effort to develop public institutions in the city have made it an interesting destination. Lake Burley Griffin divides central Canberra with the central shopping and commercial area, known as 'Civic', situated on the north side while the parliamentary triangle and embassy zone is on the south side. National institutions are likewise divided, examples being the National Museum of Australia, the Australian War Memorial and the National Botanic Gardens on the north side and the National Library, National Gallery of Australia the High Court and old and new Parliament Houses on the south side. The majority of these are passed by runners on the marathon course.

Few cities do well when they begin as a compromise and having recently celebrated its centenary, Canberra, like many other purpose-built administrative capitals (Brazil's Brasilia, Pakistan's Islamabad) with its high-design layout hasn't managed to capture the heart and soul of the country it rules. No Australian city divides public opinion quite like Canberra does. 'Canberra is like going to grandma's house,' says Jenna

Clarke, life and entertainment editor of the Canberra Times. 'Other Australian cities are doing brash, creative things but here everything is wrapped in plastic.' 'Canberra: Why wait for death?' was Bill Bryson's blistering judgement in his 2000 travelogue Down Under. 'Pyongyang without the dystopia,' was the verdict of the Economist in 2009. Not everyone shares these ideas. In 2014 the OECD (Organisation for Economic Co-operation and Development) decreed Canberra was the best place in the world to live in terms of the wellbeing of its citizens. Likewise, Lonely Planet chose Canberra as the 3rd Best City in Travel for 2018 coming in behind Seville in Spain and Detroit, USA. Canberra's ranking is the highest any Australian city has ever received from Lonely Planet that on its website asserts that that Canberra is 'criminally overlooked' and 'packs a big punch for such a small city.' Inhabitants of other Australians cities might find this ranking hard to believe. My own experience, having stayed there for extended periods in 2000 and 2001, is that like most other cities Canberra has both its good and bad points. I particularly enjoyed its proximity to nature and my long morning runs along the Cooleman Ridge Nature Trail and around the shores of Lake Burley Griffin. On the other hand I found the city centre to be soulless, without atmosphere and a big disappointment. As someone who prefers to walk everywhere when possible I also found the seeming over-dependence on cars somewhat unsettling. Quite often I'd be the only pedestrian on the streets of Chapman while walking the mile or so through deserted suburbia to collect the morning paper.

Getting to the marathon from other Australian cities is pretty straight forward. On the few occasions I've been to Canberra I've usually travelled from Sydney with Murray's coaches. Murrays operate up to 10 daily express services between Sydney Central Station and Canberra with extra services on peak days. Together with Greyhound they are the main operators on this route. The journey takes just over 3 hours with online fares available from as low as $15 depending on the time of travel. Popular services or last-minute booking cost around $35. The service is non-stop and some services operate via Sydney International Airport. If travelling by train, NSW Countrylink Xplorer runs between Sydney and Canberra three times a day on Monday, Wednesday, Friday and Sunday, and twice per day on Tuesday, Thursday and Saturday. The trip takes just over 4 hours, which is slower than a bus or driving, but the train takes a very scenic route through the Southern Highlands and the Molongolo Gorge, compared to an unexciting freeway journey by road. Canberra International Airport is also well served by flights from other Australian capital cities. It's always been known as Canberra International Airport, although international flights only resumed in 2016 after a long absence. There are flights almost hourly to Sydney and frequent flights to Melbourne. Other capitals are serviced less frequently. A flight from Sydney to Canberra only saves an hour or so over driving from Sydney and for those who are not coming from an area close to Sydney Airport, air travel offers only a marginal time saving. At the time of writing the following airlines fly to Canberra daily: Virgin Australia flies to and from Sydney, Brisbane, the Gold Coast, Townsville, Melbourne, Adelaide and Hobart. Qantas flies to and from Sydney, Brisbane, Melbourne, Adelaide, Darwin and Perth. FlyPelican flies to and from Newcastle and Dubbo. International Services operating to and from Canberra include Singapore Airlines which flies from Singapore to Wellington via Canberra International. Qatar Airways is also planning to operate services from Canberra to Doha via Sydney from

2018. The local public bus company, ACTION buses, has recently added an airport service. Routes 11 and 11A leave the airport at least every half hour during operating times and travel directly to the City Bus Station. Tickets are currently $4. There is also a private bus service provided by the Royale Group for $10 each way between the airport and the city. Taxis are available in front of the terminal towards the Qantas end for around $25 to the city centre.

The Canberra Marathon is small in comparison to other capital city races with just over 1,000 people completing the 2017 event. A further 2,020 finished the Half Marathon, a mere 167 ran the Ultra Marathon while there were 1,384 and 1,039 finishers in the 10km and 5km Fun Runs. Marathon Adult Individual entry in 2018 for those aged 18 or older on race day was $150.00. Race numbers are available for collection in the out-of-town Woden Westfield shopping centre all day Friday and in the Festival Village on West Lawns, Canberra from 6am to 5pm on the Saturday. The Ultra Marathon is the first to start at 6am on Sunday. This is followed by the Full Marathon at 6.25am and the Half Marathon at 7.45am. All events start in front of the Old Parliament House approximately 30 minutes' walk from the city centre via Commonwealth Avenue.

The Canberra Marathon course is sure to delight even the most discerning of Marathon Tourists, taking them past the majority of the city's important national institutions beginning with Old Parliament House. After Federation in 1901, and for the next 26 years, the Australian Parliament was held in Melbourne, while plans for a Federal Capital were made. It wasn't until 1927 that the first purpose-built home for Parliament was opened in Canberra. For 61 years from 1927 to 1988 Old Parliament House served as the seat of national political power. It sits in centre of the cultural landscape known as the Parliamentary Triangle—reflecting the design for Canberra by Walter Burley Griffin. Its central positioning is said to symbolise the primacy of the parliament over the executive. This iconic building has been central to Australia's development as a nation, reflecting Australia's democratic values, and political and social rights. Over the years, the building's entrance portico and lawns have been the settings for countless gatherings, protests, celebrations and demonstrations, including the Aboriginal Tent Embassy which was established in January 1972 and remains in place today. Old Parliament House holds a strong connection with many Australians, and its importance was clearly demonstrated when they rallied for its preservation when it was threatened with demolition in the 1970s. Pressure from various bodies persuaded the Government to restore and return it to the public domain and it was reopened in December 1992. Old Parliament House now serves as a living museum of social and political history as well as an important symbol of the nation's political heritage.

The course then runs along Federation Avenue on the Centenary Trail to circumvent the new Parliament House in the first 3km. Opened in 1988 this cost more than $1.1 billion to build, to a design which involved burying most of the building under Capital Hill, and capping the edifice with an enormous spire topped by a large Australian flag. The facades included deliberate imitation of some of the patterns of the Old Parliament House, so that there is a slight resemblance despite the massive difference of scale. The new Parliament House contains 4,700 rooms, and many areas are open to the public. Runners continue past Senate Garden and Magna Carta Place. Magna Carta Place is an open-space venue located in the centre of the Parliamentary Zone. It commemorates the history of Magna Carta and its relevance to the freedom and laws of Australia. The Magna Carta Monument featuring a bronze dome pavilion was the gift of the Australia-Britain Society and the British Government for Australia's Centenary of Federation.

Heading to the lake shore at 4km, the course passes by the National Rose Garden and Questacon. For many years, the Parliamentary gardens could only be accessed by Parliamentarians and their staff. Following Parliament's relocation to the new Parliament House in 1988 and subsequent developmental work, the gardens were opened to the public in 2004. Questacon is the National Science and Technology Centre, on the southern shore of Lake Burley Griffin containing more than 200 interactive exhibits relating to science and technology. It has many science programmes that are devoted to inspiring the children of Australia to love Science. The eight interactive exhibitions cover a range of science topics, from astronomy to zoology and everything in between.

A short lakeside stretch along Queen Elizabeth Terrace next sees runners passing, in succession, the High Court of Australia, the National Portrait Gallery and the National Gallery of Australia – all before reaching the 5km mark. The vast building housing Australia's highest court contains a vast lobby and three main courtrooms that are open to the public. Tours are available, though restricted when the court is sitting. The National Portrait Gallery displays some 400 portraits of people who have shaped and who continue to shape the nation. Galleries are themed by era. The public areas include a café, shop, function room, theatre, education and school group areas. The modern structure of the National Gallery of Australia houses one of the country's largest art galleries. It has a vast collection of paintings and sculptures collected from Australia and the rest of the world and has excellent Aboriginal artwork. A gift store and a large bookstore are on the ground level and entrance is free except for special exhibits. The Gallery also offers free public one-hour tours.

After heading along Bowen Drive to a looped section around Telopea Park School the route returns to the National Gallery at 10km. After a right turn into State Circle the course then goes through the 'Embassy Zone' – an area in which the majority of foreign embassies to Australia have their base. At 13km The Lodge is visible on the left hand side. This building, as I'm sure most readers will be aware, is traditionally the official residence of the Australian Prime Minister. The Lodge is one of two official prime ministerial residences, the secondary official residence being Kirribilli House in Sydney. The building was completed in 1927 in the Georgian revival style, and has been renovated several times since then. It was not initially intended to be used as a permanent official residence, and several prime ministers have chosen to live elsewhere during their terms in office.

The Lakeshore is reached again at Alexander Drive at 15km. taking the runners on an out-and-back section past the headquarters of various rowing groups to the turning point at Kurrajong Point at 17.5 km. The 20km mark is reached at Yarralumba Bay. 22km sees runners passing the Canberra Nara Peace Park before heading along Flynn Drive past the Katie Bender Memorial and over the Waterloo Bridge across the Molonglo River at 24km. The simple memorial to Katie Bender is located at the point where she was killed in a tragic incident in July 1997 when over 100,000 people (nearly half the population of the city at that time) gathered on the south shore of the western basin of Lake Burley Griffin to watch the 'implosion' of the old Royal Canberra Hospital, 400 metres away across the lake on the Acton Peninsula. It was being removed to make way for the National Museum of Australia. The demolition had been planned for some time, and the ACT Government decided to turn the building's demolition into a spectator event. Things went badly wrong and the implosion became, in part an explosion and a 1kg piece of steel was catapulted across the lake striking 12 year old Katie Bender in the head and killing her instantly. Nine other people sustained serious injuries from flying debris. The ACT Government came in for sustained criticism and a number of official inquiries were held. Many people complained the event should never have been made a public spectacle, as this was inviting disaster while others felt that this was unfair, as implosions around the world generally excited local interest and had had an enviable safety record. For numerous reasons the whole event remains controversial to this day.

Runners are now on the North side of Lake Burley Griffin. What follows is yet another out-and-back section along the usually very busy Parkes Way from 25km to 33km with the vast expanse of the National Botanic Gardens to the north. Located at the base of Black Mountain in Acton, the ANBG, to which entry is free, has the largest collection of Australian native flora in the country. The route continues along Parkes Way this time to the east of the city before eventually re-crossing the lake over Kings Avenue Bridge at 37km. It makes a left turn at Charles Sturt University Campus to again follow Bowen Drive to the turning point at Telopea School before returning to the finish close to the King George V Memorial.

Despite the fact that thousands of Canberra residents regularly walk, run and ride around the city's Lake Burley Griffin there's very little in the way of places to eat and drink close to its foreshore where runners can adjourn to post-race. Only a couple of places spring to mind from previous visits. These are the Water's Edge Restaurant just off Queen

Elizabeth Terrace and the Snapper on the Lake in Mariner Place. The former in particular is quite expensive with a 2-course lunch costing $55 (3-courses are $66) and main dishes of lemon sole fish finger, lamb back strap, quail and pumpkin risotto. Maybe not really what you're wanting after a marathon. Situated on Lake Burley Griffin, Snapper on the Lake is the Southern Cross Yacht Club's fish and chip shop. Voted by locals as Canberra's best fish restaurant, it offers fresh fish and chips for around $25 along with tranquil lake views and a fairly relaxed atmosphere. As an alternative, pizzas and burgers can be ordered off the Bar Menu for $20 and $18 respectively. The Yacht Club also serves a good selection of draught beers from between $7.50 and $9 per pint. (Cascade Light is $7.50, Carlton Draught cost $8 while 4 Pines Kolsch can be had for $9 a pint). If you're looking for somewhere a little more down-market and a little less expensive you could always walk across the bridge in to the city centre and visit P. J. O'Reilly's Irish bar on Alinga Street. From memory this serves a decent pint of Guinness along with a range of craft beers plus the usual cheap but filling pub grub.

.

ROTORUA MARATHON

NORTH ISLAND, NEW ZEALAND

MAY

May 2018 saw the 54th edition of the Rotorua Marathon, Australasia's oldest major marathon event. A Round the Lake Rotorua Relay for teams of 6 preceded the first individual event. First held in 1949, this was a club-only event hosted by the Rotorua Athletic Club. Then in 1953 the event became an open race which over the years attracted teams from throughout the North Island. With traffic congestion, teams were reduced to five persons and the event was last held in 1977. The first recorded group run around Lake Rotorua was in 1961 when 8 Rotorua runners attempted the circuit – only two finished the 26 mile 385 yards distance. Three official Club marathons followed but it was not until 1965 that a sponsored event began, supported for 35 years until 1999 by Fletchers, hence the name Fletcher Marathon seen in some years' results. In the 1965 race a mere 16 runners started the event of which only 11 completed the course, an anti-clockwise journey around Lake Rotorua. For reasons of traffic management the race direction was changed to clockwise in 1977, as this made it easier to negotiate several road crossings. What makes the Rotorua event unique is its geographical identity. One of the quirks of the full marathon is that one lap of Lake Rotorua is almost exactly the full marathon distance (give or take a few hundred metres). No more. No less. Almost perfect.

The Rotorua Athletic Club, Rotorua Joggers and the Ngongotaha Track Club joined together in 1991, to form the current Lake City Athletic Club who continued as organiser of the event. Fletcher's long-standing sponsorship, along with good organisation attracted a veritable 'Who's Who' of New Zealand's greatest distance runners as evidenced by a look at the event's Hall of Fame. Foremost among these is Olympian and legendary runner Jack Foster, a four- time winner of his home town event. A total of 6364 entries were received for the 25th event in 1989: 5967 started and 5859 finished that race. This was (and I believe still is) a record field for the full marathon distance in New Zealand. There was no such thing as chip timing in those days and, somehow or other, the organisers managed to record all finishing times by hand. Ten years later in 1999 the organisers faced the disappointment of what may have been an unfortunate world first when the 35th event was cancelled on race morning only 10 minutes before the start because of a torrential downpour over the Rotorua basin causing flooding throughout the city and washouts on the course. All entrants who had collected their race numbers were forwarded their finishers T-shirt, suitably overprinted with the words 'rained out', together with their 35th commemorative medal also stamped 'rained out'.

During the years since Fletcher's involvement with the race ended other sponsors have included Bartercard New Zealand Ltd (2000-2001), Fletcher Challenge Forests (2002-2003), Tenon (2004), The Lion Foundation and New Zealand Community Trust. Athletics New Zealand took over ownership of the event in 2000 until they were joined by in 2011 by Event Promotions Ltd, Rotorua, who were appointed as the event managers (with Athletics New Zealand retaining ownership). The new management team introduced a half marathon that year and a 5km and a 10.55km quarter marathon have also been added to encourage people to gradually step up towards completing the full circuit of the Lake. Race records for the marathon are held by Paul Ballinger, who ran 2:16:05 in 1988, and Nyla Carroll, who recorded 2:37:37 in 1994. In recent times, however, it has been disappointing that the men have not broken the 2:20 barrier since 1994 and over the same period no woman has run faster than 2:40. In 2018 Christchurch-based Blair McWhirter won the men's marathon with a time of 2 hours 28 minutes 59 seconds minutes while Alice Mason won the women's marathon with a time of 2 hours 46 minutes and 45 seconds. There were 941 finishers in the Marathon Run (there was also a Marathon Walk) with the slowest finishing time in the Run recorded at 9 hours 3minutes and 5 seconds (almost 23 minutes slower than the last finisher in the Marathon Walk!)

One of the features of the Rotorua Marathon is the numbers who return each year to complete the race. This has led to the formation of The Rotorua Marathon Survivors Club in 1993, when 29 runners were inducted in to the Club in recognition of them each having completed a minimum of 15 Rotorua Marathons. Membership has since grown steadily, and by 2017 had reached a total of 517 surviving members. (A further 37 are now deceased). Colin Smyth, 'Mr Rotorua Marathon', has run the event over 40 times while a number of others have more than 30 finishes to their name. In 2017, 123 members of the Rotorua Marathon Survivors Club returned to run the event once again. They were joined by another 23 who were attempting to complete the marathon for the 15th time and achieve induction into the Survivors Club.

Lake Rotorua, around which the marathon is run, is the second largest lake in the North Island having been formed from the crater of a large volcano in the Taupo Volcanic Zone. The volcano's last major eruption was about 240,000 years ago after which the magma chamber underneath the volcano collapsed. The circular depression left behind is the Rotorua Caldera, which is the site of the lake. Owing to the geothermal activity around the lake (including still active geysers and hot mud pools), the lake has a high sulphur content. This gives the lake's waters an unusual yellowish-green hue. Two kilometres from the eastern shore of Lake Rotorua and visible for much of the marathon route lies Mokoia Island, a wildlife sanctuary since 1921. This small, cone shaped island, is a haven for endangered New Zealand birds and remains predator free. It is also the home of a famous Maori legend. According to the legend Tutanekai was a young Maori man who loved Hinemoa. Unfortunately, she was of higher birth than Tutanekai, the daughter of a powerful chief, and the young lovers were destined to be kept apart by her family. Determined not to be thwarted in her love, Hinemoa bravely swam to Mokoia Island under the cover of night, lured by the music of Tutanekai's flute, to be with her beloved. According to legend, once Hinemoa's family discovered where she was, they accepted her choice of husband and the two tribes were united forever more.

Located on the southern shores of the lake from which the city takes its name, Rotorua is the seat of the Rotorua District, a territorial authority encompassing Rotorua and several other nearby towns in the Bay of Plenty Region. Rotorua is in the heart of New Zealand's North Island, 60 kilometres south of Tauranga, 80 km north of Taupo, 105 km east of Hamilton, and 230 km south east of the nation's most populous city, Auckland. Rotorua has an estimated permanent population of

58,800. The area was initially settled by Maori of the Te Arawa Iwi in the 14th century. The first European in the area was probably Phillip Tapsell who was trading from the Bay of Plenty coast at Maketu from 1828. A 'special town district' was created in the 1883, to promote Rotorua's potential as a spa destination. When the town was connected to Auckland with the opening of the Rotorua Branch railway and commencement of the Rotorua Express train in 1894, it resulted in the rapid growth of the town and its attraction as a tourist destination.

The name Rotorua comes from Maori whose full name for the city and lake is Te Rotorua-nui-a-Kahumatamomoe. Roto means 'lake' and rua means 'two' or in this case 'second' – Rotorua thus meaning 'Second lake'. It is the largest of a multitude of lakes found to the northeast, all connected with the Rotorua Caldera and nearby Mount Tarawera. Geologically, Rotorua is in the middle of the Taupo Volcanic Zone, which is named after Lake Taupo, the largest volcano in the area. There are four major volcanic calderas, which now contain lakes, and several more recognisable volcanoes in the surrounding area. It is this geologically active zone that produces the heat that is needed to drive all the geothermal activity. The area has become known as the thermal wonderland of New Zealand and its hot springs and geysers have attracted tourists for well over a hundred years with the tourism industry by far the largest industry in the district. Rotorua itself is built over a geothermal hot spot and there are numerous natural vents, hot pools and other geothermal features in and around the city. A common nickname for Rotorua is 'Sulphur City' due to the hydrogen sulphide emissions, which gives the city a smell similar to rotten eggs. Another common nickname is 'Rotten-rua' - a combination of its legitimate name and the rotten smell prevalent. Strangely,

I have been unable to find any complaints by runners regarding smells on the course.

Those travelling by road to the marathon will find that Rotorua is about a 3-hour drive south from Auckland, with several nice towns and villages along the way. Regular bus services between Auckland and Rotorua are provided by InterCity. For air-travellers, Rotorua Regional Airport is located 9 km northeast of the city centre, off State Highway 30. Air New Zealand provides daily turbo-prop flights between Rotorua and Auckland, Wellington, and Christchurch airports. Previously Qantas also operated Boeing 737 aircraft from Christchurch, but upon their departure from domestic flights in New Zealand this was discontinued. The airport is serviced by shuttles, taxis and bus services. The cheapest option is the public bus company, Cityride Rotorua that provides regular daily bus services to the airport, apart from public holidays. The same company also operates several routes from one side of the city to the other, including the outer suburb of Ngongotaha. The standard fare is $2.50 regardless of how far you travel. Official Hotels are the 4.5-star Millennium Hotel and the 4-star Copthorne Hotel Rotorua. An accommodation code is provided on the website for entrants to receive a discount at these.

Entries to the Marathon range from $124 until the end of November, rising to $134 from December up to $144 after April 1st. Online entries close at 7am on the Friday morning before race day (Saturday) though entries still are available on the Friday and Saturday at Registration held at the Rotorua Energy Events Centre. Late entries will close at 8.30am on Saturday morning. Half Marathon runners start first at 8:00 on Saturday morning closely followed by those in the Half Marathon Walk. The Marathon leaves next at 8:20am with the Marathon Walkers setting-off 5 minutes later. 8:40am sees the start of the Quarter Marathon runners and walkers with 5.5km runners and walkers leaving at 8:50am. The Prize Giving ceremony for all events closes proceedings at 5pm.

The start and finish to all events is based at the Government Gardens outside the Energy Events Centre. While the full marathoners will complete one full circuit of the lake, competitors in the Half Marathon head out towards the airport, along Te Ngae Road for a loop through Whakarewarewa Forest and back through the Government Gardens to the finish line. Government Gardens is an immaculate park near the CBD which also contains the city museum and the famous Blue Baths. The marathon course heads out through Rotorua's CBD, along Arawa St before heading around Kuirau Park. The park contains a series of hot bubbling mud pools in which visitors can soak their feet. Lake Rd and and Fairy Springs Rd take runners to the suburb of Fairy Springs at 5km. The larger suburb of Ngongotaha is next up at around 8km. Known locally as the 'Sunny side of the mountain,' Ngongotaha sits on the northwest shores of Lake Rotorua. With a pretty town centre, it has a distinct village feel and character built around a strong sporting identity with successful soccer, rugby and netball teams. After that there's very little else to see until runners reach the lake's northern shore at approximately 15km. The route continues along Hamurana Road, passing through the Hamurana Springs Nature Reserve. The Springs are a group of natural water springs in a beautiful reserve next to the Hamurana golf course. The main spring is the deepest natural fresh water spring on the North Island. Another spring in the reserve, the Dancing Sands spring, is named because of the effect of the emerging water on the sand on the bottom of the spring. At 25km the route turns south onto the State Highway close to the small settlement of Mourea. The Te Ngae Rd then takes runners for most of the rest of the way into town. Runners pass Lake Rotokawa on their left at around 33km and Hannah's Bay at 35km. At 36km there's a short detour to the right into Vaughan Rd before returning to Te Ngae Rd again at 40km, and finally through Prince's Arch and up the finish straight in Government Gardens.

As New Zealand's busiest tourist centre there are a variety of attractions in and around Rotorua to interest Marathon Tourists after their race. Although the city is famous for being a hot bed for geothermal activity, as well as having a rich Maori culture, there are so many adrenaline, wildife and nature experiences to be had as well. There's plenty of hot springs and volcanic activity for visitors to see, while Maori culture is likewise at the forefront with numerous cultural attractions and ceremonies for tourists to take part in. A good place to start is the Te Puia experience that brings everything Rotorua is famous for together experience. Te Puia is home to the Whakarewarewa Valley of geothermal activity including bubbling mud pools and geysers. The highlight of the visit is seeing the iconic Pohutu Geyser that erupts up to 20 times a day, spurting hot water up to 30m skyward. General admission is $40, but once inside there are regular, free guided tours throughout the park, including the geothermal areas and the kiwi house. There are also Maori cultural experiences like traditional dances and meals available for an additional charge. Also worth a mention is the self-descriptive Buried Village, swamped with ash by the nearby Mt Tarawera in the massive 1886 eruption which killed 153 people. Now open to the public, The Buried Village takes visitors through the excavated ruins of the village, a recreated cottage and a museum with recovered relics, tracing back the history of one of New Zealand's biggest volcanic eruptions.

Other attractions worth visiting include The Skyline Gondola ride from Fairy Springs Road up to Mt. Ngongotaha. This is a cheap half day activity that involves taking the cable car to the top of Skyline Rotorua on Mount Ngongotaha. You will be rewarded with epic views over Rotorua and Lake Okataina. Make sure you purchase a Luge + Gondola Ride package so that you can whizz around the mountain on a toboggan. At the top there is also wine tasting, a restaurant and the must-do Rotorua activity for adrenaline junkies - the Sky Swing. Keen mountain bikers can also try out the downhill trails from the top of the gondola. Likewise, Agroventures in Paradise Valley Road offers adventure lovers a choice of activities from jet boating, bungy jumping, freefalling and giant swinging– a bit like an extreme fun fair. For a spot of self-pampering afterwards, another place to visit in Hinemoa Street right in the centre of Rotorua is the Polynesian Spa. Here you can relax in a huge complex of pools. Whether you choose the luxury option or the main pools, either way, you have a wide range of temperatures, minerals and views to enjoy. Finally, no visit to Rotorua is usually complete without a visit to the Hobbiton Movie Set. The movie set is located just a short drive from the city close to a town called Matamata. Tours depart from Rotorua daily and will allow you to explore the movie set as featured in the Lord of the Rings and the Hobbiton films. The tour includes a visit to the Shire's Rest where you can visit The Green Dragon Inn, The Mill, Hobbit Holes and the double arched bridge – all feature prominently in the Lord of the Rings Trilogy

As for food and drink, my sons assure me that the hungry and thirsty marathon runner need look no further than two traditional pubs: The Pig and Whistle and Hennessy's Irish Bar situated close together in Tutanekai Street near the Government Gardens. The Pig & Whistle is the closest thing to a historic pub you'll find in Rotorua. Originally set up in the 1940's as a Police station, the pub's architecture makes it one of Rotorua's outstanding landmarks. It serves Monteith's, Heineken, Black Dog, Tiger, Erdinger as well as three Ciders on tap and a good range of New Zealand wines. It also provides classic New Zealand pub meals with favourites like Seafood Chowder, New Zealand Lamb Salad and Pork Spare Ribs. An added bonus is that The Pig & Whistle also has live bands every Thursday, Friday and Saturday nights. Hennessy's Bar is a traditional style Irish Pub that was totally rebuilt in 2016 after the building failed earthquake prone building assessment. It's received the prestigious Beer Masters Award, an award that recognises excellence in presentation of tap beers and service, every year since opening. As well as old favourites like Guinness and Kilkenny, the pub is said to serve decent pints of Emerson's (brewed in Dunedin) and Panhead APA Super Charger. Hennessy's has a reputation for serving Rotorua's favourite pub food, including traditional fare like mussels, lamb shanks and bangers & mash, steaks and stews, supported by burgers, sandwiches and fresh salads. I particularly liked the sound of the Beef & Guinness Casserole and the Hennessy's Irish Stew, both for $25.90, as well as the Murphy's Chicken for $19.90.

HAWKE'S BAY MARATHON

NORTH ISLAND, NEW ZEALAND

MAY

This is a recent edition to the New Zealand marathon calendar. Inspired by the success of the Air New Zealand Queenstown International Marathon, the Air New Zealand Hawke's Bay International Marathon started in 2016. The event incorporates 42km, 21km, 10K and 3K Kids' Run options. The inaugural event attracted 780 finishers in the Full Marathon distance with 2,259 runners completing the Half Marathon event and 1,252 finishing the 10K race. Numbers participating across the programme have remained at around the 4,000 mark each year and, as hoped by the organisers, have provided a major boost to the region's tourist economy in what is generally a quiet month of the year. Though the event has become a popular competition for people all over New Zealand, with 75 per cent of participants coming from outside the Hawke's Bay area, a look at the results would suggest that it has yet to fulfil the 'international' tag attached to its title.

All events start in the city of Napier on courses that are said to make for flat, easy running. They each offer a unique mix of running terrain, with a combination of running on-road, bike trails and through vineyards. The courses take in the highlights of the Hawke's Bay region which overall include running along the waterfront in Napier, Hawke's Bay cycle trails and quiet country roads, with the last 10km of the courses running through private vineyards. The finish line for all events is set in the beautiful surroundings of Sileni Estates Winery. The Winery is a major vineyard and winery development in Hawke's Bay, New Zealand's oldest established vineyard area. The first vintage at the winery was in 1998 and since then their wines have won world wide acclaim. Sileni offer sampling and wine specials at the event's Expo, while all competitors in the three main events receive their own wine glass in their race pack with which to sample The Apple Press and Sileni Estates Wine at the finish line. An encouragement to enter, if ever there was one.

For those unfamiliar with New Zealand's geography, Hawke's Bay is not a city – it's a region of New Zealand on the east coast of the North Island, known for its award-winning wines. It bears the former name of what is now Hawke Bay, a large semi-circular bay that extends for 100 kilometres from northeast to southwest from Mahia Peninsula to Cape Kidnappers. Hawke Bay was named by Captain James Cook in honour of Admiral Edward Hawke who decisively defeated the French at the Battle of Quiberon Bay in 1759. Hawke's Bay was one of the provinces when New Zealand was colonized by British settlers in the mid nineteenth century. The Hawke's Bay region includes the hilly coastal land around the northern and central bay, the floodplains of the Wairoa River in the north, the wide fertile Heretaunga Plains around Hastings in the south, and a hilly interior stretching up into the Kaweka and Ruahine Ranges. The region is renowned for its horticulture, with large orchards and vineyards on the plains. In the hilly parts of the region sheep and cattle farming predominates, with forestry blocks in the roughest areas. The climate is dry and temperate, and the long, hot summers and cool winters offer excellent weather for growing grapes. The vineyard industry has developed strongly in recent years and the area is now New Zealand's second-largest wine-producing region (behind Marlborough). Hawke's Bay produces some of New Zealand's finest wines, in particular excellent Bordeaux-style reds, shiraz and chardonnay and once a year Harvest Hawke's Bay celebrates that fact by hosting a popular three-day wine and food festival.

Napier and Hastings are the two largest cities in the Hawke's Bay region. Napier is a seaport at the south-eastern edge of Hawke Bay about 320 kilometres north-east of the capital city of Wellington. 18 kilometres south of Napier is the inland city of Hastings. These two neighbouring cities are often called 'The Bay Cities' or 'The Twin Cities' of New Zealand. With just over 63,000 inhabitants, Napier has a smaller population than its neighbouring city of Hastings (70,000) but is seen as the main centre due to it being closer in distance to both the port and the main airport that service Hawke's Bay. The two cities experienced tragedy in February 1931 when most of Napier and nearby Hastings was levelled by an earthquake. It measured 7.8 on the Richter scale and rumbled for approximately 150 seconds and remains, ahead of the Christchurch quake of 2011, New Zealand's deadliest natural disaster. The collapse of buildings and the ensuing fires killed 256 people. The centre of Napier was destroyed by the earthquake, and later rebuilt in the Art Deco style popular at that time. The demolition rubble was dumped along the eastern foreshore and turned into gardens and a recreational reserve. The earthquake also raised the land by several metres and, interestingly, some 4000 hectares of today's Napier were undersea before the earthquake raised it above sea level. The reconstruction operation took two years and as the prevailing architectural style at the time was Art Deco many of the new buildings were constructed in this style. The stunning results remain to this day. As a result, Napier's architecture is strikingly different from any other city. It's said that no other notable Art Deco city, not even Miami Beach, can lay claim to the uniformity of Napier's design. The best examples of the region's Art Deco architecture are reported to include the Daily Telegraph Building and Municipal Theatre in Napier, and the Hawke's Bay Opera House in Hastings. The Art Deco Trust protects the town's architecture and, on the first weekend of February hosts the Art Deco weekend with period costumes, vintage cars, planes and music luring 40,000 visitors. Napier is also home to the Mission Concert held early each year since 1993. The event, held at the Mission Estate Winery in Taradale, has attracted performers of the calibre of Kenny Rogers, Shirley Bassey, Rod Stewart, Ray Charles, and Eric Clapton

Most marathon runners will probably prefer to stay in Napier as opposed to Hastings during the event. This is because Registration and Expo are both held at the Napier Conference Centre in Marine Parade on the day prior to the event and the Full Marathon starts in the same street with shuttle buses provided to return them to the same spot after their race. These shuttle buses will also take 10K competitors to their start line at Gimblett Gravels Wine District and Half Marathoners to their start at Pakowhai Regional Park both before and after the race. A similar pre and post-race shuttle service is available for all events from Hastings and return.

InterCity operates daily bus services to Napier from Auckland, Hamilton, Wellington and many other towns and cities in the North Island. Hawke's Bay Airport just north of Napier also serves the region with domestic flights. Air New Zealand, Jetstar, Sounds Air, and Air Napier fly to Hawke's Bay Airport and together provide direct flights to Auckland, Gisborne, Wairoa, Wellington, Blenheim and Christchurch, with connections across New Zealand and internationally. On top of their normal services, Air NZ, the event's major sponsor, has arranged three extra return flights between Auckland and Napier to support the Marathon Unfortunately, for those who prefer travelling by train, the rail line in and out of Hawke's Bay has not had a passenger service since 2001. Accommodation is plentiful in Napier and the surrounding area and ranges from luxury to budget; hotels, self-catering apartments, motels, holiday parks and motor camps with self-catering units, budget cabins and campsites. There is also a beachfront youth hostel for backpackers. If booked from the UK on booking.com, prices for a double/twin room for three nights over the Marathon weekend in 2019 ranged from £108 in the Toad Hall Backpackers, to £221 in both the Shoreline and Beachfront Motels rising to £260 in the 4-star Art Deco Masonic Hotel in the centre of town.

Entry fees for the 3rd edition of the race in 2018 started at $150.12 for Early Bird entrants rising to $158.76 and then to $169.56 shortly before the race (these prices include an 8% service fee). T-shirts and shuttle bus costs are not included. I was surprised to read that of the 4,200 plus competitors who completed their respective events, the ratio was 66% female to 34% male. Of these, there were 436 finishers in the marathon (a considerable drop in numbers from the inaugural race) 1850 in the half marathon and 1483 in the 10K. Race day starts with the departure of the shuttle buses from 5:45am and 7:30am. Start times for the various races are: 10K Run at 7:45am; Half Marathon at 8:15am; Marathon at 9:00am and Kids Run at 1:00pm. Due to course management and road closure restrictions there is a cut-off point at the 10km mark into the marathon race which all participants should have passed by 10:40am. The course is officially closed at 4:00pm.

Following the start on Marine Parade in Napier the course heads south running along the waterfront, turning onto Te Awa Avenue before heading inland at Kenny Road. Athletes then head towards Meeanee via Eriksen Road and Awatoto Road. A left turn onto Brookfields Road leads athletes all the way to the first trail section along the North side of the Tutaekuri River towards the coast. Organisers advise that runners do not need to wear trail shoes as the course is smooth, easy, hard packed trails. After crossing underneath the State Highway, runners catch a glimpse of Cape Kidknappers, a headland at the south-eastern extremity of Hawke's Bay. The headland was named after an attempt by local Maori to abduct the servant of a member of Captain Cook's crew aboard HMS Endeavour, during a landfall there in 1769. The cape has been identified as an Important Bird Area by BirdLife International because it is a breeding site for over 3000 pairs of Australasian gannets. The course then turns back inland along the South side of the Ngaruroro River. This trail section leads all the way to the halfway point where athletes take a small diversion through the Pakowhai Country Park before re-joining the trail heading west towards Twyford. Placed approximately equidistant between Napier and Hastings, Pakowhai is an attractive country-style park that has become a popular recreation destination for inhabitants of both cities. Runners then leave the trail back onto tarmac to wind through Twyford before entering the Gimblett Gravels Wine District. The Gimblett Gravels winegrowing area planted on the former bed of the Ngaruroro River, is a small sub-region in the Hawkes Bay area defined by a very unique stony soil type. It is reputed to produce an excellent quality Syrah. From this point it's largely trail all the rest of the way through a combination of the vineyards, and farmland finishing through the Bridge Pa wine district to the finish line at Sileni Estates Winery.

With this being a fairly new event, I haven't been able to find too many online comments from finishers though, after much digging, I finally came up with an opinion for each of the years that the race has been run to date. Posting on the site 'Jog around the Blog' in 2016 W. Le Roux wasn't too complimentary stating that 'The finish area was good. Lots of stalls to buy food and drinks and just relax under the trees after the run. So, it's not a bad event. But it's not a great event either. And it certainly didn't live up to the expectations of fantastic scenery as advertised on their website. Marketing hype like 'Running through a natural wonderland of wineries, orchards, and late autumn Hawke's Bay countryside' oversold it a little.' Writing in the Guardian in 2017 Kate Carter penned, 'What better prize could there be on crossing the line than a medal and a bottle of limited edition Sauvignon Blanc.' Finally in 2018 a contributor to runningmumsaustralia.com wrote, 'I absolutely loved running at Hawkes Bay. I couldn't fault the event for its scenery, the route, the organization, the finish area and the medal. Every bit of it was amazing!'

Apart from the must-see Art Deco buildings there are a number of other attractions in and around Napier that might be of interest to fellow Marathon Tourists. Foremost among these is the statue of Pania on the Reef located at Soundshell on Marine Parade. Pania is a figure of Maori mythology that has become the symbol of the city. Reputed to be one of the most photographed landmarks in New Zealand the statue is regarded in Napier in much the same way that the Little Mermaid statue is regarded in Copenhagen. In October 2005 the statue was stolen, but it was recovered a week later, largely unharmed. Also worth a visit is the MTG Hawke's Bay (the museum, theatre and art gallery) which features information on both the 1931 earthquake and Napier's redesign as an Art Deco city. Likewise the historic Napier Prison, New Zealand's oldest, opened in 1862 and shut down in 1993. During its history the site has hosted a prison, an insane asylum and orphanage. Visitors can learn about the history of prisons as well as witness the path of the 1931 earthquake. It is the only place in Napier where some of the earthquake damage has been left in place. The prison is open daily for self-guided audio tours. Also on Marine Parade is the National Aquarium of New Zealand, the country's premier aquarium. It offers a reef tank, a viewing tunnel for marine life which spirals its way beneath the enormous Oceanarium creating the impression of a true underwater experience, and a typical New Zealand rocky shore environment. Visitors can see sharks, stingray and hundreds of fish species. Also on display are eels, trout, sea horse, turtles, octopus, tropical marine fish, kiwi, tuatara, water dragons, native frogs and crocodiles. For lovers of the outdoors, nearby Te Mata Peak standing 400 metres above sea level has nature trails and panoramic views from its summit. Visitors can see Napier and the Mahia Peninsula to the north and east, hill country to the south and east, and the Ruahine, Kaweka and Maungaharuru ranges beyond the fertile Heretaunga Plains. It's possible to drive to the top via Te Mata Peak Road or run, walk or mountain bike through 99 hectares of beautiful parkland on a series of well graded tracks.

It's probable that having tasted the wines at Selini Estates at the end of the race, some people might want to see more of what's on offer. There's a variety of tour operators waiting to help you with that. Bay Tours and Charters Hawke's Bay offer a door-to-door service Classic Wine Tour aimed at showing visitors a cross-section of Hawke's Bay wineries. For around $85 you can visit and taste at 3 or 4 winery cellar doors, discover the 'roots' of winemaking with a trip into the vineyard itself and finish off with a mid-afternoon Cheese Platter at one of the wineries. Alternatively, you can do-it-yourself by hiring a bike and simply cycling between the 72 vineyards and wineries in the area via a dedicated cycle path that links many of them. Most have cellar door tastings with a cover charge of about $5 that typically gets you a taste of five or six wines and is usually waived if you make a purchase.

The place for post-race food and drink appears to be the village-like atmosphere of Ahuriri, home to a range of bars and restaurants on the waterfront at West Quay. Most frequently recommended is Shed 2, a converted storage shed goes right back to the days the square-riggers tied up just metres from its front deck. Dinner for 2 costs around $45 from an extensive menu featuring a wide variety of seafood dishes, pork belly, pork ribs, farm steak, pizzas, Guinness Pie and burgers. Nearby, Mexi Mama is said to offer excellent Mexican fare for around $17 per head, including margaritas. Apparently, the locals' favourite drinking places on the quay are Gintrap and the Thirsty Whale, though I prefer the sound of the nearby Speights Alehouse. The Alehouse is the only bar in the bay serving all seven of the Dunedin brewery's beers on tap, from top-seller Speight's Gold through to the crafted pilsner, pale ale, porter and old dark. As someone who spends a fair bit of his time searching for the perfect strong dark beer the last two sound right up my street.

.

GREAT OCEAN ROAD MARATHON

VICTORIA

MAY

Now part of The Great Ocean Road Running Festival weekend held in May each year, the Great Ocean Road Marathon offers one of the most spectacular marathons in the world in a beautiful and unique area of Victoria with panoramic views of the Southern Ocean. Along with the 44km Marathon (note the distance) the Great Ocean Road Festival of Distance Running also features a 60km ultra marathon, a 23km Half Marathon, a 14km run, a 6km run and The Kids' 1.5km Gallop. The event has been held annually since 2005 with the longest distance category, the 60-kilometre Ultra Marathon, going along the coastline from the idyllic town of Lorne and ending in Apollo Bay, where the shorter runs take place and where all runs end. As the course stretches along the coastal towns between Lorne and Apollo Bay runners of all distances can soak up some of Australia's most scenic beaches and breath-taking views. The marathon reminds me in many ways of California's famous Big Sur Marathon, in that it's a point-to-point race that runs follows a rugged and undulating coastline along an iconic stretch of road. The annual two-day running festival attracts over 7,000 participants of all ages and abilities.

The Great Ocean Road is an Australian National Heritage listed 243 kilometres road along the south-eastern coast of Australia between the Victorian cities of Torquay and

Allansford. Built by returned soldiers between 1919 and 1932 and dedicated to soldiers killed during World War I, the road is the world's largest war memorial. Winding through varying terrain along the coast and providing access to several prominent landmarks, including the Twelve Apostles limestone stack formations, the road is an important tourist attraction in the region. The Great Ocean Road was first planned towards the end of the First World War, when funds were provided for returned soldiers to work on roads in sparsely populated areas in the Western District of Victoria. At the time, the rugged south-west coast of Victoria was accessible only by sea or rough bush track. Besides being dedicated as a memorial, it was also envisaged that the road would connect isolated settlements on the coast, and become a vital transport link for the timber industry and tourism. Construction on the road by approximately 3,000 returned servicemen began in September 1919. An advance survey team progressed through dense wilderness at approximately 3 kilometres a month. Construction was done by hand using explosives, pick and shovel, wheel barrows and some small machinery. The job was perilous at times and several workers were killed on the job with the final sections along steep coastal mountains being the most difficult to work on. The soldiers were paid 10 shillings and sixpence for eight hours per day, also working a half-day on Saturdays. The section of road used by the Marathon was the last to be finished.

    Much of the road hugs coastline affectionately known as the 'Surf Coast' between Torquay and Cape Otway and the 'Shipwreck Coast' further west of Cape Otway, providing visibility of Bass Strait and the Southern Ocean. The road traverses rainforests, as well as beaches and cliffs composed of limestone and sandstone, which is susceptible to erosion. It travels via Anglesea, Lorne, Apollo Bay, and Port Campbell, the latter being notable for its natural limestone and sandstone rock formations including Loch Ard Gorge, The Grotto, London Arch and The Twelve Apostles. At the stretch of the Great Ocean Road nearer to Geelong, the road meanders along the coast, with tall, almost-vertical cliffs on the other side of it. Over its life, the Great Ocean Road has been susceptible to natural elements; in 1960 the section at Princetown was partially washed away by water during storms. It experienced landslides in August 1964, and in 1971; both closing sections of the road near Lorne. Because of the terrain surrounding the road, it was also closed due to bushfires in 1962 and 1964. In January 2011 a section of the overhanging cliffs collapsed due to heavy rain.

For runners arriving at Tullamarine Airport, Melbourne there are several ways to get to Apollo Bay and Lorne. The airport has Skytrain shuttle buses to the city, as well as a taxi service. Lorne is 146km from Melbourne CBD and will take approximately 2 hours to drive. V-line operate regular train services from Melbourne to Geelong from where there are several daily bus services to both Apollo Bay and Lorne. Alternatively, it's possible to take the regular airport transport service operated by Gull from Tullamarine to Geelong and then to both destinations via a V-line bus service.

Lorne, a popular destination on the Great Ocean Road tourist route, is a seaside town on Louttit Bay located around the Erskine River. At the 2016 census it had a population of 1,114 but this figure grows during the holiday season. With a lush, hilly hinterland descending to sandy beaches that frame a horseshoe-shaped bay Lorne, the largest resort town along the Great Ocean Road, has an idyllic setting. Considered by many as Melbourne's answer to Byron Bay, Lorne is popular summer holiday destination for Melburnians, offering beach, bush and cultural attractions to suit all tastes. It is described as having a quintessential Aussie beach-town vibe plus waterfalls, wilderness and wildlife in its hinterland, as well as a thriving festival and sports calendar.There's accommodation options to suit all budgets with many quaint bed-and-breakfast lodges alongside grand hotels as well as newer resorts and motels. It also boasts what is described as 'one of the best beachfront and riverside campgrounds in Australia.'

Apollo Bay is the main location for all the running events, being the finishing point for the Ultra Marathon, the 44-kilometre Marathon and the 23-kilometre Half-Marathon, as well as the start and finish line for the 14-kilometre Paradise Run, the 6-kilometre Mizuno Run and the 1.5-kilometre Kids Gallop. Apollo Bay is midway along the Great Ocean Road in the shelter of Cape Otway and on the lowest slopes of the beautiful Otway ranges. The town had a population of 1,598 at the 2016 census. Though it is smaller and quieter than other nearby places such as Lorne it is also host to the annual Apollo Bay Music Festival and the Great Ocean Sports Festival. As a popular tourist destination, Apollo Bay offers both swimming and surf beaches, as well as a large boat harbour and marina which is home to a major fishing fleet. The town's commercial centre, featuring a good selection of restaurants and cafes, is situated along one side of the Great Ocean Road, overlooking a wide, grassy foreshore which fronts the main swimming beach. Another popular beach is located at the mouth of the Barham River in Mounts Bay. The rugged and bushy Great Otway National Park, which includes a lighthouse at Cape Otway, is easily accessible. This makes Apollo Bay a great place to enjoy the coast and the bushy hinterland of the Otway Ranges. In winter to spring, southern right whales come to the area mainly to breed, to give birth their calves, and to raise them in the warmer, calm waters of South

Australia during their migration season. Less frequently, humpback whales can be seen off the coast.

Runners are required to collect their Race Packs from the Race Week Offices at either Lorne or Apollo Bay provided that they chose one of these options upon entering. Registration also gives participants free access to a range of activities across the weekend. Lorne and Apollo Bay host a kite festival, live music and yoga sessions so that spectators too can enjoy the festivities. Entry fee for the Marathon was $139 in 2018. Entrants are given 6 hours and 30 minutes in which to complete the event. Finishers in 2017 included 959 marathon runners, 62 in the Ultra Marathon and 2,839 in the Half Marathon event. There were a further 897 in the 14km (plus 4 Wheelchair competitors) 722 in the 6km event and a further 434 in the The Kids' Gallop. Quite a busy weekend!

The event kicks off with the 1.5km Kids Run and 6km Run on Saturday morning with the Geelong Advertiser 14km Paradise Run starting after lunch at 1:00pm. For those who enjoy shorter distances, the latter is described as a beautiful run that starts in the main street of Apollo Bay and heads inland across quiet farmland before dipping into the temperate rainforest that is a major feature of the Otway Ranges and finishing at Apollo Bay Pub in the afternoon. Running on Sunday, the second day of the Great Ocean Road Running Festival is a little more uniform. Competitors for the 23km Half Marathon, the 44km Great Ocean Road Marathon, and the 60km Ultra Marathon, all leave at 8am sharp. The half marathoners leave from Kennett River and the marathoners leave from Lorne Pub. A shuttle bus service runs from Apollo Bay to Lorne to get Marathon runners to the start line. This morning service runs between Apollo Bay, Kennett River and Lorne in the morning (departing Apollo Bay and Lorne at 5:45am). There are two departure points in Apollo Bay (Main

St) with one bus heading for Lorne for the marathon runners and the other bus for Kennett River for the start of the half marathon. Obviously, it's important that you make sure to get on the right bus. Return buses travel from Apollo Bay back to Lorne after the event with the final bus leaving at 2.30pm. Runners are required to purchase a bus pass $10 charge during the online event registration process to enable them to use these buses. All the competitors on Sunday finish at the Apollo Bay Pub – said to be one of the most picturesque and iconic pub locations in the country. The atmosphere in Apollo Bay on the second and final day of the festival is reported as 'high energy' especially with an entertaining Pub To Pub Waiters' Challenge, featuring waiters from various food and beverage outlets running in their aprons, balancing bottles on their trays racing each other. After the event buses leave from Apollo Bay from approximately 12pm onwards to Skenes Creek, Kennett River, Wye River and Lorne

Following the start outside the Lorne Surf Lifesaving Club, the opening sections of the marathon course include a series of steady climbs and descents as the road winds from creek crossings at sea level to cuttings on the cliff tops, offering spectacular views over the ocean along the way. Both water and Endura Sports Drink are provided on the 12 drink stations en route. It's spectacular scenery all the way and because there are only about 1,000 entrants in the full marathon, it's never too crowded at the start, but always enough runners so you never feel isolated The field also tends to spread out a lot faster than a city race, meaning access to aid stations is much easier.

Marathon runners pass through a series of small townships en route from Lorne to Apollo Bay. The first of these is Separation Creek which is both a small creek and a settlement of the same name located on relatively gentle slopes, right on the Great Ocean Road. A 250 m long beach lies on the east side of the road, with forested bluffs and rock platforms bordering each end. The creek drains across the southern end of the beach. Next up is Wye River, situated on one of the most spectacular sections of the Great Ocean Road. This is a small coastal town, located on the river it's named after, with a rugged and bushy mountain backdrop. It's where the rainforest meets the sea and is well-noted for its wildlife, beaches and scenery. There's a general store located beside the river, and the town's hotel is perched high above the beach, offering visitors great views while eating and drinking. Scenic views can be enjoyed from Point Sturt, at the southern end of Wye River. The remains of piers built between 1899 and 1910 over the beach and rocks can be observed from here.

Further along the course, the settlement of Kennett River has become known as one of Australia's koala-spotting capitals, thanks to the large numbers of these native animals that make their home in the blue gums that line the main road. Sugarloaf Hill, a prominent, 30 metre high knoll, around which a platform beach runs for 1.3 km is next visible on the right. Runners continue along the coastline through Wongarra, with Sunnyside Road the only road running inland in the area. Much of the northern area of Wongarra is either state forest or lies within the Great Otway National Park. The locality contains scenic tourist destinations: Cape Patton and the Carisbrook Falls. The final settlement encountered is that of Skenes Creek, an idyllic township located 6km east of Apollo Bay on a popular surf beach. If you're camping, your can literally set your tent up right next to the beach, on crown land - offering a safe swimming beach without having to cross a road. As the course progresses towards the finish in Apollo Bay, the hills fall away, the roads flatten out before the streets of the town lined with cheering families, friends and locals provide a contrast to the serenity of most of the run

The Great Ocean Road Running Festival is a very different event to your standard city running festival experience. It's a unique kind of race that you won't get at any of the big-city marathon festivals in Australia. Even the distances are different, most noticeably the 44km Marathon and 23km Half Marathon distances, slightly longer than the standard of 42.195km and 21.096km, respectively. Though, for those aiming to improve their PB, there is an official marathon timing point at the standard distance of 42.195km at the entrance to the Apollo Bay township. There is also the opportunity to stop here and walk the rest of the way to the Apollo Pub! Many follow their run with a dip in the sea, only 100m from the finish line, and after freshening up, re-gathering for the traditional 'Can Too' celebration at one of the local hotels for dinner. Rather than being all about fast times, the event is mainly all about enjoying the festival experience. The fact that it starts outside the iconic Lorne Pub (of Pier-to-Pub fame) at one end and the home stretch lands runners across the finish line outside the Apollo Bay Pub at the other end says it all. Like its Big Sur counterpart in California, it's not a designer-fast course measured to the nearest millimetre without hills or challenges. But as any runner knows a challenging course usually makes it a rewarding course. This is confirmed by the comments from race finishers on marathonguide.com. For example S. R. from Melbourne wrote, 'Don't be put off by the hills and weather - it is a wonderful course with enthusiastic organizers. And if it were easy it would not feel so good!' J. A. from Singapore posted, 'This race is beautiful - truly one of the best roads I have ever run on,' while D. W. from Lorne describing his hometown marathon added, 'The scenery is steep cliff on the left, with million dollar view of the ocean and forest on the right. Amazing really. Everyone should run/drive this road at least once.' It's now on my Bucket List.

ADELAIDE MARATHON

SOUTH AUSTRALIA

MAY

I last visited Adelaide many years ago in the mists of time; 1974 to be precise. In those days the city was known as the 'City of Churches' (though locals kept telling us that there were many more pubs than churches) and was considered something of a rustic backwater by residents of its nearest big-city neighbours in Sydney and Melbourne. Not being particularly interested in religious architecture, I recall spending most of the time sitting in the sun while staying with friends in the beachside suburb of Glenelg, making only the occasional foray into the city centre. The place seemed as dull as ditch-water in those days. The Lonely Planet guidebook has a theory about this, feeling that 'The stuffy, affluent origins of the City of Churches did more to inhibit development than promote it. Bogged down in the old-school doldrums and painfully short on charisma, this was a pious, introspective place.' It would seem things are different nowadays. Adelaide has had a resurgence in the past few years and is now a vibrant and cosmopolitan city with a lively small bar scene reinvigorating the city's laneways. Famous chefs and high-end boutiques have also made Adelaide their new home and it's now full of up-market cafés and multicultural restaurants as well as host to a strong festival calendar. My youngest son

Ross holidayed in Adelaide last year and came home enthusing about his experiences in the city.

Adelaide does not share the convict settlement history of other Australian cities. It was established as a planned colony of free immigrants, promising civil liberties and freedom from religious persecution, based upon the ideas of Edward Gibbon Wakefield. This vision of religious tolerance initially attracted a wide variety of religious practitioners – hence the accolade of 'The City of Churches' - referring to its diversity of faiths rather than the piety of its citizens. Named in honour of Adelaide of Saxe-Meiningen, queen consort to King William IV, the city was founded in 1836 as the planned capital for a freely-settled British province in Australia. Colonel William Light, one of Adelaide's founding fathers, designed the city and chose its location close to the River Torrens in the area originally inhabited by the Kaurna people. Light's design set out Adelaide in a grid layout, interspaced by wide boulevards and large public squares, and entirely surrounded by parklands. Early Adelaide was shaped by prosperity and wealth—until the Second World War, it was Australia's third-largest city. It's now the fifth-most populous city of Australia with an estimated resident population of around 1.35 million, more than 75% of the South Australian population, making it the most centralised population of any state in Australia. The city is noted for its many festivals and sporting events, its food and wine, its long beachfronts, and its large defence and manufacturing sectors. It ranks highly in terms of quality of life being consistently listed in the world's top 10 most livable cities out of 140 cities worldwide by The Economist Intelligence Unit. It was also ranked the most livable city in Australia by the Property Council of Australia in 2011.

Geographically, Adelaide is north of the Fleurieu Peninsula, on the Adelaide Plains between the Gulf St Vincent and the low-lying Mount Lofty Ranges which surround the city. Adelaide stretches 20 km. from the coast to the foothills, and 94 to 104 km. from Gawler at its northern extent to Sellicks Beach in the south. Though not as isolated as, say, Perth, Adelaide is nonetheless a difficult pace to get to when travelling overland. It's at least a one day drive away from any capital cities on the Australian east coast. For those travelling to the marathon, Greyhound Australia run services to Adelaide from Sydney, Melbourne and Alice Springs. The shortest route from Adelaide to Melbourne takes 8-9 hours while The Overland train service to Melbourne takes over 10 hours. For those arriving by air, Adelaide International Airport is around 7km to the west of the city centre. The airport has scheduled international services to Auckland, Hong Kong, Denpasar, Kuala Lumpur, Singapore, Guangzhou China, Doha and Dubai, though it is the only major Australian airport that does not have Qantas international flights. Domestic services and connections are available to most major Australian cities and regional centres via budget airlines Virgin Australia, Jetstar and Tigerair. JetBuses J1, J1A, J1X and J3 link the airport with the city, operating every 15 minutes throughout the day. The city centre can be reached from the airport in 15-25minutes with a ticket costing $5.10 during peak, $3.30 off-peak and includes unlimited transfers within a 2-hour period. Taxis are available outside the terminal, at around $16-20 to the city centre. An extra $3 is added to fares starting at the airport.

    Once in the city centre, the Adelaide Metro bus system is quite comprehensive, and extends out to the Adelaide Hills in the east, down to Maclaren Vale in the south. For the new arrival, the best way to familiarise yourself with your surroundings is to hop on one of the two free 'city loop' bus services providing a scenic tour of the city. These buses weave through the city in opposite directions and are as frequent as every 30 minutes. The clockwise and anticlockwise routes each make about 30 stops taking in all the major cultural and commercial centres, beginning at Victoria Square and including Adelaide Railway Station. Another option for getting around town is the 'Adelaide Free Bikes' system run by Bicycle SA. Just bring a form of photo ID as your deposit in exchange for a rental bike – complete with helmet, lock and maps – and pedal around the city. There are several pick-up hubs around town, the only catch being you must return the bike to the same location you borrowed it from. Those who prefer to walk could consider Adelaide City Council's free downloadable Adelaide City Explorer self-guided walking tours. There are 19 themed trails available; on subjects like historic pubs, flora and fauna, art-deco architecture and public art.

Adelaide has hosted a Marathon since as far back as 1979 when the first event was held as part of the surge of interest in long distance running which spread throughout the world during the 1970s. Numbers in the first Adelaide Marathon almost matched the total number of finishers of a marathon in South Australia to that date, which was 548 from 37 events since 1920. There were 695 entries in the first Adelaide Marathon: 525 starters and 463 finishers of whom 14 were female. For its next edition the race attracted nearly a thousand entries and the numbers kept rising to a peak of 2750 entries for the 1986 event, which was promoted for several years as the 'big one' given that it was the State's sesquicentenary (150 years) of European settlement. However this boom could not last and from 1987 the decline in participation began with 763 finishers in Adelaide, falling to under 500 by 1990. There were only 448 finishers in 2018.

Throughout its history the event has been organised by the South Australian Road Runners Club (SARRC). SARRC was originally established in 1980 specifically for people interested in running the Adelaide Marathon. The Marathon is still its flagship event with 2018 being the 40th running of the race. Distances in the 2018 Adelaide Marathon Festival event included the Full Marathon, Half Marathon, 10km, 5km and 2km Fun Run with all distances receiving Finishers Medals. Largely due to the Adelaide Marathon the club has grown from a local running group to the largest running group in South Australia. SARRC's vision is that every man, woman and child should have an opportunity to run. As an organisation SARRC is modelled on the New York Road Runners where club and events serve runners and walkers of all abilities from beginners to competitive runners. It follows a 'not for profit' model, earning income from hosting a range of 10km, half and full marathon running events, its membership base, and its club and event sponsors.

In 2018 the race moved from its traditional August date to the last weekend in May. It included a new, faster AIMS Certified course that had yet to be finalised less than two weeks before race day. For the first time and due to, what we were informed, was an overwhelming interest in entries, the Marathon was capped at 600 participants and the Half Marathon at 1300 with 50% of entries said to having already been allocated. I found the event website short on detail – particularly for a race organised by a running club whose Committee must, through experience, be aware of runners' need for information. I found it surprising that the course had not been published so close to the event. I wasn't the only one who thought so. Posts by Forum members on the Cool Running, Australia website suggested that others were dissatisfied with the paucity of information on offer. For example one would-be entrant posted, 'Just looked at website as I'm interested in it. Thin bare on information, how can they open registrations for an event with hardly any information except the date!!' and 'I'd prefer things like courses finalised before opening registrations - no problem with announcing a confirmed date as soon as available, but taking money without a course and with a no-refunds policy is a bit rich for mine.' When eventually a course map did appear on the site I couldn't make head nor tail of it. It showed a series of convoluted laps starting and finishing at Adelaide Oval with not a single direction arrow in sight to indicate the direction in which runners were headed. As a serial Marathon Tourist interested as much in what I'm going to see en-route as in running a decent time, I always want to know before entering what a course has to offer. If it offers nothing then I simply don't enter. I'd certainly have been interested in 2017 when the pre-race publicity suggested that the course would, 'showcase Adelaide to approximately 3000 local, national and international runners who will run past the iconic landmarks of the Adelaide Zoo, Adelaide Botanic Gardens, River Torrens and Adelaide Oval.' As it happened that's what the new, revised course did in the end. But, it would have been nice to know this in 2018 before committing to entering.

Entries opened for the Adelaide Marathon Festival 2018 in September the previous year. Super Early Bird entries to the marathon were available for two weeks at $100. These rose to $140 closer to race day. Finishers' medals were included in the entry fee with event T-shirts and singlets costing a further $40 to purchase. Race Bib collection took place at Adelaide Oval on the Friday and Saturday before the event. There was also a Marathon Gala function at the Adelaide Town Hall on the Friday evening, hosted by the Lord Mayor and with a range of special guests to celebrate the successful years of the Marathon and the Future of the event in Adelaide. Entry to this cost $15.

Race day started with the Marathon setting out at 7.30am. Half Marathon runners left at 7.45am with the 10K and 5K runners leaving at 8am and 11.00am respectively. (The event's Flamingo Fun Run takes place on the Saturday.) Marathon runners are given a huge 8 hours in which to complete their course for which pacemakers are provided at 15 minute intervals from 2 hours 30 minutes to 5 hours. Water and Powerade are available at 17 drink stations along the course. All four Sunday events start and finish at the Adelaide Oval – the start is outside the stadium in War Memorial Drive while runners have the pleasure of finishing within the stadium itself. The Adelaide Oval has hosted sporting events at the highest level since Colonial times and its iconic, historic and cultural presence remains today. Hailed as the world's prettiest cricket ground, the Adelaide Oval hosts interstate and international cricket matches in summer, plus national AFL football and state football matches in winter. A wholesale redevelopment has boosted seating capacity to 50,000 and has been a major success story for a footy mad city. Guided 90-minute tours run on non-game days, departing from the Riverbank Stand (south entrance), off War Memorial Drive. The tour includes admission to the famed Bradman Collection which tells the story of Australia's greatest ever cricketer and provides an insight into life in Australia from the 1920s to the 1970s. The venue also plays hosts to a number of other major functions, events and concerts with big name acts like The Rolling Stones, AC/DC, Guns N' Roses and Ed Sheeran appearing there in recent years. The iconic oval can be reached a short walking distance from Adelaide's CBD on a new foot bridge which links from the Festival Centre crossing the River Torrens

Virtually all of the marathon route is confined within the broad area of unique parklands bordering both sides of the

River Torrens, north of the Adelaide Railway Station. It is predominantly on road, but also uses the wide, sealed paths along the beautiful river. Runners pass close to both Old and New Parliament House as well as such important buildings as the Adelaide Convention Centre, the Adelaide Exhibition Centre and the city's Casino as well as the stately mansions that overlook the Adelaide Golf Course. Highlights of the course are largely confined to the eastern section of the course. Foremost among these are Elder Park, Adelaide Zoo and the city's Botanic Gardens. Situated on the southern bank of the River Torrens and bordered by the Adelaide Festival Centre and North Terrace, Elder Park is a beautiful urban park with an iconic rotunda erected in 1882, plus walking trails and a lake with paddle boats. The idea of a rotunda by the River Torrens was suggested in the early 1880s as part of a plan by the Adelaide City Council to improve the river and its surrounds. The council proposed to dam the river, create a lake and construct a public esplanade to the west of City Bridge. Wealthy businessman, pastoralist, parliamentarian and philanthropist Sir Thomas Elder heard of these plans when he was holidaying in the United Kingdom and ordered a rotunda to be made and sent to the colony, asking the council to accept it as a mark of his appreciation of the improvements they had carried out and his interest in the city. The popular Popeye boat offers a 40 minute round trip cruise departing from Elder Park, travelling west to the Torrens Weir, turning around and travelling back up to the Adelaide Zoo before returning to the landing. The Park is also the home of the annual Christmas Carols by Candlelight for Adelaide and also hosts Symphony under the Stars and the Adelaide Festival of Art.

Further to the east the course bisects two of Adelaide's most popular tourist attractions: Adelaide's Zoo and Botanic

Garden. The zoo is the second oldest zoo in the nation and represents a significant part of South Australia's heritage and social history. Since Adelaide Zoo first opened to the public in 1883, generations of South Australians have shared in the wonder of a visit to its facilities. The zoo retains many of its original buildings, garden design and features, some of which are state heritage listed places on the South Australian Heritage Register including the front entrance on Frome Road and the former Elephant House. The zoo is also a botanical garden and the grounds contain significant exotic and native flora, including a Moreton Bay fig planted in 1877. It was established at a time of great resurgence and interest in natural history and was modelled on the major European zoos of that time, particularly, Regents Park Zoo in London. The zoo contains around 1800 exotic and native mammals, birds and reptiles. There are free walking tours half-hourly feeding sessions and a children's zoo. Wang Wang and Fu Ni are Australia's only giant pandas and always draw a crowd. Other highlights include the nocturnal and reptile houses. The zoo's most recent enclosures are in the second phase of the South-East Asia exhibit, known as Immersion, providing visitors with the experience of walking through the jungle, with Sumatran tigers and orangutans seemingly within reach. The Zoo is open from 9:30am – 5pm every day of the year, including Christmas and all public holidays. Adult entry is $36, a child ticket costs $15. Family tickets are $91.50.

Opposite the zoo, runners will see The Adelaide Botanic Garden, a 51-hectare public garden at the north-east corner of the Adelaide city centre. It encompasses a fenced garden on North Terrace (between the Royal Adelaide Hospital and the National Wine Centre) and behind it the Botanic Park (adjacent to the Adelaide Zoo). The Garden is part of Colonel William Light's vision for the planned city. However, it wasn't until 1854, after a public appeal to Governor Sir Henry Young that gardens were established at the current location. The garden's design was heavily influenced by the Royal Gardens at Kew, England and those in Versailles, France. The Garden is described as an oasis of beautiful landscaped gardens with majestic avenues leading to stunning architecture. This includes: the 1989-built Bicentennial Conservatory, the largest single span glasshouse in the Southern Hemisphere, home to a number of endangered rainforest plants and the beautiful Palm House, one of the last of its kind remaining in the world, featuring an interesting variety of plants from the island of Madagascar and the Amazon Waterlily Pavilion, whose design was influenced by the leaf structure of the plant of the same name. Visitors can discover the best of what the Gardens have to offer on a free guided walk with an expert on most days of the year.

I've been advised that the best place to head to for post-race refreshment is the area around Gouger Street This offers a wide range of tastes to suit many budgets in a variety of Asian, Italian and seafood restaurants as well as upmarket French, Argentinian and many other choices. Gouger Street incorporates Adelaide's 'Chinatown Arch' which fronts a large number of budget eating options. Market Plaza Food Court, located within the historic Central Market in Adelaide's Chinatown is a favourite among locals and tourists. Here you can find a wide variety of Chinese, Japanese, Singaporean, Malaysian and Korean food under one roof. Gouger Street is also home to an increasing number of bars and pubs. Finding somewhere for a decent beer in Adelaide presents no problem. It has a higher per capita density of pubs than any other major Australian city, with more than 70 pubs in the city centre alone. There are pubs and bars dotted all around the CBD, but a few districts are worth singling out. Rundle Street and its neighbouring area known simply as 'The East End' have a number of popular pubs. Hindley St used to be notorious as the seedy home of Adelaide's strip clubs and biker bars, but it, and 'The West End' have undergone a renaissance. The eastern end of Hindley Street is more mainstream, whereas the western end, west of Morphett Street has a few trendier and more alternative venues. The seedy places are still there, but so too is a university campus and a number of trendy bars and clubs. To the north, O'Connell Street is home to a few of North Adelaide's popular pubs. While you're there you must try Cooper's Sparkling Ale – 5.8% of pure pleasure – the first beer I look for on my visits to Australia.

WESTERN SYDNEY MARATHON

NEW SOUTH WALES

JUNE

I hadn't heard of this event before travelling back to Australia in 2014 with intentions to run in both the Sydney and Melbourne Marathons that year. It came as a pleasant surprise to see that, at the time, this relatively new event had been conveniently placed exactly two weeks after the main Sydney event and two weeks before the one in Melbourne. Though I wasn't entirely sure in what part of Western Sydney the race was taking place the opportunity to run it couldn't be missed. For those unfamiliar with the geography of New South Wales, Sydney is subdivided into a number of regions which are administered as Sydney's boroughs. Currently there are 18 of these boroughs one of which is known as Western Sydney. This is a major region of Sydney covering 5,800 square kilometres with an estimated resident population of over 1.5 million people. The term 'Western Sydney' has a number of different definitions, although the one consistently used is that the region is composed of the nine local government authorities which are all members of the Western Sydney Regional Organisation of Councils (WSROC). Penrith City Council, one of the of the Western Sydney Marathon's major supporters, is among these nine local government authorities. The whole region lies in the Cumberland Plain, a relatively flat area lying to the west of

Sydney CBD stretching westwards towards the Blue Mountains. European settlement in the area dates from 1788 when the first farms were established. Gradual growth took place during the early 1800s, with land used mainly for timber-getting, sheep and cattle farming, crop growing and market gardening. Growth increased in the late 1800s and the early 1900s, aided by the opening of railway lines, improved access, the establishment of many industries and tourism. Significant residential development occurred during the 1950s and 1960s, spurred by immigration, industrial growth and the construction of public housing estates. The population continued to increase from the early 1990s, rising from about 1.06 million in 1991 to nearly 1.52 million in 2016.

Results for The Western Sydney Marathon are shown on the website from 2013 onwards so I'm led to surmise that this was the first year in which the race was held. The venue is the Sydney International Regatta Centre on the outskirts of Penrith with the programme now consisting of a number of races intended to cater for all ages and abilities: Marathon, Half Marathon, a 10km 'Lap the Lake,' a 5km Family Fun Run and a 2.5km Youth Dash. Originally held in October the event has now changed to a June date. According to the organisers, the NSW Government Office of Sport, 'The Western Sydney Marathon celebrates health, fitness and active lifestyles.' The promotional literature reports that it's intended as a fun and festive day out for the whole family with a health and fitness expo, activities for the kids during races, a jumping castle, entertainment, massage, market and food stalls. The event is described as, 'About bringing the community together.' It did this in 2017 by attracting 150 runners to the Marathon, 324 finished the Half Marathon with 368 completing the 10K race and 415 in the 5K Fun Run. A total of 1,257 participants on the day – a much higher number than on my visit three years earlier, so the event is making progress in achieving its aims.

Purpose-built for the 2000 Sydney Olympics and Paralympics, with one of the best rowing and sprint kayak courses in the world, the International Regatta Centre site sprawls over 178 hectares and boasts scenic views of Penrith Lakes, the Lower Blue Mountains and surrounding parkland. The Centre was built on land that used to be a quarry for gravel and sandstone until it was redeveloped as part of the Penrith Lakes Scheme. The goal of the scheme was to turn the area into a recreational space for the local community The naturally beautiful setting offers a large selection of event facilities including outdoor and undercover exhibition areas, a 1,100-seat spectator pavilion, giant LED screen, multiple meeting and private function rooms and a village green with natural amphitheatre. The Centre also hosts 5km walking and cycling paths for recreational use and launch pontoons for water access making the Centre an important venue for outdoor entertainment and recreation both on and off the water.

Mo and I travelled to this one from our son's apartment in Manly on the day before the event. It is possible to get there and back on the same day (Saturday) via trains leaving from Sydney's Central Station at the ungodly hours of 04:24 and 04:56, arriving in Penrith at 05:14 and 06:06 respectively. We preferred to take the more leisurely option of sailing upriver on one of the River ferries that leave at regular intervals from Circular Quay to Parramatta. The ferry ride under the Harbour Bridge and up the Parramatta River makes the trip to Parramatta worthwhile simply for the journey itself. This allowed us time for a good look around Parramatta, a city in its own right within the Sydney Metropolitan Area and the second oldest European settlement on the Australian mainland. We were impressed by what we saw and wished we could have had a longer stay. Parramatta is on the upper reaches of the Parramatta River that flows into Sydney Harbour. Located 24 km from Sydney CBD it was the earliest vice-regal home of colonial Sydney. An agricultural settlement was established there within weeks of the first fleet arriving from Britain. The present day Sydney CBD was established as the colony's port settlement to service the more desirable Parramatta which became the preferred home of governors and the privileged free settlers in the early years of the colony. Most of Australia's earliest colonial buildings remain standing and open for visiting. In fact, there are more heritage listed buildings in Parramatta than Sydney's historic Rocks quarter. The city has a vibrant multicultural community, lively bars and restaurants along the trendy Church Street, elegant parks, Riverside Theatres and other attractions that make it a worthwhile visitor destination within Greater Sydney.

From Parramatta we continued by train to Penrith and our overnight accommodation at the Nepean River Holiday Park. Situated at the foot of the Blue Mountains, Penrith is located on the banks of the Nepean River about 50 kilometres west of the Sydney central business district on the outskirts of the Cumberland Plain. It's the administrative seat of the local government area of the City of Penrith and one of only four cities within the Sydney metropolitan area. We were as unimpressed by the place as we had been impressed by Parramatta. A Friday evening trolling up and down Penrith High Street looking for somewhere suitable to eat and drink is not my idea of fun. In the end we settled for one quick drink in a dead-end pub and a take-out pizza before heading back for an early night. While the city centre itself had little of interest if we'd be staying longer I'm sure we would have made the effort to investigate some of the river-based activities on offer. For example, The Nepean River has an interesting walking track, including a 7km loop, which is part is part of the larger 'Great River Walk' a planned larger walk which in future will cover 570km, linking the river's mouth at Broken Bay to its headwaters at Lake Bathurst, south of Goulburn. Walkers can stop along the way at one of the lookouts or seating areas to watch the boats, birds and other wildlife. I also like the idea of a cruise along the Nepean River on a romantic old-world style paddle wheeler the Nepean Belle. Designed on the traditional Mississippi sternwheelers, the Belle has just celebrated 35 years of cruising the Nepean River up to the World Heritage listed Nepean Gorge in the Blue Mountains National Park. Next time maybe – I'd like to think that I'll do this marathon again someday.

Entry fees for the marathon start at $75 before the end of March rising to $95 on race day. The entry fee includes a finisher's medal, race number with timing chip, downloadable certificate, a recovery area with bottled water, fruit and lolly bag, drink stations around the course, access to the expo and on-site medical services and free parking or return transfer from Penrith railway station. The latter is important. If you're without your own vehicle don't make the mistake that I did and travel to Registration the day before the race. I wished I'd ignored the organiser's warning that this is necessary to avoid congestion and long queues and simply registered on the morning of the race. There was no congestion and no long queues. One of the negatives of the event's location is that The Regatta Centre is around 7km from central Penrith and inaccessible by public transport. We forked-out unnecessarily for expensive return taxi fares to Friday registration when we could have just as easily have taken the free shuttle bus on the Saturday morning. On race day these buses operate a continual loop between Penrith Station and the Regatta

Centre. The bus departs from the northern side of the Station approximately every 15 minutes. The first bus will depart Penrith Station at 5.00am. The last bus will depart Penrith Station at 1.00pm.The bus stop is located at Penrith Station Northern exit. Again, don't make the same mistake as a bunch of us did in 2014 when we stood for ages outside the southern main entrance to the station wondering why the buses hadn't shown up. The Registration Area is located at the Centre, adjacent to the Lakeside Restaurant, behind the grandstand. Just make sure that you arrive at least 30 minutes before your race. The venue's gates open at 5am and it's approximately a 15 minute walk from where the shuttle bus parks to the event expo area.

I found The Western Sydney Marathon to be very much a case of 'after the Lord Mayor's Show' compared to the hype and excitement of its big city neighbour 50 kilometres down the road. With a field scarcely reaching a hundred as to the tens of thousands in the Sydney Marathon, it's one of those low-key, minimum-fuss events that I much prefer to run. In 2014, of the various events on the day, the marathon started at 7am with a 6-hour time limit, the half marathon at 7.30am, the 5K Family Fun Run at 9am and the 10K at 9.30am. (I believe that a fifth event, the 2.5K Youth Dash, has been added in recent years) This meant that there was always fresher legs charging past you on the multi-lap course. The marathon was a 6-lap course around the Regatta Centre with the first 2km of each lap being up and back around an artificial loop outside the park. The next 5km of each lap took us round the pancake-flat stretches of the man-made rowing lake. The big concern for most of us was the weather. Sydney had been enjoying its hottest spring for 100 years and temperatures of 28 degrees were forecast on the day. As things turned out, cloud cover kept conditions sensible for the first two laps.

Once this burned off conditions became uncomfortably hot and the best we could do was to take a 'runner's shower' (pouring cold water over the head) at each of the four water and electrolyte drink stations on each lap.

The boredom of the long stretches around the lake was alleviated by sparkling blue of its water and the magnificent views of the Blue Mountains to the west. An added bonus was that the repetitive nature of the course meant that supporters were able to hand us extra drinks and gels on our way around. Just as in Sydney two weeks earlier, I was able to maintain a steady 6 minute per kilometre pace for most of the way – slowing down to 7 min per km in the final stages as the heat took hold. It was a great experience finishing in front of the Grandstand where Redgrave and Pinsent created Olympic history in 2000. I was in Sydney at the time watching athletics at the nearby Olympic Stadium and clearly recall the respect afforded to the pair by the Aussie public (traditionally never ones to appreciate a British victory). For our efforts we received a rather nice hat that I still wear, a rather tacky medal and were treated at the finish to a welcome Aussie BBQ to conclude a memorable day in the sun. It was then back on the shuttle bus to Penrith for a couple of beers before catching the train to Katoomba to stay with long-term friends at their home in the Blue Mountains. Marathon Tourism at its best – you can't beat it!

CHRISTCHURCH MARATHON

SOUTH ISLAND, NEW ZEALAND

JUNE

The city of Christchurch has been in the news a great deal during the past few years due to the terrible series of earthquakes that decimated the city in 2010 and 2011 resulting in the deaths of 185 people inhabitants and the wholesale destruction of thousands of buildings in Christchurch city centre. Apart from the obvious fact that Christchurch's citizens have had more important things on their minds than running marathons, it goes without saying that the ongoing rebuilding and redevelopment work has greatly affected the organisation of the Christchurch Marathon. Seven years on from the earthquakes Christchurch hosted the 38th edition of the event to which runners are beginning to return in increasing numbers. More than 4300 runners and walkers from 19 countries entered the various events on 2018's ASB Christchurch Marathon programme, up 300 from 2017. Around 1000 entrants were visitors to Christchurch, ensuring that the event brings significant economic benefits to the city as it recovers from the devastation. 'We're really pleased with the entry,' says race director Chris Cox. 'It shows that the event is finally starting to recover following the earthquakes.'

Christchurch Marathon's history is well documented on the event's website. It's a story worth telling. I wish more race organisers would do this – it helps satisfy the curiosity of us marathon enthusiasts who like to know how an event has developed over the years. What follows is an attempt to summarise what's written there.

The first Christchurch Marathon was inspired by the 1974 Christchurch Commonwealth Games event, often described as one of the greatest races in history. I remember it well – mainly because I was cheering for pre-race favourite, Great Britain's Ron Hill, an inspiring figure in UK marathon history at the time. Hill didn't win, instead fellow Brit. Ian Thompson ran what was then the second fastest marathon of all time. Behind him New Zealander Jack Foster was dragged along to a New Zealand record of 2hrs 11min 18secs to secure the silver medal meaning that, at 41, Foster became the fastest Masters Marathoner in history. More than 44 years later, Thompson's effort still remains the fastest marathon run on New Zealand soil. The race inspired something of a running boom in Christchurch and in 1978 local long distance runner Don Cameron and the Long Distance Running Club of New Zealand decided to harness that inspiration into an annual marathon. The race, which attracted 500 entrants, was called the Sedley Wells Midwinter Marathon, the first New Zealand marathon to combine a half marathon and the first New Zealand marathon to welcome recreational runners alongside official club runners. The event was still not quite what Cameron had envisaged. Council traffic restrictions had forced them to run a two-lap course from QEII stadium around Horseshoe Lake, then alongside the Avon River on River Road before returning on Avonside Drive. By 1981 the event was almost up to 1000 participants and so successful that the City Council allowed Cameron and co-organiser Rod Rutherford to resurrect the original historic Commonwealth Games course. The race was rebranded as the 'City of Christchurch International

Marathon.' This started at QEII Stadium and followed the Avon River through the central city and Hagley Park, then up Memorial Avenue to Christchurch Airport and back. It was flat, fast and scenic and the same basic route that the event used until the 2010 earthquakes.

From 500 runners in 1978, by the year 2000 the event had grown to 3500 participants. In 1996 the event had been reinvigorated with a shift of the start/finish venue from QEII Stadium to the iconic Christchurch Town Hall. Based in the central city, the event created more presence in the community and also became a destination event for the running tourist. The introduction of a 10k fun run, walking events and Kids options saw the event grow every year to 2010, when 5800 participants from 12 countries toed the start line. The earthquakes of 2010 and 2011 that had created havoc in the city effectively ruined the Avon River route of the traditional Commonwealth Games course. The Christchurch Town Hall start/finish venue was condemned and the Avon River roads that the event used were ruined, as were the neighbourhoods the course passed through. At the time they were part of The Central City Red Zone, a public exclusion zone in the city implemented following the earthquakes. In 2013, the area was officially renamed the CBD Rebuild Zone by government agencies, but remained known as the Red Zone. It gradually shrank in size and the last cordons were removed on 30 June 2013, 859 days after the last earthquake. The challenge for the organisers was to find a new course that didn't add to the City's stresses but that also had a venue big enough to host the event. In 2011 the race was moved to Lincoln University, on the outskirts of the City. 3759 participants lined up at Lincoln, less that the record 5800 entries of the previous year, but given the eight week build up and earthquake stresses, it was a huge success. In 2015, after four years of hard work behind the scenes, the Christchurch Airport Marathon (as it was then known) returned to the central city when approval was given for a fast, flat and spectator-friendly route that toured famous Christchurch landmarks such as Cathedral Square, Hagley Park, Oxford Terrace, Canterbury Museum and the Avon River. With minor modifications to fit in with ongoing redevelopment work, the course has remained basically the same since then. I can find no specific, detailed description of the course on the 2018 website, just the following rejoinder: 'Due to ongoing Christchurch rebuild parts of the course may change prior to race day. So check back during race week & check the race programme. Participants do need to be aware that parts of the course run through the Red Zone where road surfaces are not first rate. We will make improvements where dangerous, but there may be short sections of gravel where roads have been left unsealed since the earthquakes.'

Christchurch is the largest city in the South Island of New Zealand and, with a population over 350,000, is the third largest city in New Zealand after Auckland and Wellington. Known for its English heritage shown in its fine older buildings, especially the neo-gothic buildings in the cultural precinct along Worcester Boulevard and Rolleston Ave, the city was established on the edge of the Canterbury Plains in 1850 by Anglican English settlers. The agricultural industry based on the surrounding farming country has always been at the economic core of Christchurch and is responsible for much of its prosperity. The beautiful River Avon, followed by marathon runners both out of and back into the city, meanders through the central city and disrupts the otherwise regular rectangular layout of the city streets. On its banks are cycling paths, the green expanse of Hagley Park and Christchurch Botanic Gardens. The large number of public parks and well-developed residential gardens with many trees have given Christchurch the name of 'The Garden City.' Both the Park and the 30-hectare Gardens feature prominently on the marathon route. Hagley Park is well known as a site for sports such as golf, cricket, netball, and rugby, and for open-air concerts by local bands and orchestras. Hagley Oval, located within the southern portion of Hagley Park, has been used on-and-off as a venue for local, national and international cricket matches for decades, and was upgraded in 2014 as part of preparation for the 2015 Cricket World Cup. Nearby, close to The Arts Centre, is one of the most significant collections of heritage buildings in New Zealand with the city's award-winning Christchurch Botanic Gardens offer a relaxing inner-city escape. The Central City, which was fully closed off following the earthquakes, opened in stages and was reopened in June 2013 - though there are still some streets closed off due to earthquake damage, infrastructure repair work, and damaged buildings. After the major rebuild most areas are now accessible and the city remains a major gateway to the rest of the South Island.

Christchurch International Airport is a major transit airport for international and domestic travellers. There are international services to and from Australia, China, Cook Islands, Fiji, Singapore, Thailand and United Arab Emirates. For those who want to see more of the country before or after the marathon there are also frequent daily, direct, domestic flights to and from Auckland, Dunedin, Invercargill, Nelson, Queenstown, Rotorua and Wellington. There is a regular public bus service from the airport to the city centre costing around $8 for the 20-30 minute trip. These operate half-hourly during the week and at least hourly on weekends. A door-to-door shuttle bus service to all parts of Christchurch is also available for about $25 for the first person and $4 per subsequent passenger. Taxis from outside the terminal building cost about $45 to the city centre. The other two large cities in New Zealand, Wellington and Auckland, are both situated on the North Island and both are considerable travelling distances from Christchurch: 440 kilometres and 1,704 kilometres respectively. If you don't have your own vehicle, the journey to Wellington could take as long as 9 hours: 5 hours by train to Picton and then 4 hours by ferry across Picton Sound. In fine weather both legs are said to be incredibly scenic. The first half of the train trip hugs the coast, crossing the weird landscape of the Grassmere salt ponds & then in and out of tunnels and across rocky beaches where New Zealand Fur seals can be seen. Only about an hour of the ferry trip is in open water, out of sight of land while the last hour is through the beautiful Marlborough Sounds where dolphins occasionally accompany the ferry. From Wellington it's approximately a further 12-hour journey by bus or train to Auckland.

Entry to the 2019 edition of the Christchurch Marathon was set at $95. Race Pack Pick Up is on the Saturday at the Event Village, Cathedral Square, Christchurch. Participants driving from out of town on race morning are permitted to pick up the race pack on race morning from 7:00am to 7:45am. All activities on race weekend are based at the Christchurch Town Hall on Kilmore Street. This includes the pre-race registration, start, finish and prize giving. A secure bag storage area is also available inside the Town Hall. Entertainment, sponsor displays, event merchandise and vendors with food and beverages available all weekend. On race day the three main events: Marathon, Half Marathon and 10K start simultaneously at 8:00am. There are also a variety of Kids' Fun events from noon onwards. All events Start outside the Christchurch Town Hall, on Kilmore Street, facing east with the start area divided up into zones based on runners' predicted time. All events finish outside the Town Hall, heading west on Kilmore St. Officially, Marathon runners are given 6 hours in which to complete their race. Participants on the course after this time will be marshalled on to footpaths and will from then on be running unofficially without course controls and at their own risk and responsibility. No pacers are provided for the full distance event but Pace Teams are available to aid the Half Marathon with the expectation being that 10k and Full Marathoners will also benefit until they turn off. To give you some idea of numbers participating, 442 completed the Marathon in 2018, there were 1,702 finishers in the Half Marathon, 92 in the Half Marathon Walk, 1,315 completed the 10K race with a further 223 in a 10K Walk.

The course is difficult to describe without the assistance of a map for readers to follow. Basically, it consists of 3 loops, all of about 10km, one of which marathon competitors have to run twice. After leaving Christchurch Town Hall runners in all three main events first complete an initial loop of 10km close to the centre of town. This goes through the city centre initially before heading west for a circuit of North Hagley Park and return. After the 10K runners finish both the Full and Half marathoners head off out of the city following the river along Kilmore Street and Avonside Drive to around the 16km mark where the Half Marathoners turn and 'loop' (this is the 2nd of the loops) back to their finish. Full marathoners continue eastwards on a 3rd loop which takes them around Avondale Golf Course and Avondale Park before returning back along the river to around the 26km mark. Here they turn into the 2nd loop at McBratney's Road, running back towards the finish before turning again at approximately 32km to re-run the 2nd loop (are you still with me?) to the finish in Cathedral Square.

Apart from what they can see on their way around the course most runners will be interested in finding out what else Christchurch has to offer. Cathedral Square is one of the best places to start. Known locally simply as the 'Square,' Cathedral Square is the geographical centre and heart of the city where the city's Anglican Cathedral is located. The Square is regarded as the very centre of Christchurch, attached to the historic Worcester Boulevard, the metropolitan Colombo Street and close to the meandering Avon River. Sitting right at its centre is the statue of John Robert Godley, the founder of Christchurch and Canterbury. Recently, to commemorate the new millennium and its coincidence with the 150th Anniversary of this Foundation, an 18m high sculpture named 'The Chalice' was erected in the square. Forty-two leaf patterns featuring different native plants make up the Chalice, designed by prominent New Zealand artist Neil Dawson. The area around the Square is a good place to eat while in the city with a variety of restaurants as well as food stalls, cafes and bars. There's also a daily market in the Square selling everything from Possum Fur garments, to affordable clothes and greenstone. Historic trams leave from here taking visitors on a loop circuit of the best central city attractions. Your ticket allows you to hop on-and-off at different stops over two consecutive days. The romantic-at-heart can dine on board in the evening.

For those on a budget, I'm told that the token attraction to visit is the city's admission-free Canterbury Museum adjoining the Botanic Gardens. The Museum includes colonial, Maori and natural history sections, an Antarctic exploration display as well as visiting exhibitions. Visitors can experience New Zealand's rich cultural and natural heritage, see rare Maori artefacts and the stories behind them and tour Antarctic Gallery celebrating the heroic age of discovery and exploration. There's also a replica of an early Christchurch Street that transports you back in time with the sights and sounds of pioneering days. Another free-entry option one block east of the Botanic Gardens is the Christchurch Art Gallery. This spectacular facility opened in 2003 is the largest in the South Island, with over 5000 items and visiting exhibitions.

At the time of writing, the recent earthquakes have opened up a whole new tourism experience catering for those curious to find out more about their impact on the city. Earthquake Tourism Tours of affected sites are now available, although visitors can also make their own way to sites of significance such as Christchurch Cathedral, the Catholic Basilica and the Cardboard Cathedral. A new visitor attraction, the Quake City Museum provides a deeper understanding of the aftermath of the 2011 and 2012 earthquakes via objects, photos & first person audio accounts. Quake City (entry $20) charts the extraordinary response of the emergency services, international rescue teams, the thousands of volunteers who pitched in to help and the incredible resilience of Canterbury's communities. Exhibits include some of the objects which have defined the Canterbury earthquakes including the spire of Christchurch Cathedral and the railway station clocks which stopped at 1.51 pm on 22 February 2012. The rebuild section of the exhibition brings the visitor up to date with progress in regenerating the city and the recovery projects underway.

An even more poignant reminder of the earthquakes can be seen by visiting the 185 Empty White Chairs Earthquake Memorial - a simple but moving memorial to the victims of the quake located on a site where a church once stood. The story behind the chairs is an interesting one. On the day of the earthquake's first anniversary, local artist Peter Majendie arranged 185 empty chairs that he had painted white on the site of the demolished Oxford Terrace Baptist Church. Envisaged as a short-term installation, this unofficial memorial has become a major tourist attraction in Christchurch. The day after the installation, the local newspaper The Press reported that the artist's intention was for the memorial to stay for a week. The artist himself said later that he thought the chairs should stay for three weeks. As things turned out, it preceded the official earthquake memorial—the Canterbury Earthquake National Memorial—by five years. It's said that Majendie's main inspiration for the installation came from paintings by Vincent van Gogh of empty chairs, representing their owners' different personalities. Further inspiration came from the Field of Empty Chairs, part of the Oklahoma City National Memorial, and the chairs in New York's Bryant Park. It's reported that many locals would prefer to turn the temporary installation into a permanent fixture.

Runners looking for an immediate carbohydrate load after the event simply need to walk south from the finish and turn right into Hereford Street to find two of the best burger joints in the city: BurgerFuel (a chain described elsewhere in this book) and Wendy's Hamburgers – another fast-food chain offering, among other things, a Low Carb Burger for $9.20, a Big Bacon Classic for $9.50 and a huge Triple Burger for $13.70. Not much farther away in Lichfield Street is the Pot Sticker Dumpling Bar. Apparently, Pot sticker comes from the street name for pan fried dumplings. The café/restaurant offers dumpling dough around fresh cooked prawns or free range meats, ready to dip into hot chili sauce. Dumplings with names like Porkie Coriander, Chick'n Cori and Beef Root sell at 6 for $10 or 12 for $18. They make a change from the usual fare. For those looking for somewhere a little more formal Francesca's Italian Restaurant a short walk north-east of the finish in Gloucester Street offers a range of thin base pizzas cooked in a wood fired pizza oven for between $22 and $25. Keep on walking northwards towards the river and you'll find Pomeroy's Old Brewery Inn. This is described as a comfortable and traditional English-style pub that offers an unsurpassed range of hand-picked beers including the best of New Zealand's craft beers complemented by imported favourites. It also serves its own craft beer on tap. I liked the sound of their 5.5%ABV Oatmeal Stout for $11.50. There's also a 7%ABV Unconditional Love IPA from Wellington's Garage Project micro-brewery for $13 and Pomeroy's own 4.8%ABV American Amber Red Ale for $10 per pint. No guesses as to where I'll be heading after the marathon.

TRARALGON MARATHON

VICTORIA

JUNE

Though there's not a great deal at this event's location of interest to Marathon Tourists, I can't leave this one off any description of Australian marathons– its longevity deserves respect. The Traralgon Marathon is the oldest continuously running marathon in Australia having been first run in 1968 as the sanctioned Victorian Country Championship. The race has been put on by the Traralgon Harriers Club from the very beginning and while there were earlier marathons in Australia none of them are still being held. 34 runners paid 30 cents each to enter the 1968 event of which 18 finished, including five local Harriers. The inaugural race was an all-male affair, won by Barry Sawyer in 2:26:53. On the second running, competitors were greeted by awful weather with visibility reportedly down to a few metres. Of the 26 starters only 14 finished. It wasn't until a decade after the first race, that women began competing with Patricia Cooper being the first official female runner and winner of the event. For the 50th anniversary in 2017 around 600 runners participated across the events on the programme with virtually an even split between male and female competitors.

The Traralgon Marathon has attracted a dedicated following of athletes who continue to run it year-on-year. The event has had some well-known runners take part including famous Australian Boxer Johnny Famechon, Ultra-marathon runner Cliff Young and World Champion distance runner, Derek Clayton who still holds the race record of 2:13:39 in 1970. Clayton apparently also did the race as a warm up for the Mexico Olympics in October 1968. He broke the world record for the second occasion in 1969 at Antwerp in a time of 2:08:33 and it stood for almost 12 years afterward. 2018 saw the 51st edition of the event and though the course has changed a number of times throughout its history it has been run in an out and back format to Toongabbie for many years. In 2016, for what the organisers describe as, 'In a bid to overcome safety issues, attract more people to the event and promote the region,' it moved away from the main road onto the Gippsland Plains Rail Trail but essentially still follows the same out and back format.

Traralgon is a city in the Latrobe Valley, West Gippsland, Victoria around162 kilometres south-east of Melbourne via the Princes Highway. With a population of just over 25,000 it's the largest and fastest growing city in the greater Latrobe Valley area, which is home to most of Victoria's power generation facilities. First settled in the 1840s, the origin of the name Traralgon is uncertain. It is popularly believed to be derived from words from the Gunai language: tarra meaning 'river' and algon meaning 'little fish' though I've also read that its name is Aboriginal for 'crane feeding on frogs.' The area around Traralgon was first settled by Europeans in the 1840s soon after being explored by Count Paweł Strzelecki on his return from exploring the Snowy Mountains. Due to the Latrobe Valley having relatively high rainfall, the land is very fertile, and farming was quickly established. As with much of central and western Gippsland, this was mainly dairy farming. The area was originally settled in the 1840s as an agricultural and pastoral centre but grew during the gold rushes due to its important location on the road from Melbourne to Sale. In 1877 the railway line from Melbourne was completed with a railway station at Traralgon giving the town a major economic boost. Further development resulted from the expansion of the power generation industry following World War II. This included large expansions at Yallourn and Hazelwood Power Stations and the construction of the massive Loy Yang Power Station in the 1970s and 1980s. The latter, together with an open-cut coal mine, is a short drive south of the town. The Hyland Highway passes right through the complex and a couple of visitor lookouts are provided for visitors to marvel at the massive scale of coal mining and electricity generation. The power station's two chimneys at 260 metres high - roughly the same height as Melbourne's Rialto Towers – are a major feature of the landscape. In recent years Traralgon has grown to service Victoria's energy, and the local surrounding agricultural, pastoral, papermaking and timber industries. It's described as the region's entertainment capital with an expanding choice of dining options and a thriving pub and club scene with sidewalk cafes, restaurants and shopping arcades marking the commercial centre of the city.

The best way to get from Melbourne to Traralgon is by V-line train from Flinders Street station. Direct services depart hourly, and operate every day. The journey takes approximately 2 hours 11 minutes and costs between $13 and $25. Alternatively, for around the same price, V-Line also operates a bus from Melbourne to Traralgon 3 times a day. The journey takes approximately 2 hours and 20 minutes. Accommodation options include central motels such as the 3.5-star City Gardens Motel and the 3.5-star Connells Motel & Serviced Apartments both of which charge around £170 for a 3-night stay (Friday to Monday) over the marathon weekend. The 4-star Bridges on Argyle Hotel a 10-minute walk from the train station costs around £270 for the same period (all booked online in advance by UK visitors)

The 51st Traralgon Marathon and Running Festival in 2018 included three events: the Marathon, a Half Marathon and a 10K race. There was also a Kid's 2K run. Marathon entry costs ranged from $80 until the beginning of May, then a standard entry of $100 until June with entries climbing to $140 on race weekend. Bib Pickup was available at Traralgon Recreation Reserve from 5:00 to 7:30pm on the Saturday and from the same venue between 6:30 to 7:40am on race morning. One of the features of this event is that it offers an early start to slower marathon runners. This is because the events traffic management permit is only approved until 12:35pm. Runners who will run the marathon in slower than 4:30 hours are to make an early start at 7:05am following a race briefing at 6:55am. Bib collection for these entrants is available from 6:30-6:50am. Anyone who intends to take advantage of the early start option must inform the organisers in writing prior to race day. I had a wry smile at the following note posted on the event website: 'Due to likely cloudy and dark conditions early starters should wear appropriately light/visible clothing so that they are visible by motorists. The race directors reserve the right to prevent early starters from starting the race if clothing isn't considered appropriately visible for the weather conditions on the day.' It concludes, 'The final and most important rule of all is to have fun!' This is definitely not a large event in terms of numbers of participants. In 2018 only 76 competitors 'had fun' finishing the Full Marathon (53 males and 23 females), 171 finished the Half Marathon, 193 completed the 10K race and a further 24 enjoyed the Kid's Run

After the early starters have left, the remaining marathoners leave at 8:05am, followed by the Half Marathon at 9:05am, the Kid's Race at 9:15am and 10K runners at 9:40am. The start and finish location for all events is at the Traralgon Recreation Reserve which incorporates parking, toilets, change rooms and spectator access. All three events are an out and back format. Only the first and last 5km or so are on road with the remainder of the course being run on a hard packed grave surface. All runners will head around the south east side of the Traralgon Oval before leaving the Recreation reserve on to Howitt Street. The course turns right at the Princes Highway and another right along the footpath in an easterly direction towards the rotunda in the middle of Victory Park. It turns left at the rotunda and winds through Victory Park in a northerly direction and under the Princes Highway Bridge. This course here is a very flat one with some lovely scenery through Victory Park and along Traralgon Creek. The route continues to follow the path along the creek and through residential streets before heading up a small hill where runners from the two longer events will cross the Traralgon-Glengarry Road and join the Gippsland Plains Rail Trail, turning left towards Glengarry. (The 10K event midpoint is located along Marshals Road where participants will turn for the run home).

The half and full marathon travel along the Gippsland Plains Rail Trail, a 67km long recreational trail following the former historic Gippsland Plains railway line route between Traralgon and Stratford. The half marathon turns just prior to reaching the neighbouring township of Glengarry while the full marathon continues heading along the rail trail towards Glengarry. On this first section of the trail between Traralgon and Glengarry runners pass through the scenic Latrobe River floodplain and over four restored bridges. The next 9km on the Glengarry to Toongabbie section is a smooth, well packed gravel path that leads to the Eaglehawk Creek and continues through farming country before arriving at Toongabbie. Just prior to the Traralgon-Maffra Road runners turn right leaving the Rail Trail for a short period and onto Stringers Road. Continuing along Stringers road towards Traralgon they arrive at a junction with Henderson's Road where the turnaround point is marked at the traffic island. Runners then retrace their steps towards the finish back at the Traralgon Reserve to be welcomed by a variety of food and drink.

I've searched thoroughly for reports and opinions on this event without much success. The following two comments sum up much of what is written. Posting on marathonguide.com S. P. from Melbourne states, 'For a small country marathon this one is a ripper. Fantastically run and the runners are looked after unbelievably well with a spread that I have never seen beaten anywhere. A race organised by runners for runners. Highly recommended.' These sentiments are echoed by Tasmanian Road Runner B Davis, who having completed the 50th anniversary race in 2017, was impressed enough to write, 'It was the friendliest and most encouraging marathon I have ever run. Everyone supported one another. The residents came out and cheered; and the volunteers offering refreshments were beautiful souls full of encouragement…. Traralgon will forever be a special marathon for me and I highly recommend it to others. It was incredibly well organised far exceeding the organisation of a recent international event I competed in.'

I've also searched extensively for the sort of things in the Traralgon area that might be of interest to fellow Marathon Tourists – again hitting the proverbial brick wall. The best I can come up with is travellercom.au's recommendations that include a visit to Victory Park Gardens (part of the marathon route) to see a giant mountain ash, a time capsule and a quaint band rotunda. South of the town, Hazelwood Dam, a man-made lake where water sports can be enjoyed, and Tarra-Bulga National Park are also said to be worth a visit. The latter covers 1,625 hectares of temperate rainforest in the Strzelecki Ranges and features giant mountain ash trees, beautiful fern gullies, ancient myrtle beeches, and several nature walks crossing a graceful suspension bridge and visiting the Tarra Falls. Other nearby attractions include the father and son operated Narkoojee Winery in Glengarry, described as, 'An outstanding winery regularly producing wines of exemplary quality and typicity' by the Australian Wine Companion 2018. Pre-arranged visits are welcome on weekends to sample its chardonnay, cabernets and merlot. There is a picnic and barbecue area and a basket lunch is available by arrangement. For those with their own vehicle, further north of Traralgon are extensive alpine ranges which include such attractions as the ski resort of Mount Baw Baw, the Thomson Dam (which provides Melbourne with its largest supply of water), a number of state and national parks, and the historic town of Walhalla. Further south are the Strzelecki Ranges that offer a number of scenic tourist drive routes, including the Grand Ridge Road and the route to the Tarra Bulga National Park.

For post-race food and drink Traralgon is well served by the typical array of fast food outlets – McDonalds, KFC, Domino's Pizza, Hungry Jack's, Nando's, Subway etc, as well as a good range of ethnic and Australian restaurants. There's even the ubiquitous Irish Bar, Flanagans on Princess Street, sitting right next door to the Royal Exchange Hotel. Both are said to serve a decent beer as well as the usual range of pub grub.

PERTH MARATHON

WESTERN AUSTRALIA

JUNE

I look back on this event with a great deal of affection. My wife Mo and I lived in Perth during the 1970s and 80s and in 1985 the race provided my first introduction, not only to the world of marathon running, but also to the world of marathon tourism. This was something I knew little about at the time as there weren't too many marathons around in those days. I entered the Perth Marathon simply because it was being held on the date of a landmark birthday - my 40th. The experience taught me a lot – mainly about the dangers of over-confidence, starting too quickly and not treating the distance with the seriousness it deserved. As a sub-1 hour 30 half marathoner I naively thought that it would be a simple matter to run double that distance for around a 3-hour finish. How wrong could I be? Very wrong, in fact. Despite having made a solo 6-hour walk around the course to get the feel of the distance on the weekend before the race, I came in almost one and a half hours outside my predicted time with Mo, my heavily pregnant wife, waiting anxiously at the finish line with our 3-year old son in tow wondering if she should call the nearest hospital. Having taken on board lessons learned it was still another three years before I plucked up the courage to try again. Second time around I knocked well over an hour off my Perth finishing time.

The 1985 version of this marathon was a very different creature to today's event. When the first Perth Marathon (known at the time as the Perth People's Marathon) was conceived in 1979 it was never envisaged that the event would attain international status. Western Australia, because of its isolation, had always suffered from the lack of outside competition. Race organisers WAMC (Western Australia Marathon Club) who still organise the event today had hopes to rectify this. The WAMC was formed in 1971 by a small group of distance runners who wanted to provide a more extensive and varied programme of distance running. The club's growth was slow during the early 70s but took off later that decade and in the early 80s. This coincided with a worldwide boom in marathon running and the WAMC became involved in promoting mass participation events such as the Bridges Fun Run in 1978 (an event in which I cut my running teeth) and the first People's Marathon the following year.

The first Perth Marathon is the oldest marathon held in Western Australia and, in fact, was only the third public marathon held in the whole of Australia. It was organised by the WAMC as their contribution to the State's 150th anniversary of European settlement as well as to test the air for an event of this nature. Response was overwhelming with 580 runners starting the inaugural race – a huge anti-clockwise circuit of the Swan River. The course followed the Stirling Highway from Langley Park to Fremantle where it crossed the Swan River before continuing on its southern bank around Preston Point Road to Canning Highway and through South Perth before re-crossing the river over the Narrows Bridge back to Langley Park. In 1980, when the success of the first event had convinced the WAMC that the run should be held annually, the course was modified to make it flatter and more scenic. Entry numbers were around 500 in the following years and the course was changed again in 1983 when the start and finish was moved across the river to Richardson Park close to the South Perth zoo. I can well recall the noise of the zoo animals becoming increasingly louder as I made my slow way to the finish line on my marathon debut in 1985. The programme for that year shows that there were 584 West Australians in the race listed separately from the 14 'International Athletes' and 21 'Eastern States Athletes.' Out of that little lot I can only find 3 female entrants – one of whom was from Belgium. My how things have changed. Contrast this with results from 2017 which show that out of the 635 finishers, 187 were female (29.4%) Unfortunately, the same results reveal that the marathon has failed in its objective to increase competition from outside Western Australia. I can find only three overseas competitors (from Portugal, Netherlands and USA) listed among the finishers while the number of interstate athletes hardly reached much over double figures. I wonder how much this is due to the fact that in recent years the event has had some of its thunder stolen by a rival marathon in the city. August's annual City to Surf 'fun run' has now been expanded to incorporate the marathon distance. The Chevron City to Surf Perth Marathon was held for the first time as part of the 2009 event when over 40,000 competitors took part in all five events in the series. The marathon itself attracted 698 marathon finishers in 2017, slightly more than the number that completed the original Perth Marathon that year.

 As the capital of Western Australia, Perth is the most isolated capital city of over 1,000,000 people in the world. The nearest city with a population of more than 100,000 is

Adelaide, 2,130 km away. The city is geographically closer to both Dili, East Timor (2,785 km), and Jakarta, Indonesia (3,002 km) than to Sydney (3,291 km), Brisbane (3,604 km), or Canberra (3,106 km). Perth is located along a flat coastal plain, centred along the Swan River and bounded by the Darling Scarp to the east and the Indian Ocean coastline in the west. The Greater Perth area has a population of over 2 million, making it the fourth largest city in Australia. The Perth region had been home to the indigenous Nyoongar people for at least the past 40,000 years before British settlers established a free settler colony there in 1829 as part of the Swan River Colony. The settlement was given the name 'Perth' after the Scottish city of Perth, the hometown of Sir George Murray, the British Colonial Secretary at that time. From 1850, an influx of convicts boosted the size of the colony and their labour helped shape the early architecture of the city. The discovery of gold in the 1890s triggered a boom which, with subsequent mineral discoveries, has been key to the city's economy. Once a small, isolated city, the mining boom in Western Australia following the end of World War 2 has led to a high rate of migration to Perth, which allowed its population to overtake that of Adelaide in the 1980's. While the actual mining takes places in distant, more remote parts of the state, much of the mining-related services sector is based in Perth. Today, Perth remains Australia's fastest growing city, and in recent years has transformed from a relatively laid back city to a fairly vibrant one.

These days, tourism in Perth is an important part of the state's economy. Tourist attractions are generally focused around the city centre and nearby Kings Park, the coast to the west, and the Swan River that flows through to meet the Indian Ocean at Fremantle. If I were to make recommendations from my experiences of living in Perth I would definitely suggest concentrating on these three areas. (Though the port of Fremantle to the south of the city is also an important tourist attraction in its own right and well worth a visit by anyone travelling to the marathon.) Kings Park was the first place I made for on my arrival in 1972 – it's scarcely changed a bit since then. Located in central Perth between the CBD and the University of Western Australia, Kings Park is huge. As one of the biggest inner city parks in the world, it dwarfs Central Park in New York City. Yet it's very easy to explore on foot or, even better, by hiring a bike within the park. There are many landmarks and attractions on offer, including the State War Memorial Precinct on Mount Eliza, Western Australian Botanic Garden, and children's playgrounds. Other features include the DNA Tower, a 15m high double helix staircase that resembles the DNA molecule and Jacob's Ladder, comprising 242 steps that lead down to the Swan River at Mounts Bay Road.

For beach lovers, the many uncrowded beaches along the Perth coastline define the city's outdoor lifestyle. With more sunny days than any other capital city in the world, Perth has perfect beach-going weather with almost perfect beaches to match – all a short bus ride away from the city centre. My own particular favourites are Cottesloe and Scarborough – both suburbs in which I've lived for extended periods of time. The former has more sheltered, safer waters for swimming while the latter is one of Australia's best surf beaches. Go to both of them! The other great water-based attraction is the Swan River. You can't go to Perth without spending some time on it – even if it's only to take the short ferry ride across from Elizabeth Quay jetty to Mends Street in South Perth. There are a number of other longer-distance excursions available if time allows. For example, during our years in Perth we always took overseas guests on one of the scenic 2 hour 45 minute cruises offered by Captain Cook Cruises between Perth and Fremantle. Costing $40 and running three-times daily, these sail past such key sights as Perth's impressive Bell Tower, the restored Swan Brewery, Kings Park, Royal Perth Yacht Club, the magnificent homes overlooking the river plus Fremantle's busy inner harbour before returning to Perth.

Away from the water, culture vultures might prefer to visit The Perth Cultural Centre, an area of central Perth, which includes the Art Gallery of Western Australia, the Western Australian Museum Perth, the State Library of Western Australia, and the Perth Institute of Contemporary Arts (PICA). A walkway connects the Cultural Centre to Perth railway station. The nearby Scitech Discovery Centre is an interactive science museum, with regularly changing exhibitions designed to inform and educate visitors on a large range of science and technology based subjects. Scitech also conducts live science shows, and operates the Horizon planetarium located next to the Discovery Centre.

Most interstate and overseas visitors to the marathon will arrive in the city by air. All scheduled international and domestic flights arrive and depart from Perth Airport. This has four terminals, which for ground transport purposes can be regarded as two precincts. T1 and T2 (international plus certain regional and domestic flights) are side-by-side to the east of the runway, while T3 and T4 (domestic and Qantas Group domestic) are side-by-side 9km by road to the west. A free bus plies between the two precincts, taking 15 minutes. Give yourself plenty of time if travelling between terminals. As we found to our cost while arriving on a domestic flight from Brisbane to connect to an international flight to the UK in 2015, the shuttle buses are not always there when you want them and sometimes they're too full to board. We were forced to take an expensive taxi ride between terminals and, after a nerve-wracking journey, only made our connection with seconds to spare. I've heard similar stories from other disgruntled passengers – some of whom have been put-off visiting Perth because of the situation. It's time the Perth Airport Authority got its act together on this one. The city and major hotels can be easily accessed by taxi or commercial shuttle buses from all terminals though, for more than two people, it is often cheaper and faster to take a taxi into the city (waiting time and drop off other passengers can make a shuttle bus service to the city very long). A taxi by meter to the city will cost approximately $40 from the international airport; the shuttle costs about $15 per person. Transperth runs a limited-stops express bus service number 380 servicing T1 and T2. Tickets are at standard public transport prices ($4.50 adults, $1.80 concession) Transperth buses also serve T3 and T4 via bus routes, 37 and 40.

The current edition of what is now branded as 'The Running Warehouse Perth Marathon and Relay' is again being organised by the West Australian Marathon Club. It's billed as a community event with the proceeds being donated to CanTeen - the only organisation of its kind supporting 12-24 year olds who are either living with cancer or who have a family member with the disease. As always, the WAMC's aim is 'to promote the sport of distance running.' When I last considered running this event in 2018 Marathon entry cost $95 for a member of the WAMC and $110.00 for the general public. The race Expo and Bib Collection is held at the WAMC Clubrooms at The Camfield, Burswood on the Saturday before the race. These premises can easily be reached by public transport from the city centre. The Perth-Armadale rail line runs through the area and is serviced by Burswood and Perth Stadium railway stations. Buses from the Victoria Park transfer station along Great Eastern Highway and Craig Street service the area. Burswood is an inner south eastern suburb of Perth, located immediately across the Swan River from Perth's Central Business District while The Camfield is named after Henry Camfield who was granted 1,000 acres of land in the area when he emigrated from England to the Swan River Colony in 1829, with two indentured servants and their families. During much of my time in Perth the land was considered something of a swampy backwater, ripe for redevelopment given its proximity to the city and the growing high demand for riverside land. In 1985, the development of the Burswood Island Resort, including a casino, rehabilitated the area and changed its image completely. Burswood can now boast facilities that include Belmont Park Racecourse, Perth's winter thoroughbred racing track; Perth Stadium, a new 60,000 seat multi-purpose venue for all football codes, cricket and entertainment events; the State Tennis Centre; and Crown Perth (formerly the Burswood Entertainment Complex), with three hotels, a casino, a convention and function centre, a theatre and many restaurants and bars. Nearby Burswood Park has popular walking and cycling trails along the Swan River. It's also a great place for training runs.

These days the Marathon starts at The Camfield at 7.30am on the Sunday morning with the Relay starting 30 minutes later. A marathon cut-off time of 6 hours 30 minutes applies with all participants required to be off the course by 2:00pm. Aid stations are on average every 2.5km along the course and at each station there is water, Shotz re hydration drink and the option to have your own drinks available for collection. The current version of the course barely touches the wider reaches of the Swan River west of the Narrows Bridge around which I ran in 1985, though it still manages to hug the river shoreline for much of the way. This time it runs on both banks east and west of the Narrows Bridge, mainly between the city and the eastern suburb of Maylands. The route is best described by following the Relay course from leg to leg.

The first leg consists of an approximately 10km stretch from The Camfield to Victoria Avenue in the city. The course first runs south along Camfield Drive, passing the various building in the Crown Perth resort before going through an underpass below Albany Highway as it crosses Heirisson Island and The Causeway (another bridge over the Swan). This takes runners onto the cycle and pedestrian track through McCallum Park following the southern foreshore of the river downstream through South Perth, past the Mends Street jetty and then over the Narrows Bridge. The bridge is Perth's busiest and most important river crossings, carrying nearly 200,000 vehicles every weekday. Until its completion 61 years ago The Causeway Bridge had been the only river crossing between Perth and Fremantle.

The Narrows Bridge has an interesting story as it took more than a century of procrastination and debate before its construction finally began. Even then, it remained a contentious project with people condemning the reclamation of parts of the Swan River to support the bridge - a plan described by some as vandalism. The government's announcement that it would be called Golden West Bridge on completion created a backwash of public protest. Ultimately, people power won and it was named after the stretch of water between Mill Point and Point Lewis which had become known as 'The Narrows.'

After heading over the bridge runners turn right towards the city centre below the Perth Convention and Exhibition Centre and past the new Elizabeth Quay development and the iconic Bell Tower. Opened in January 2016, Elizabeth Quay is a mixed-use riverside development project involving the construction of an artificial inlet on what was previously the

Esplanade Reserve, and modifications to the surrounding environs including Barrack Square. The planner's vision of a cityscape flowing seamlessly to the waterfront under the slogan 'The river The city Together again,' has aroused considerable controversy. The waterfront development has been described by supporters as a jewel in the city's crown and by detractors as a luxury that the state, which during construction was $31bn in debt and heading to a deficit of $2.7bn, cannot afford. Dubbed by some as a palace built as a vanity project by Premier Colin Barnett (nicknamed 'The Emperor') many of Perth's residents have never been convinced about its viability. Some are angry that the government dug an inlet in the middle of Riverside Drive, a major cross-city road, forcing motorists to do a slow dog-leg around the development. Others resent the state spending so much on a luxury development ahead of more popular projects such as a proposed light rail line. And, many fear that despite the best intentions the development will succumb to the same eerie emptiness that haunted the Docklands development in Melbourne. Early signs were ominous: The water park was closed in Feb 2016 due to widespread contamination and a proposed triathlon leg to be swum in the inlet was cancelled in March 2016 due to high levels of fecal bacteria in the water. Included on the site and worth visiting in their own right are The Swan Bells - a set of 18 bells hanging in a specially built 82.5 metre-high copper and glass campanile. Twelve of the set are historic bells are from St Martin-in-the-Fields church in Trafalgar Square in London donated to the State of Western Australia as part of the 1988 Australian bicentenary celebrations. They are reputedly one of the largest sets of ringing bells in the world.

Runners continue eastwards past the first relay change-over point at the foot of Victoria Avenue (where I used to rendezvous with Mo after her shift at the nearby Royal Perth Hospital all those years ago) and to a turn-around loop at the northern end of the Causeway Bridge. Returning along Riverside Drive, back past Elizabeth Quay, the route goes under the Narrows Bridge into Mill Point Road to a turn close to The Blue Boat House on the river. This iconic Boatshed, built in the 1930's, has provided stunning backdrops for thousands of photographers around the world. This out-and-back section provides runners with two opportunities to take a look at the historic Old Swan Brewery Building – yet another source of recent controversy concerning redevelopment. The brewery buildings constructed from 1879 on the Swan River foreshore beneath Mount Eliza became one of Perth's dominant landmarks. The brewery ceased production at the Mounts Bay site in 1966 moved all brewing operations to the Emu Brewery site in Spring Street, and then in 1978 to Canning Vale. In 1989, the West Australian government leased the site to building company Multiplex for a peppercorn rental, so it could be redeveloped as a commercial precinct. The Noongar community, concerned about the site's ancient and sacred Aboriginal heritage, established a protest camp on the site. The on-site protest endured for many months and culminated in a bitter but non-violent confrontation with police in January 1990 at which several arrests were made. In August 1992, police had to break through picket lines to allow development work to proceed. Ultimately, the Noongar's claims were turned down and the development of the property went ahead. The renovated 1879 building now contains a restaurant and function centre which re-opened in 2001. The site also has a microbrewery which produces malt ales and lagers.

The course then re-crosses the Narrows Bridge to a second relay change-over point at approximately the half-way mark of the race. Runners now re-trace their steps for approximately 6.3km along the South Perth foreshore before returning to The Camfield and the third relay change-over. The final 14.8km or so of the course heads north from there, across the bridge carrying the Graham Farmer Freeway and then along the northern foreshore of the Swan to the Maylands Yacht Club. Here, the route turns inland through the Berringa Reserve and past Lake Bungana and Lake Brealey to Maylands Waterland, described in the brochure as 'a water play paradise, with lots of shallow pools and play features… perfect for under 5's.' The final turnaround arrives shortly afterwards on the nearby Tranby Reserve. All that remains is for runners to re-trace their steps back to the bridge and a circuit around the Perth Stadium to the Finish line.

The Perth Stadium, also known by naming rights sponsorship as Optus Stadium, was officially opened on 21 January 2018. It has a capacity of over 60,000 people, making it the third-largest stadium in Australia (after the Melbourne Cricket Ground and Stadium Australia). Perth Stadium is primarily used for Australian Rules football and cricket. Perth's two Australian Football League (AFL) teams – the Fremantle Dockers and the West Coast Eagles – relocated their home games from my beloved Subiaco Oval to Perth Stadium. The Perth Scorchers now play their Big Bash League cricket matches at the venue, having previously played at the WACA Ground. It's rumoured that Australia's national soccer team (the Socceroos) will play some World Cup Qualifiers and friendlies at the venue in the coming years. The Stadium is also capable of hosting major concerts and other entertainment events with Ed Sheeran and Taylor Swift recently performing there. Unfortunately, unlike in 1985 there doesn't appear to be any post-race functions to look forward to on finishing. Not that I managed to make it to the post-race meal on finishing. I simply zonked out on returning home and slept right through the following morning's alarm.

I last visited Perth in 2015 en route to the Brisbane Marathon to celebrate yet another landmark birthday – this time my 70th. Whilst in the city I took the opportunity to run the new Perth Marathon course in stages in preparation for the Brisbane event. Though preferring the original course around the river taking runners to Fremantle and back it's nonetheless one I'd really like to complete someday. I have plans to finish my marathon career, as I started it, with this race. Hopefully there's a few more years of marathon running ahead before I reach this stage. The only criticism I could find about the course came in the following post on the website marathonguide.com, 'The race location was gorgeous along the river although not ideal because we were running on a shared bike path. During the whole race we had to dodge cyclists, dogs, kids, walkers with prams which became more and more frustrating as the day progressed.' I've run a number of marathons on shared courses like this and can understand the runner's frustrations.

Apart from 2015, I've revisited Perth on a regular basis since selling-up home and returning to live in the UK in the late 1980s. Plans to return on a permanent basis were thwarted by the explosion in real estate prices making it impossible to re-settle in the areas in which I once lived: namely the beach suburbs of Mosman Park, Cottesloe and Scarborough. The soulless uniformity, dependence-on-car culture of Perth's outer suburbs, the only places that I could afford a property, does nothing for me I'm afraid. On my last visit I found the city centre to be tired and run down with most of its beautiful old colonial buildings having been replaced or overshadowed by chrome and glass skyscrapers. The emphasis once placed on the central shopping area has now been surpassed by drive-to American-style shopping malls that have mushroomed in the outer suburbs. Sadly, the Northbridge eating area, one of my favourite haunts for the variety and quality of its ethnic restaurants now seems to specialise mainly in Chinese take-aways. (Though old favourites like the Roma and Cicerellos in Fremantle and the Witch's Cauldron in Subiaco still remain – though I've heard the latter is shortly to close) Perhaps the new Elizabeth Quays development next to the river will re-vitalise the city centre over time. I really hope so. I consider Perth as my second home and somewhere I always look forward to revisiting.

BROOME MARATHON

WEST AUSTRALIA

JULY

This is neither one of Australia's traditional marathons nor one of its largest. It's a fairly recent addition to the Australian marathon calendar that, so far, has attracted very few participants. I've included it in this book firstly because of its enormous potential and secondly, because it's run on one of my all-time favourite beaches. The Broome International Airport Marathon is held on the town's famous Cable Beach, often described as 'The most picturesque beach in Australia.' I first encountered the beach on my one and only visit to Broome way back in the 70s when the organisation I was working for at the time opened a new office there. As a committed beach runner it wasn't hard to be impressed by the seemingly never-ending stretch of pure white sand, fringed by the turquoise Indian Ocean, heading far off into the distance. What struck me most about it was the fact that, for much of the time, I had the beach entirely to myself. While it was a great place for training runs during my visit I never really expected that one day someone would have the foresight to organise a marathon in this exotic location.

The Broome International Airport Marathon Festival incorporating a variety of races including the 10.5 kilometre Matso's Dash, the 21.1 kilometre Phoenix Fitness Half Marathon and the full 42.2 kilometre marathon distance is the brainchild of Race Director Glen Taylor, founder of FitEvents - a company specialising in 'Exciting Sports Events in Amazing Locations'. Glenn has always been an active adventurer and keen sportsman, having completed 9 Ironman Triathlons and represented the New Zealand elite team in the 1999 World Championships. In 2007, he and his wife cycle-toured Australia and settled in the Kimberley, where he is based. His company also organise other events in the region including: the First National Kimberley Lake Argyle Swim, the Kununurra Half Marathon, the Lake Argyle Adventure Race and the Ord River Dragon Boat Marathon. According to Glen, the running events on Cable Beach emphasise participation, fun and enjoyment. 'With our aim of attracting visitors to run in the marathon, a partnership with Broome Airport is a perfect match. Last year half our participants were visitors, who spent an average of 7.74 nights in Broome. Visitor numbers will continue to grow along with the event.'

Disappointingly, there were only 25 finishers out of 29 entrants in the marathon race in the inaugural event in 2013. This is still the largest number of finishers to date with only 18 completing the distance in 2018. The majority of these were from West Australia with only a smattering runners from other Australian states and even less from overseas. This is despite the event appointing Australian Marathon legend Steve Monaghetti as event ambassador in 2016 and opening a stall at the 2017 Melbourne Marathon Expo. Glen is realistic in facing the difficulties in attracting large numbers to such a remote location explaining that while flights can be as much as $800 one-way from Melbourne to Broome it's possible to fly Melbourne to Bali for as little as $100. He's optimistic that a trial of direct flights from Singapore to Broome in 2019 might open up the potential to attract runners from the Asian countries. Broome also has a strong historical connection with

Japan (more of which later) that has yet to be fully exploited. I feel strongly that, as the event becomes more well-known particularly throughout Asia, participant numbers will inevitably increase.

Broome is a coastal, pearling and tourist town in the Kimberley region of Western Australia, 2,240 km north of Perth. When I last visited in the 1970s it was a sleepy outback town known mainly for its unsavoury association with the pearling industry. These days the urban population of around 14,000 grows to over 45,000 per month during the peak tourist season (June to August). Marketed under the slogan, 'Where the Red Desert meets the Sea,' Broome is renowned for its relaxed atmosphere and unique character and acts as a gateway to the West Kimberley region with all of the wilderness adventures that area has to offer. The town is surrounded by the tropical waters of the Indian Ocean, with the white sandy stretch of Cable Beach contrasting with the red rocks of Gantheaume Point (both feature on the marathon route) and the darker sands of Roebuck Bay.

British explorer William Dampier first visited the region in 1688 and his meticulous journal from his travels is what later inspired the first official voyage of discovery. Dampier returned briefly in 1699, following which accounts of his voyages began to stimulate interest in the areas rich pearl shell beds. By the late 1870s there was a growing pearling industry in the waters off north-western Australia with the largest base of operations being located in Cossack, about 700km from what was to become Broome. In 1879, Charles Harper suggested to the Legislative Council that Roebuck Bay be set up as a port with facilities for the pearling industry. Subsequently, in 1883, John Forrest selected a town site on Roebuck Bay just east of Dampier Creek where three native wells existed and predicted this site would become the Capital of the Kimberley. Later that year, the townsite of Broome was proclaimed and named after the colony's Governor, Frederick N. Broome.

The pearling industry started in Broome with the harvesting of oysters for mother of pearl in the 1880s and has continued to the large, present-day, cultured pearl farming enterprises. In the early years, local aborigines especially women and girls were enslaved and forced to dive for pearls with little or no equipment. Pregnant girls were preferred as they were believed to have a superior lung capacity. In 2010 the Shire of Broome and Kimberley commissioned a Memorial to the Indigenous Female Pearl Divers. After slavery was abolished in the British Empire in 1883 and diving suits were needed for deeper diving, Asians and islanders were given the dangerous job instead. The Japanese were especially valued for their experience but they were only one of the major ethnic groups who flocked to Broome to work on the luggers or the shore-based activities supporting the harvesting of oysters from the waters around Broome. They were specialist divers and, despite being considered enemies, became an indispensable part of the industry until World War II when Broome was attacked at least four times by Japanese aircraft. During these attacks 86 people (mostly civilian refugees from the Dutch East Indies) were killed and twenty-two aircraft were destroyed, the remains of which can still be seen in the harbour at low tide. The town's Japanese cemetery also contains the graves of 919 Japanese divers who lost their lives working in the pearling industry. Each year Broome celebrates the fusion of different cultures brought about by the industry in an annual cultural festival called Shinju Matsuri (Japanese for 'Festival of the Pearl').

Very easy to explore on foot, Broome's two main areas are Chinatown in the heart of old Broome, and Cable Beach, home to resorts and restaurants. Chinatown has long been a multicultural hub that developed from the pearling crew camps and corrugated tin sheds which ranged along the Roebuck Bay foreshore, and the area around Dampier Terrace and Carnarvon Street. It quickly became the commercial and nightlife heart of the new town. Visitors to Chinatown today can still see the distinctive corrugated iron style of building reminiscent of Broome's early days in a stroll along Carnarvon St, where the corrugated iron buildings that housed noodle restaurants, boarding houses and shops are still home to cafés and retail businesses, as well as the world's oldest operating picture gardens, Sun Pictures. The beautiful bronze statues and plaques in the centre of the street honour Broome's pearl divers, pearling master and crews while, on Short Street, the Streeter & Male buildings and nearby Streeter's Jetty provide a visual connection to Broome's pearling past. While Chinatown's buildings were small, densely packed and accessible only by walkways and lanes, the more spacious pearl masters residences stretched out along Weld, Walcott and Robinson Streets in the area known as Old Broome.

Most visitors to Broome will usually arrive at Broome International Airport, the regional air hub of northwestern West Australia and the tourism gateway to the Kimberley region. Virgin Australia and Qantas fly regularly to Broome from Perth and it is serviced by most Australian capital cities. Additionally, Airnorth also flies to Darwin and Kununurra while Skippers Aviation connects Broome to Fitzroy Crossing and Halls Creek. In 2018 SilkAir also operated 4 seasonal charter flights to Broome from Singapore. Hotels in Broome tend to fill up quickly during the peak tourist season so it's sensible to book well in advance. I looked up a range of 3 to 5-star accommodation for 3 nights from Friday to Monday over the marathon weekend. Prices varied from $642 in the 3-star Mercure Broome to $717 in the 4-star Blue Seas Resort Cable Beach $717 and $881 in the 5-star The Pearle of Cable Beach.

The entry fee for the Marathon is $120 (Half Marathon $95). Number & Race Pack Collection takes place the day before the event from 10am to 2pm on the grass between the Surf Club and Café on Cable Beach. On the morning of the event there are Race Briefings on the Start Line 15 minutes prior to the start of each race. The briefing for the Full Marathon is at 05:45am with those for the Half Marathon and Matso's Dash following at 06:45am. Tide times are a critical part of selecting the perfect date and start time to ensure competitors have super firm sand on which to run. Broome has huge tidal movements so the run time is designed to ensure a low tide with hard packed sand for the duration of the course. Cut-off times for the events are 6 hours for Marathon runners and 3.5 hours for those in the Half Marathon. All events run along the beach starting and finishing close to the Surf Club. According to the race website, 'The beach finish ensures a festive atmosphere where families can come and cheer and have fun on the beach.' Post-Race Presentations are held at 12:00 noon at the Finish Line, Cable Beach. The beach is very much a part of Broome's history, earning its name from the telegraph cable laid between Broome and Java in 1889, connecting Australia's North West with the world. It's internationally known for its long, flat 22 kilometres of sun-kissed white sand with gentle rolling waves perfect for swimming, rich red soil and spectacular Indian Ocean sunsets. Cable Beach is also home to one of Australia's most famous nudist beaches. The clothes-optional area is to the north of the beach access road from the car park and continues to the mouth of (would you believe it) Willie Creek, 17 km away. Though much more crowded these days then when I first visited, sunset over Cable Beach is still spectacular. With colours ranging from purples and golds to fiery reds, the skies light up as the sun slowly sinks into the sea, providing picture perfect photo opportunities. One of the most popular activities is riding a camel along the beach around sunrise and sunset on the northern parts of the beach. At the southern end of the beach is Gantheaume Point where at low tide, you can see 130-million-year-old dinosaur footprints. Gantheaume Point Lighthouse is a wonderful place to watch for dolphins and migrating whales in season.

The route of each event is easy to describe. There's not a great deal to see except sea and sand – perfect for those of us who enjoy running in these conditions. Starting from the Surf Club, marathon competitors will run to Gantheaume Point and turn around and run to Coconut Wells. They turn again at Coconut Wells, run back to Gantheaume Point, before one last turn around back to the start/finish area at Cable Beach. The Half Marathon Course simply runs to Coconut Wells and back while those in the 10.5 km Matso's Dash run to Gantheaume Point and return. (Incidentally, in case you're wondering about the name, Matso's is the Kimberley's award winning microbrewery described as 'a true Broome treasure' whose main objective is said to be to create beers of individuality that will reflect the region). Drink stations with both electrolyte drink, bottles of water and jelly beans are located at 5km intervals at the Gantheaume Point Turn, Cable Beach Access Ramp, half way to Coconut Wells, and at the Coconut Wells Turn. Unique 'Zebra Rock' medals were awarded in all distances at the 2018 event where finishing times of the 18 runners who completed the Marathon ranged from 3hr 12 to 5hr 55 minutes. A further 52 runners finished the Half Marathon and 50 completed the 10.5km Dash – a total of 120 over all three events.

At the end of the event there's a number of attractions that Marathon Tourists might enjoy while in Broome. The town's natural environment draws visitors from around the world. The contrast between its turquoise waters and the intensely coloured red earth continues to inspire artists and photographers. Roebuck Bay, on which Broome is situated, is a haven for thousands of migratory birds, and the waters around Broome attract fishing enthusiasts keen to try their hand at catching some of the tropical species. Whales, dolphins and turtles all populate local waters, and the dinosaurs that once roamed the area have left their mark, with their footsteps preserved in reef rock in Roebuck Bay and along the coast towards the Dampier Peninsula. You'll probably never notice them without local help but for around $128 it's possible to take a one-hour hovercraft tour over tidal flats and have some of the best examples pointed out to you by an expert guide. If you've any money left you might also consider joining Broome Whale Watching on a three hour morning or sunset Roebuck Bay Eco Tour ($95) on an ocean cruise to spot rare Subfish Dolphins (a rare type of dolphin, with a rounded nose and fins). Broome has the largest known population on earth of these cute-looking mammals.

Of course, no visit to Broome would be complete without exploring the reason for its existence. Without the discovery of pearl shells here in the 1800s, Broome might not even exist - that's how vital the pearling industry has been to this town. A visit to Willie Creek Pearls, a working pearl farm can include a guided two hour boat tour ($90) of its aquatic beds and information about the industry's often brutal history. Also, for those who want to learn more about Broome's past, Narlijia Cultural Tours, offers two hour walking tours through the heart of Broome. Using historic maps, the local Aboriginal guide explains the history of the town's main street and

Chinatown district, the importance of the pearling industry and the significance of the landscape to his people. After that you could always watch a movie in the oldest working open-air cinema in the world. Heritage-listed Sun Pictures is one of the most iconic places in Broome. Featured in the box office hit 'Australia' and in the local movie 'Bran Nue Dae,' Sun Pictures still shows current release movies under the stars every night of the week. I recall a wonderful balmy evening there many years ago watching (if my memory can be trusted) 'The Deerhunter.' I'd love to go back. Another experience I'd like to repeat is seeing the Staircase to the Moon. This is a natural phenomenon caused by the full moon rising over Roebuck Bay at low tides, creating a beautiful optical illusion of a staircase reaching to the moon. The best thing about this one is that it's free and can be seen from several vantage points around town. I think I'll give the Camel Rides a miss though. It's just a bit too touristy for me and with day rides costing from $35 and sunset rides from $85, I'd prefer to spend the money in one of Broome's many hostelries.

Despite its small size, the large number of visitors that come to Broome ensures a vibrant nightlife scene. Entertainment usually revolves around bars and restaurants, plenty of which are to be found in the town centre. The Roebuck Bay Hotel, is a popular meeting spot that sprawls across several bars. The terrace bar at the Mangrove Hotel has ocean views. Captain Murphy's Irish Pub is another drinking spot favoured by many. The town's only microbrewery, Matso's Broome Brewery also has a bar and restaurant, and offers a cocktail menu. Occupying a 1910 building overlooking Roebuck Bay with wide verandas and a big beer garden, this pub and restaurant serves a wide range of handcrafted ales. Fans of Matso's beer go for the Hit the Toad Lager, Pearler's Pale Ale, Bishop's Best Dark Lager and a recently released IPA. The brewery offers Tasting Sessions between 11am and 12pm Wednesday and Friday. Away from the town, much of Cable Beach's nightlife centres on the bars and restaurants in resort hotels, but you don't have to be a hotel guest to enjoy them. Cable Beach Club Resort & Spa has several bars and you can drink by the pool, or watch the sunset from a beachfront terrace. Somewhat different to the resorts, Divers Tavern is a lively sports bar featuring live music several nights a week as well as a bistro that serves steaks and seafood dishes.

WELLINGTON MARATHON

NORTH ISLAND, NEW ZEALAND

JULY

This event had its origins in what was then called the Harbour Capital Half Marathon. Established by the Wellington Marathon Clinic in 1986, this was a popular but modest midwinter event attracting less than 1000 entrants for almost 20 years. However, since 2003, when they shifted the race base to Westpac Stadium and established a safer and more scenic waterfront course, entries have grown some 400 percent to become central New Zealand's premier event with a Full Marathon now part of the proceedings. The change was prompted by the fact that original half marathon course run from Taranaki Street Wharf over to Island Bay had become too traffic congested and there always seemed to be some sort of road works or other organisation problem going on. The Westpac Stadium venue and new central city and waterfront route around the harbour bays and return now takes runners past some of Wellington's most popular landmarks and attractions. A Marathon was introduced to the programme in 2005 and in recent years between 4000 and 5000 runners and walkers from more than a dozen countries have lined up for the various events under the Wellington Marathon umbrella. Runners from as far afield as Argentina, Canada, France, French Polynesia, Germany, Indonesia, Japan, China, Malaysia, Netherlands, Niger, Oman, Singapore,

Taiwan, UK, USA, and Australia were among 3,622 entrants in 2018. Of these, there were 341 in the Marathon, 25 in the Marathon Walk, 1,291 in the Half Marathon, 208 in the Half Marathon Walk, 1,212 in the 10K race plus a further 253 in the 10K Walk while 292 entered the Kid's Magic Mile.

The Wellington event is now firmly established among the 'Big 5' of New Zealand marathons alongside Auckland, Christchurch, Queenstown and Rotorua. American Dan Lowry and Wellington-born Alice Mason set the current records for the marathon in 2017, posting times of 2hrs 22min 43secs and 2hrs 48min 36secs respectively. One of the event's attractions is that this is a race where anyone can be a winner. While every finisher wins a medal, the 2018 edition of the race saw one lucky finisher win a Volkswagen Polo courtesy of principal sponsor, the Wellington-based motor company Gazley Volkswagen. Alongside the Volkswagen Polo, every finisher also had a chance to win a trip to the New Caledonia Marathon and the first Wellington woman in the Full Marathon won a trip to Japan's Senshu Marathon. The Japanese prize is part of Wellington's sister city relationship with Sakai city in Osaka. Both cities have strong running traditions and have annual exchanges whereby the first Wellington runner from the Wellington Marathon and the first Sakai runner from their Senshu Marathon win trips to each other's events. The exchange alternates annually between the first male and female.

Wellington, the capital city and second most populous urban area of New Zealand, with 412,500 residents, sits near the North Island's southernmost point on the Cook Strait. The city is synonymous with both wind and water. Both are major components of the marathon. Strong winds through the Cook Strait, which can often affect the quality of runners' performances, have given the city the nickname 'Windy

Wellington.' The city core lies along the western shore of the highly-protected Wellington Harbour with the city's suburbs ringed by mountains spreading out in all directions. The majority of the marathon course follows a route around the harbour shoreline. Wellington Harbour ranks as one of New Zealand's chief seaports and serves both domestic and international shipping. Named in honour of Arthur Wellesley the first Duke of Wellington and victor of the Battle of Waterloo, Wellington is the southernmost capital city in the world. It is also the most remote capital city, being the farthest away from any other capital. Situated near the geographic centre of the country, Wellington is well placed for trade. In 1839 it was chosen as the first major planned settlement for British immigrants coming to New Zealand. As the nation's capital since 1865, the New Zealand Government and Parliament, Supreme Court and most of the civil service are based in the city. Architectural sights include the Government Building—one of the largest wooden buildings in the world—as well as the iconic Beehive. Despite being much smaller than Auckland, Wellington is also referred to as New Zealand's cultural capital. The city is home to the National Archives, the National Library, the Museum of New Zealand Te Papa Tongarewa, numerous theatres, and two universities. Wellington also plays host to many artistic and cultural organisations, including the New Zealand Symphony Orchestra and Royal New Zealand Ballet. It has a reputation as one of the world's most livable cities with the 2014 Mercer Quality of Living Survey ranking Wellington 12th in the world.

While the Government sector has long been a mainstay of Wellington's economy, its central location meant it was chosen as the site for the head offices of various sectors – particularly finance, technology and heavy industry. In recent years, tourism, arts and culture, film, and ICT have played a bigger role in the economy. Tourism is a huge contributor and Wellington was ranked fourth in the Lonely Planet Best in Travel 2011's Top 10 Cities to Visit in 2011. Fellow New Zealanders make up the largest number of visitors with 3.6 million visits each year. These are joined by an annual influx of around 540,000 international visitors, many of whom arrive on the increasing number of cruise ships arriving into Wellington Harbour The city promotes itself as 'Absolutely Positively Wellington' and is also marketed as the 'Coolest little capital in the world' by Positively Wellington Tourism, an award-winning regional tourism organisation. Popular tourist attractions include Wellington Museum, Wellington Zoo, Zealandia and the Wellington Cable Car.

Wellington International Airport is the arrival point of the vast majority of overseas entrants to the marathon. Located in Rongotai, about 5 km from the city centre, the airport has frequent domestic flights to Auckland, Christchurch, Palmerston North, Rotorua, Hamilton, Nelson, Blenheim and many other destinations. International flights from Australia (Sydney, Melbourne, Brisbane, Gold Coast and Canberra) arrive about twice daily. There are also flights from Wellington to Fiji and Singapore. There is a regular airport bus known as the Flyer that departs from the south end of the domestic terminal until 9pm. Shuttle van services, taxis are directly outside the terminal. For those travelling by bus, InterCity operates services to Wellington from across the North Island. Daily services operate between Auckland, New Plymouth, Napier, Hastings and Palmerston North, as well as overnight services between Auckland and Wellington. All InterCity Wellington bus services depart and arrive at Platform 9 at the Wellington Railway Station. There is also a train service between Wellington and Auckland and regular ferries between Wellington and Picton, connecting with buses and the train to Christchurch.

Accommodation options on arrival range from 3-star hotels at £58 per night to 5-star at £102 per night (booked in advance by UK visitors). Runners might want to consider the Special Marathon Rates and Services section on the event website. This promotes the historic 3-Star-Plus Comfort Hotel and the modern 4-Star-Plus Quality Hotel, located next to one another in the heart of Wellington. The Comfort hotel offers marathoners special rates of $99 per night while the Quality Hotel can be booked for $135 per night. Both provide Marathon Pre-Race Pasta Menus, Marathon Breakfast buffets served from 5:30am on race day as well as free race day shuttle bus services for guests to & from Westpac Stadium. Late check-out is also available for in-house participants until 12:30pm after the event with showers and bag storage for in-house participants until 5pm after the race.

Entries for the Gazley Volkswagen Marathon (as it's now called) Run and Walk cost from $80.00 to $100.00 after mid-June. Race T-shirts are an extra $40. Registration takes place at the Gazley Volkswagen premises in Kent Terrace, Wellington from 9am to 6pm on the day before the race. Runners' Race Pack includes: programme, race number & timing chip, any T-shirts purchased and Stadium parking tickets already purchased. Number pick up on race morning is only available for entrants driving from outside greater Wellington on the day. Those participants can collect their race pack on race morning at Westpac Stadium between 7:00am and 8:30am in the Pavilion Bar. All race day activities are held at Wellington's Westpac Stadium, a much-loved Wellington landmark and one of the busiest stadiums in New Zealand hosting an array of events. The 34,500-capacity sports stadium opened in 2000 offers international-standard multi-purpose facilities and hosts four sporting codes - Rugby Union, Rugby League, Football and Cricket - as well as providing a venue for numerous functions, concerts, exhibitions, corporate functions and other non-sporting and community events. It is the home of the Wellington Lions Mitre 10 Cup rugby team and the Hurricanes Super Rugby team. The stadium also hosts the Wellington Sevens, one of the events in the annual World Rugby Sevens Series for national rugby sevens teams. The stadium also regularly serves as a home venue for All Blacks rugby matches and, during the summer, generally hosts international and occasionally domestic limited overs cricket. AC/DC, Bon Jovi, Elton John and Guns N' Roses are among some of the 'big name' acts that have appeared at the venue in recent years.

All events start and finish on Sunday on the Fran Wilde Walkway outside Westpac Stadium with secure baggage storage available inside the stadium, on the main concourse. Marathon Walkers are the first to start at 7:00am, followed by runners in the full marathon at 7:30am. Half Marathon Runners and Walkers leave together at 8:45am with 10K Runners and Walkers setting off at 9:15am. The final event on the programme, The Kid's Magic Mile leaves at 9:30am. To help get runners to their starts on time the organisers, in conjunction with CQ Hotel Wellington, provide a free participant bus service on race day from CQ Hotel Wellington through the CBD to Westpac Stadium. A Tranzit branded bus drives a continuous circuit, leaving from CQ Hotel Wellington on Dunlop Terrace at 6:00am, 6:30am, 7:15am and 8:00am. Post-Race the bus returns back through the CBD to the CQ Hotel at regular intervals. At 1:00pm, the course controls will cease and though the finish remains open participants are on the course at their own risk. This effectively gives marathon runners 5.5 hours in which to complete their race.

The Wellington Marathon course follows a fast, flat and scenic route around Wellington's spectacular waterfront. All events are out and back, although the course over the last 2.6k is a little different to the first 2.6k. On the return leg, runners follow the waterfront walkways, as opposed to the roads which means some tight corners and possible congestion. Every kilometre is marked sequentially on the outward journey. But on the return journey all events count down the kilometres remaining to avoid confusion between the different events on the same out and back route. After the initial 300 metres from Westpac Stadium on the Fran Wilde Walkway the course turn left over the Waterloo Quay footbridge down onto Waterloo Quay. It then continues south toward Wellington CBD into Customhouse Quay, Jervois Quay and Cable Street. This is possibly the area of most interest to Marathon Tourists as the route takes in Wellington Railway Station, the busy ferry terminals, the New Zealand Academy of Fine Arts, Wellington Museum and the city's Underground Market.

The course continues along Cable Street past the Circa Theatre, the Museum of New Zealand Te Papa Tangarewa and Waitangi Park to the end of Cable Street before turning onto Oriental Parade. Te Papa Tongarewa is New Zealand's national museum. Known as Te Papa, or 'Our Place', it opened in 1998 after the merging of the National Museum and the National Art Gallery. More than 1.5 million people visit every year. Te Papa Tongarewa translates literally to 'container of treasures'. A fuller interpretation is 'our container of treasured things and people that spring from mother earth here in New Zealand.' Te Papa's philosophy emphasises the living face behind its cultural treasures, many of which retain deep ancestral links to the indigenous Maori people. Visitors can discover the treasures and stories of New Zealand's land and people under one roof on six floors of interactive displays. They are able to see Maori and Pacific cultural artefacts, New Zealand's extraordinary natural life, its most important works of art, and its unique history via the museums five main collections areas: Arts, History, Taonga Maori, Pacific Cultures, and Natural History. It's a must-visit attraction before or after the marathon.

Once in Oriental Parade runners will see the Carter Memorial Fountain, a distinctive feature 150 metres out in Wellington Harbour from Oriental Bay. Eight floodlights are used to light and colour the fountain which spouts water 16 metres into the air. Installed in 1973, it was originally to be named the Oriental Bay Fountain until the untimely death of its benefactor Hugh Carter. Carter had wanted to give something back to his home city and, inspired by the famous Jet d'Eau fountain in Geneva, forked out $75,000 for a replica to be built in honour of his parents Tragedy struck just days after the fountain was officially opened. Carter was about to sail to Nelson on his launch Kualani when he slipped and drowned in Wellington Harbour. The fountain was subsequently named the Carter Fountain as a mark of respect.

All events then follow the coastline all around the waterfront past Point Jerningham to Balina Bay. After the 10K and Half Marathon runners turn back towards the city at their respective half-way points the Full Marathon continues on Shelly Bay Road past Shelly Bay and Point Howard to the first of its three turns at approximately15.5km at Scorching Bay on the Miramar Peninsula. Close to the Point Halswell headland (originally known by its Maori name, Kaitawharo meaning 'to eat jellyfish') around which runners make their way to Scorching Bay is the Point Halswell Lighthouse and the Massey Memorial. The Memorial is the mausoleum of William Massey, Prime Minister of New Zealand from 1912-1925, and his wife. The land on which it's built had been used for defence purposes during World War I and an unused fort on the site was converted to a crypt and a gun-pit lined with marble to serve as a vault. It's interesting place to go if you want to see a large memorial in the middle of nowhere, with an excellent view of the surrounding harbour. Further round the headland is the former coastal artillery battery, Fort Ballance, built in 1885 following fears of an impending war with Russia, The fort is one of the best preserved of a string of nineteenth century coastal defences constructed to protect New Zealand's main ports from a naval attack. The 1880s layout of Fort Ballance is largely unaltered and a good impression of the original nineteenth century fort remains leaving a permanent reminder of the technology used in the coastal defence network of the 1880s. It is now listed as a Category I Historic Place.

After the first of the turns at Scorching Bay, marathon runners return on the opposite side of the road almost as far as Miramar Cutting for the 'Full Marathon Turn 2' at around their half-way mark. Full Marathoners then repeat this out and back section to Scorching Bay and 'Turn 3' at 26.5km. Marathon runners are given a wrist band at every turning point to indicate that they have completed each of the turns. The wrist bands must be worn until the finish and handed back. After this final turn, it's all the way back home along the by-now familiar section of coast to the finish line. The only difference is that instead of returning to Cable Street the course turns 150m earlier into Herd St and the Wellington Waterfront area. It then follows the waterfront, past the Marina, behind Te Papa Museum, Frank Kitts Park and Ferg's Kayaks to Queens Wharf. At Queens Wharf the course passes under the sails then follows a car parking lane north approximately 500m to Bluebridge Ferry entrance. At

Bluebridge the course continues north on Waterloo Quay and up the footbridge for the final 800m to finish back on the Fran Wilde Walkway at Westpac Stadium.

As to sightseeing, as capital cities go, Wellington is really rather small but, being the capital, it's endowed with museums, theatres, galleries and arts organisations completely disproportionate to its size. The central area is surprisingly compact at just 2km across, which means it's easy to get around on foot. The Wellington's waterfront area is an attractive district right in the hub of the central city. Both Queen's Wharf and Frank Kitts Park are surrounded by fine buildings, including the Civic Centre and the Museum of New Zealand. From Frank Kitts Park, there is a good view of Wellington Harbour, and the park hosts a market every Saturday. There are also plenty of cafés and restaurants in this area, so it's a great place for a stopover while strolling around the central city.

One of Wellington's most popular tourist attractions, the Wellington Cable Car is also close at hand. This is one of the easiest way to get a nice view of the city and harbour for a $9 fare. Departing every 10 minutes, the short journey begins on Lambton Quay in the city centre, and finishes in the suburb of Kelburn. Along the way, it travels under the corporate towers of The Terrace, past Kelburn Park and Victoria University of Wellington. After emerging at the top, visitors can look out over the city's central business district, Mount Victoria and out across the harbour to the Hutt Valley before visiting the Cable Car Museum. Return trips are available or you can simply take a leisurely walk through Wellington Botanic Garden and historic Bolton Street Cemetery, to Parliament. The Botanic Garden features 25 hectares of protected native forest, conifers, plant collections and seasonal displays as well as a variety of non-native species. The garden's main attractions are the Duck Pond, Begonia House and the award winning Lady Norwood Rose Garden. A number of sculptures are also positioned around the gardens, including works by Henry Moore and Andrew Drummond. It is classified as a Garden of National Significance by the Royal New Zealand Institute of Horticulture. Entrance is free.

As Wellington is surrounded by hills, there are a number of good vantage points for anyone wanting to admire the views. Rising 196m above the city, the Mount Victoria Lookout is a Wellington must-do, rewarding visitors with stunning panoramic views of Wellington city, its harbour, and beyond. Located right next to the central business district, you can drive all the way up, or take a walkway through the bush-covered Town Belt - it takes about an hour to walk up from Courtenay Place. From the top, you can enjoy the views of Tinakori Hill, the Hutt Valley and Eastern harbour bays, Matiu/Somes Island and the Miramar Peninsula. It's described as a relaxing spot for a picnic while watching ferries and cruise ships sail into the harbour and planes fly in and out of the airport.

By far the most convenient place in the country to see rare New Zealand wildlife is Zealandia, a 225-hectare urban eco-sanctuary only two kilometres from the central city. Here, many of the country's native birds, including endangered species such as the stitchbird, saddleback, and takahe can be heard and seen as well as more than 100 kiwi (which can be spotted on guided night tours) and New Zealand's famed reptile, the tuatara. There are 32 kilometres of walking trails throughout the reserve for visitors to explore plus a museum that documents the natural history of the country. Entrance costs $17.50 for an adult plus extra for guided tours.

Finally, nature lovers looking for a secluded getaway close to the city might consider taking one of the regular daily ferries departing from Queens Wharf to Matiu Island (also known as Somes Island) in Wellington Harbour. The island offers a variety of wild New Zealand landscapes. During the pre-European era, Matiu Island was occupied by Maori. During the modern era, it was used as a quarantine station, internment camp, and military installation until being turned over to New Zealand's Department of Conservation as a nature reserve. It features a series of short hiking trails up to its highest point (complete with World War II gun emplacements) and around its perimeter, all with excellent views across to the mainland.

All this fresh air is bound to have everyone both hungry and thirsty. I'm told that Wellington is a beer lover's dream, with a thriving craft brewery scene and an abundance of bars serving the best local ales. Lonely Planet even named it 2017's best beer destination in New Zealand. The Malthouse on Courtenay Place is Wellington's original craft beer bar has been serving up craft beer for over 20 years. With a range of 29 taps and over 140 different beers, drinkers are spoilt for choice here. Lovers of craft beer might also want to try the Garage Project Taproom, just across the road from their Aro Valley brewery in Aro Street. The taproom boasts 18 taps and two cask lines. I particularly like the sound of their Garage Project Aro Noir - a 'pitch black' stout. (I've seen the photos. If it tastes half as good as it looks it'll do me).

For the budget conscious looking to find filling food to replenish lost energy, the wellingtonnz.com website offers a number of recommendations. These include the Little Penang restaurant on Dixon Street that serves authentic Malaysian flavours and attracts 5-star customer reviews. Also included is Fisherman's Plate on Bond Street – with the suggestion to ignore their fish 'n' chips and go for the best Vietnamese pho in town. Burger Liquor on Willis Street is said to serve delicious burgers and beverages, including famous boozy milkshakes. Finally, for late-night eaters, Tommy Millions on Courtenay Place is reported as serving 'New York inspired-pizza' (whatever that means) from a takeaway kiosk. This should be enough to keep you going until you get back home.

Perth Marathon (Photo courtesy of WAMC and Focused Ninja Photography)

Western Sydney Marathon. Before the Start

Cable Beach Broome (Photo courtesy of Broome International Airport Marathon)

Brisbane Marathon Expo with Mo

I'm almost finished in Sydney!

Photo courtesy of Australian Outback Marathon

Running across Rottnest Island (Photo courtesy of WAMC)

Finishing outside the MCG in Melbourne

THE GOLD COAST MARATHON

QUEENSLAND

JULY

I first visited the Gold Coast for a couple of days in 2001 while driving up from Sydney for the World Masters Marathon Championship being held that year in Brisbane. My memory is of enjoying early morning training runs alongside thundering surf on seemingly endless beaches. I remember thinking at the time that someone should organise a marathon along these beautiful beaches, without realising that someone actually had already done such a thing – not on the beach itself but as close as you can get to it for 26.2 miles. In those days, although becoming increasingly popular, it bore little resemblance to the major event that it's now become. Now branded the 'Gold Coast Airport Marathon' for sponsorship reasons, it's considered by some to be Australia's premier road race and is one of only two marathons in the country to hold IAAF Gold Label status at the time of writing, (the other is the Sydney Marathon)

The race is held on the first Sunday in July each year along with a half marathon, a wheelchair marathon and a wheelchair 15K. Shorter distance events, including 10K and 5.7K races take place on the Saturday. The marathon was first held in September 1979 as part of a health awareness campaign for the area initiated by the local Rotary Club. It's now reached its 40th anniversary so it's been going longer than London and many of the so-called bigger marathons. The inaugural race started and finished in the Gold Coast suburb of Evandale and consisted of 6 laps over Chevron Bridge, through Surfer's Paradise and back over the Isle of Capri Bridge with 124 competitors in the marathon, 144 competitors in the half marathon and a further 423 in an additional Fun Run. After a number of successful years of growth, the ownership and management of the event changed several times, falling into debt with a considerable amount of money owed including athlete prize money. This poor financial position affected the race's reputation and when major sponsor JAL withdrew its support the event seemed doomed, until the intervention of the Queensland Government with a lifeline rescue package assured its continuation. In 2001 the event was taken over by Gold Coast Events Management which had previously managed the successful Pan Pacific Masters Games. A measure of their success is that the event now attracts close to 30,000 participants and apparently an international TV audience in 150 countries.

Central to the race's popularity is the beauty of the surroundings in which it takes place. The route runs adjacent to a collection of some of the best surf beaches in Australia, if not in the world and has a reputation as one of the flattest, fastest and most scenic courses on the marathon calendar. In addition it's considered ideal for those seeking a personal best time – the weather conditions on the Gold Coast in July are traditionally suited to running, with low humidity, little wind and mild morning temperatures. In 2015, 60% of participants registered their fastest ever time at their chosen distance. Factor in the Gold Coast's status as one of the world's most popular holiday destinations with its beaches, theme parks, elaborate system of inland canals, all backed by sub-tropical rainforest and you've got the perfect package for any aspiring marathon tourist.

Many people are under the mistaken impression that the name Gold Coast simply refers to a collection of beaches in southern Queensland. It's actually the name of a city that has been in existence for over fifty years and has grown during this time to become the second most populous city in Queensland as well as the most populous non-capital city and the sixth most populous urban area in Australia. Gold Coast was originally known as the South Coast because of its location south of Brisbane. Inflated prices for real estate there in the 1950s led to the nickname 'Gold Coast.' Although those living in the area at the time considered this as derogatory, the term Gold Coast simply became a convenient way to refer to the holiday strip between Southport and Coolangatta. As the tourism industry grew, local businesses began to adopt the term in their literature and in 1958 the Town of South Coast was officially renamed Town of Gold Coast. The area was given city status one year later.

The city consists of 70 kilometres of coastline with some of the most visited surfing beaches in the world. There are also beaches along many of the Gold Coast's 860 kilometres of navigable tidal waterways so waterfront living is very much a feature of the Gold Coast lifestyle. The Gold Coast Seaway, between The Spit and South Stradbroke Island, allows vessels direct access to the Pacific Ocean from The Broadwater and many of the city's canal estates. Unsurprisingly with all this water about, Tourism is the region's biggest industry with around 10 million tourists visiting each year of which almost 1 million come from abroad. It is Australia's 5th most visited destination by international tourists. The Japanese, in particular, seem attracted to the region and large numbers of Japanese runners feature in the annual marathon. More than

$4.4 million is contributed into the city's economy by tourists each year while its 500 restaurants, 40 golf courses and 5 major theme parks, among other attractions, employ one in four of its inhabitants.

Runners travelling for the marathon have a choice of airports located both north and south of where the event begins. The Gold Coast Airport (the event's sponsor) is an international and domestic airport located at Coolangatta on the southern fringes of the city. Major Australian domestic carriers operate frequent flights from Sydney (25 per day) and Melbourne (15 per day) as well as from other cities in Australia. There are also direct international flights from New Zealand, Japan, Singapore and Kuala Lumpur. Runners flying directly from the UK will probably have to land at Brisbane Airport on the north side of the city and about an hour away from the Gold Coast. Trains run from the airport to six stations on the western side of the Gold Coast though each station is about a 15-minute taxi ride from the beach where most of the accommodation is situated. Buses are also available from each station at an approximate cost of between $5 and $20, depending on destination. If you really want to be near the start and finish of the race the 5-star Meriton Suites, Southport, less than a five minute walk away, is currently offering one bedroom suites for couples at £404 for a 3-night stay over the 2019 marathon weekend. But, you better be quick, accommodation anywhere near the race venue tends to sell out well in advance.

The Gold Coast Marathon also incorporates a number of championships in the event including the IAAF Oceania Area Marathon and Half Marathon Championships, Australian Defence Marathon Championships, Queensland Marathon and 10km Road Running Championships and Australian Masters Athletics Championships. Early Bird entry fees for the

2016 marathon are available from December through to the end of April for $135. After that it will cost you $155. Registration and number pick-up takes place at either of the two designated Check-In Centres. There's usually a selected venue in central Brisbane for Saturday pick-up only, though most visitors choose to travel to the main Expo at the Gold Coast Convention and Exhibition Centre on the Gold Coast Highway in Broadbeach. This is open Thursday 4 to 8pm, Friday 10am to 8pm and Saturday 9am to 5pm. At the Expo runners can purchase a ticket to the annual Garmin Legends Lunch where they can mingle with previous winners such as four-times champion Pat Carroll and famous former Australian marathon runners such as Rob de Castella and Steve Moneghetti.

The marathon is the final of the four events that set off on the Sunday morning from the Race Precinct (Start and Finish area) at the Broadwater Parklands. The Half Marathon leaves at the ungodly hour of 6am while the two wheelchair events start simultaneously at 7.15am with the marathon heading off five minutes later. The route the marathon takes visits a veritable What's What of iconic surfing beaches familiar to anyone who's ever spent any time on the east coast of Australia. Briefly, from the start at Southport it turns south following the main road along the Gold Coast past Main Beach, Surfers Paradise, Broadbeach, Mermaid Beach and Miami Beach to the turn at 16km at Burleigh Head. Runners then run back the way they came, this time heading a further 6km past the start line to the second turn overlooking the bay at Broadwater. It's then back along the bay to the finish in the park.

From the Start, and after crossing the bridge over the Nerang River, the route turns eastward towards the first of these beaches, Main Beach, at 3km. The name is purely literal as, situated at the northern end of the Gold Coast, it was the main surf beach to the town of Southport. A highlight of a visit here is to the beach itself, where an old bathing pavilion has been reincarnated as a trendy beach café. The old male and female changing pavilions are still there complete with loads of retro photos as reminders of what the area used to be like. The pavilion sits next to the Southport Surf Club, popular with surfers due to its open shore break and the first to make its mark on the area in 1936. Next up at 5km comes Surfers Paradise, the undisputed capital of the Coast. It's here that you'll find most of the tourist attractions, hotels and night life. Originally named Elston, the suburb was officially re-named as Surfers Paradise in 1933 when the local council decided that the new name would prove more marketable. During the past 50 years it has grown from a small beach resort typical of many on Australia's coastline to become one of the biggest tourism machines in the Southern Hemisphere. Today, Surfers Paradise is home to many attractions catering for everything from bungee jumping to ice skating as part of its laid-back lifestyle. One of the on-course highlights is passing the Q1 building which, when it was opened in 2005, was the world's highest residential tower. The observation deck on level 77 is 230 metres above the ground and a major tourist attraction providing excellent views in all directions from Brisbane to Byron Bay. But, they don't call it Surfers Paradise for nothing. The main draw-card remains the 150 metre stretch of glorious sand that extends for almost 10km in each direction. I'd still like to see someone organise a marathon along the actual beach.

Broadbeach at 8km, known as 'Broadie' to the locals, was for a long time considered the little brother to the much bigger Surfers Paradise. Development in the area today is mostly of low-rise structures with much of the suburb consisting of canal waterways, including Lake Trepid, that are linked to the Nerang River. Runners pass the Jupiter's Hotel and Casino as well as the Convention Centre that houses the race Expo. Its major attractions are the annual Blues on Broadbeach Music and Jazz Festivals. The headline act for the 2016 Blues Festival was none other than fellow Geordie Eric Burdon (of the Animals fame) who I last saw performing at Newcastle's Club A Go Go as long ago as 1966.

Mermaid Beach sits between the 10 and 11km marks. The suburb contains numerous accommodation options from caravan parks to apartments but is best known for Hedges Avenue, dubbed 'Millionaires Row.' This is where some of the Gold Coast's glitterati have bought prestigious properties along its prime beachfront location. I don't think there's any actual mermaids there, the name is derived from the cutter HMS Mermaid on which explorer John Oxley sailed when discovering the nearby Tweed and Brisbane Rivers in 1823.

Heading towards the southern end of the Gold Coast, runners reach Miami Beach at 13km. Its clean, white sandy beach lined with picnic and barbeque areas make this an ideal location for family outings. It's home to the famous Pizzey Park, a 5-star Olympic training pool favoured by leading Australian swimmers such as Grant Hackett. Another well-known Australian, the singer Johnny (now John) Farnham, chose the Miami Ice Factory as the location to film the video for his top-10 single 'Two Strong Hearts.'

Runners turn to head back north at Burleigh Heads, just after the 15km mark. Burleigh Heads is a beachfront alternative to the more touristy suburbs further north. It attracts a large number of professional surfers to its renowned surf breaks. The headland at Burleigh, locally known as The Point, is a favourite Sunday afternoon spot for local musicians. Behind it Burleigh Heads National Park is a wild, natural headland with walking tracks along the foreshore and through lush rainforest. It's said to be a great place to spot sea eagles, migrating whales and the occasional koala and wallaby roaming free.

After retracing the route back to its start point runners now have to negotiate a final 12km loop north and then south alongside The Broadwater. This is a huge shallow estuary that stretches from Southport to the southern section of the UNESCO World Heritage Listed Moreton Bay in the north. This is a beautiful part of the course. Originally a lagoon created from water deposited by the Nerang River, development since the 1970s has seen the construction of an extensive network of artificial waterways that account for up to 90% of Australia's canal estates. The Finish in Broadwater Parklands on the shores of the estuary gives hot and sweaty runners the chance to cool their feet in its sparkling blue waters.

There's also no shortage of places to eat and drink within a short walking distance of the finish. The usual chains like McDonalds, Nando's and Hungry Jacks all have outlets close by while, for those with a taste for more exotic food, there's a whole range of ethnic restaurants in the vicinity. These include: two Japanese restaurants, the Muruya and the JFX, two Korean restaurants, Café 928 and Goha Korean Restaurant, two Mexican restaurants, Casa Mexicana and Zambrero Southport, several Chinese restaurants, the Bombay Affair specializing in Indian dishes and the Absolute Thai on Scarborough Street. I've always found when I've been in Australia that the local RSL Club can be relied upon to provide quality food at value-for-money prices. Southport's RSL, only about 800 metres from the race's finish, would probably be my go-to destination after the race. Its Bistro 36 menu offers everything from salads to burgers to roasts to pasta, fish and chips and more. I like the sound of their 'Roast of the Day' for $9.90, the 'Traditional Steak and Kidney Pie' at $13.90 and the 'Chef's Liver and Bacon Casserole' for the same price. The RSL can also always be relied upon to serve up a decent beer at a competitive price. There's not really any need to look elsewhere.

Despite its stunning location, the Gold Coast has become one of those Marmite destinations – people either love it or loathe it. Some would argue that it has been ruined by crass commercialism, pointing out that the continuous development of ugly, expensive high-rise holiday apartments, cheap motels and tacky theme parks has simply been taken too far, leading to a loss of character and class. They may well be right but I retain great memories of early morning runs along beaches to-die-for, before the crowds woke up and before the acres of high-rise concrete covered the beach in their shadows. I'd like to go back for more and the Gold Coast Marathon provides the ideal opportunity to do so.

AUSTRALIAN OUTBACK MARATHON

NORTHERN TERRITORY, AUSTRALIA

JULY

The idea behind Australian Outback Marathon came from Mari-Mar Walton, the founder and Managing Director of Travelling Fit an Australian-based Sports Tour Operator, following a visit to Uluru with her husband Michael for the first time in 2004. Mari-Mar had previously taken part in adventure races around the world and she wanted to bring the concept of an 'all inclusive, fully hosted' Marathon holiday to Australia. After six years of planning, gaining permissions and working out the logistics of putting on an event such as this in the middle of the desert, the inaugural Australian Outback Marathon took place with 187 runners participating in the various events on 31st July 2010. 554 runners completed the four-event programme in 2017. Race organisers Travelling Fit started as an idea in 2000 when Mari-Mar wanted to travel to London to run the Marathon but couldn't find a suitable travel agency to help arrange the trip. Travelling Fit has since grown to become Australia's only travel company dedicated to the needs of runners and the wider running community, taking thousands of runners overseas every year to participate in some of the world's greatest races, both big and small. I believe Travelling Fit are also the only travel company in Australia offering guaranteed entries to all six of the World Marathon Majors (Tokyo,

London, Boston, Berlin, Chicago and New York). According to the company's literature, 'All the staff at Travelling Fit know what it takes to participate in and finish a Marathon, most from first-hand experience.' And, with running as a passion and not just a job, the company's core mission to 'always put the runner first' is paramount in everything they do. I guess it's reassuring to know that you're in good hands when undertaking to run a marathon in what many consider to be a hostile environment.

Anyone familiar with the geography of Australia will understand that the term 'Australian Outback' does not refer to a precise location. Far from it, The Outback, literally 'out the back' (of where we live) is the colloquial name given to the vast, unpopulated and mainly arid areas that comprise Australia's interior and remote coasts. It's used to describe the emptiness, remoteness, and the huge distances of inland Australia into which a large majority of its citizens have probably yet to venture. Australia is one of the most urbanized countries in the world with something like 87% of its population concentrated in the cities along the southern and eastern coast, or not far from it. The only other populated region is the area around the city of Perth on the southern west coast. The Australian Outback is just about everywhere else - 6.5 million square kilometres of it inhabited by less than 60,000 people! Nothing says Australia quite like its Outback. The open spaces that seem to stretch on forever tell the story of the exploration and development of its wide, brown land, and reflect Australia's pioneering spirit and unique identity. Though quite what early Australian explorers like Burke and Wills (the first to cross Australia from south to north at the expense of their lives) and others such as Stuart, Mitchell, Eyre and Giles would have made of the idea of running a marathon through such hostile territory is hard to imagine. I had my first experiences of it over 40 years ago while driving across the Nullabor Plain from Perth to Adelaide long before they ever put tarmac on the surface. I've experienced it during camping holidays in the more isolated parts of the West Australian Goldfields as well as on visits to the Kimberley Region of W.A. There's definitely something special about the place and I can fully understand why a properly organised marathon held in the Outback's harsh and unforgiving conditions might appeal to a certain type of runner. In contrast to pounding the pavement with thousands of other runners through the hustle and bustle of city streets the serene remoteness of the Australian Outback is entirely another world.

The Red Centre, in the Northern Territory, exemplifies the Outback. Its gateway is the isolated town of Alice Springs and its landmarks include Uluru, Australia's iconic red-rock monolith. In the north, Kakadu National Park has Aboriginal rock paintings and billabong oxbow lakes. The Ayers Rock Resort plays host to the ninth edition of the Australian Outback Marathon in July 2018. (The Marathon is always held on the last Saturday in July). Numbers have increased considerably over the years, although the combination of isolated location and expensive entry costs ensure that this race will never attract the numbers of the country's big-city marathons. There were 91 finishers in the inaugural marathon in 2010 compared to 166 in 2017. In the same years, the event's Half Marathon races had 48 and 171 finishers respectively. For most, it's a once in a lifetime experience. It's not every day that runners get to experience the stunning views of Uluru (Ayers Rock) and Kata Tjuta (the Olgas) during a marathon event. These represent two of Australia's most iconic landmarks, with Uluru in particular being instantly recognisable throughout the world, and are considered as the major attractions and selling points of the Outback Marathon.

One of the great natural wonders of the world Uluru, as named by the Aboriginal people (but also known as Ayers Rock) and Kata Tjuta, (also known as The Olgas), form the two major landmarks within the Uluru-Kata Tjuta National Park. On 19 July 1873, the surveyor William Gosse sighted Uluru and named it Ayers Rock in honour of the then Chief Secretary of South Australia, Sir Henry Ayers In 1993, a dual naming policy was adopted that allowed official names that consist of both the traditional Aboriginal name and the English name. It was renamed 'Ayers Rock / Uluru' and became the first official dual-named feature in the Northern Territory. The order of the dual names was officially reversed to 'Uluru / Ayers Rock' in November 2002 following a request from the Regional Tourism Association in Alice Springs. Uluru, now listed as a UNESCO World Heritage Site, is a sandstone formation towering above the surrounding landscape standing 348 metres high, rising 863 metres above sea level with most of its bulk lying underground, and with a total circumference of 9.4 km. It's not only a spectacular natural formation, but it's a deeply spiritual place. It's reported that visitors can feel a powerful presence the moment they first set eyes on it. Uluru is more than just a rock, it is a living cultural landscape considered sacred to the local Aboriginal people, the Anangu. Each feature of the rock has a meaning in 'Tjukurpa' or Dreamtime, the traditional Anangu law that explains how the world was created. The spirits of the ancestral beings continue to reside in these sacred places making the land a deeply important part of Aboriginal cultural identity Visit at sunrise or sunset for the spectacular sight of this huge monolith transforming from ochre to burnished orange and intense red.

25 km to the east of Uluru, Kata Tjuṯa, (literally meaning 'many heads') is a group of large, domed rock formations. The 36 domes that make up Kata Tjuṯa cover an area of 21.68 km2. The alternative name of The Olgas comes from the tallest dome Mount Olga which was named in 1872 by the explorer Ernest Giles, in honour of Queen Olga of Württemberg (daughter of Tsar Nicholas I). Though less spectacular, Mount Olga is actually 198 metres higher than Uluru. A number of legends surround the great snake king Wanambi, who is said to live on the summit of Kata Tjuta / Mount Olga and only comes down during the dry season. His breath was said to be able to transform a breeze into a hurricane in order to punish those who did evil deeds. The Anangu Aborigines believe the great rocks of Kata Tjuta are homes to spirit energy from the 'Dreaming', and since 1995 the site is being used once again for cultural ceremonies. Since the National Park was listed as a World Heritage Site, annual visitor numbers have risen steadily each year. While increased tourism provides regional and national economic benefits it also presents an ongoing challenge to balance conservation of cultural values and visitor needs. Admission to the park costs $25 per person.

Travelling Fit, have designed the Australian Outback Marathon programme to be enjoyed by all levels of running abilities offering four different events - a full marathon, half marathon and an 11km and 6km fun run. In addition to its beauty, the course is reasonably flat, with only a couple inclines and sand dunes. Most of the course is on unsealed roads, bush tracks and soft-sand trails, with a few small sand dunes and plenty of Australia's famed 'Red Earth' thrown in for good measure. Entries to the event are only available as part of a Package and there are no 'Entry Only' options available. The Australian Outback Marathon is what is described as a fully packaged marathon experience. This means that participants don't just enter the race but get to choose from a selection of fully hosted Outback holidays which range from a basic trip of three days and two nights up to six days and five nights. The itineraries are designed to suit all budgets and travel plans. Each package includes shuttle services, first class accommodation, and guaranteed race entry. Depending on the itinerary chosen, various different tours and meals are included as part of the event's package. All participants who have booked an accommodation package have breakfast included for every morning that they are staying at the Ayers Rock Resort. In addition, everyone who has booked an accommodation based itinerary is invited to attend the Friday evening Carbo Load Dinner plus the post-race Celebration Dinner held at a private, outdoor dining area. As an incentive to enter early anyone who books prior to mid-May receives a limited edition Australian Outback Marathon running top. Of the five different options available the most expensive 'Platinum Package' (6 days/5 nights) costs as much as $4075 single, $2960 double, $2690 triple and $2550 quadruple. The cheapest option available in the 'Red Earth Package' (3 days/2 nights) works out as $1370 single, $1010 double, $975 triple and $960 quadruple. I'll leave you to decide whether or not you're getting value for money. For those with deep pockets taking one of the longer packages or who plan on remaining in the resort after their race Travelling Fit have a number of optional tours at discounted prices to choose from. These include: Uluru Sunset and Sunrise Coach Tours, Sunset and Sunrise Camel Rides. Uluru/Kata Tjuta Helicopter Tours, Kata Tjuta 'Valley of the Winds' Walk and Ayers Rock Sky Diving.

Many participants arriving for the event choose to fly into Connellan Airport (Ayers Rock Airport), situated near Yulara, around 463 km, a 5 hour drive away from the town of Alice Springs in the Northern Territory, and a 20 minute drive from Uluru (Ayers Rock) itself. At the time of writing there are regular flights to Connellan from Sydney with Virgin Australia, Jetstar and Qantas airlines. Jetstar also has flights from Melbourne while Qantas also flies there from Alice Springs and Cairns. The original Connellan Airport at Uluru was provided by Edward Connellan, who started Connellan Airways in 1942, providing passenger transport, chartered Royal Flying Doctor Service flights and mail runs. The development of tourism infrastructure adjacent to the base of Uluru that began in the 1950s soon created adverse environmental impacts. It was decided in the early 1970s to remove all accommodation-related tourist facilities near the base of Uluru and re-establish them outside the park. In 1975, a reservation of land beyond the park's northern boundary, 15 km from Uluru, was approved for the development of a tourist facility, to be known as Yulara, along with a new airport. The new facilities became fully operational in late 1984. In 1992, the majority interest in the Yulara resort held by the Northern Territory Government was sold and the resort was renamed Ayers Rock Resort – the accommodation option for all Australian Outback Marathon packages. The ten minute transfer ride from the airport to the resort is included as part of the tour itinerary.

Race packs are delivered to all participants when checking in to the hotel. Transfer to the race start has been included as part of each package and private coaches collect entrants from outside their hotel in plenty of time to ensure that they are at the start line ready for their event. All events have a designated start time of 7:45am and must be completed by 3:45pm (an 8 hour cut-off). Each race is chip timed. In 2017 the winner's time was just under the 3-hour mark at 2:59:58

while the final finisher came in at 7:29:33. Quite a time gap! At the start runners are treated to the unmistakeable sounds of a didgeridoo as their welcoming music. As one finisher commented, 'Nowhere else in the world would you hear the words three, two, one' and then, rather than a starting pistol, have the didgeridoo blast out the Go'. The average daytime temperature in the area in July is 21 degrees whilst the night-time temperature is only 5 degrees. This means that on race day the temperature will be chilly just before and just after dawn but will be perfect once you are running. The humidity levels are usually less than 10%. The organisers advise that normal running gear will be fine for the event. Given the chilly start some participants may want to consider running in leggings and a long-sleeved running top but these are optional and very few runners have opted for them in previous years. Those that are competing in the Marathon and Half-Marathon, are able to discard unwanted clothing at any of the aid stations passed en-route. Drinks and aid stations with water and sports drinks are placed at short intervals throughout the course. The cheers and encouragement of the medical personnel and local volunteers in such a sparsely populated environment are said to be very welcome.

The Marathon itself is run on private red earth bush tracks that are a feature throughout Central Australia. The tracks are made of packed earth and are specially graded for the race meaning that they are slightly soft underfoot. The entire course is relatively flat from a topographical point of view but there are a few little inclines here and there. The course also features a couple of short sand dunes and though not long or high, it's said that they certainly feel like a challenge when running up them – with the views at the top making the effort worthwhile. The only comprehensive description I can find about the course is the one given on the event's website.

Without repeating this verbatim it seems that runners leave in a south-Westerly direction from the start/finish area. During the first 3km the ground underfoot turns from a graded bush road to a genuine bush fire-trail, with a combination of packed and soft, red earthy sand underfoot. The course then crosses the Lassiter Highway for another 3km. giving excellent views of Kata Tjuta (The Olgas) on your left. Turning in a north-easterly direction for another 2km the ground changes once again from a desert track back to an unsealed but graded road. After approximately 8km runners reach Mala Road, one of the few sealed roads on the course. This road then goes through the village of Yulara before arriving at yet more off-road trails. After crossing both Giles Road and Coote Road, a brief turn due North returns onto the red earth as the course heads up towards Connellan Airport. The turn back towards the start/finish area comes after approximately 12km. There are a few small dunes to navigate here with some spectacular views of Uluru in the distance.

The Lassiter Highway is crossed again at 15km followed by sections of sealed road and then tracks. The 5km stretch after 18.5km is reported as being 'pure Australian Outback' conditions with exceptional views, particularly from the top of Jem's Dune which is almost exactly half-way. At around 22.5km runners start the trip home along some of the tracks near the resort with the track at 26km marking the way back to the finish. After re-crossing the Lassiter Highway for the final time the course offers some fantastic views of Kata Tjuta, especially in the 30km-32km stretch. Heading back through Yulara village at around 32.5km runners once again reach Mala Road, before returning to red earth at around 36km. Here they also get to see the twin sights of Kata Tjuta on their left and Uluru on their right. From here it is described as 'plain sailing all the way to the finish line, with yet more breathtaking views to inspire you over the last few kilometres.'

At the finish line food is provided for all participants starting from as early as 9:00am. There is also electrolyte drinks, sandwiches, muffins, tea, coffee and hot soup available all day. Private coaches operate a shuttle service from the race start/finish area back to the resort so that competitors can leave whenever they have finished their event. The organisers encourage all participants to either remain at the finish to cheer in those who have yet to complete their race or to hop back on the shuttle after freshening up at their hotel in time to cheer in the last participants. I'm told that such is the sense of camaraderie engendered by the event, many finishers do just that. As one finisher commented, 'There is a certain intimacy you get in the smaller marathons, which is missing in the larger ones. The Australian Outback Marathon definitely had it.'

The Celebration Dinner held on the Sunday evening is the final highlight of the event. This takes place outdoors in the desert, with Uluru to the east and Kata Tjuta to the west. Writing in 2011 Edition 4 of Distance Running magazine, Australian marathoner Jenny Buchanan describes how under a multitude of stars in a clear, bright sky finishers were treated to a delicious meal, fine wines, a slideshow of the previous day's races and the comradeship of fellow runners. Her final comments show her appreciation of the event, 'The Australian Outback Marathon allowed us to share part of our great country along with others from the global running community. It is a truly unique experience that will long be remembered.' These sentiments are echoed by James Reimann from Minnesota, USA writing in marathonguide.com who felt that, 'If you plan on running all 7 Continents, or only one marathon/half marathon in Australia, or heck, if you live in Australia, this is the one to do on that continent. The organization was top rate…….. This will remain in my memory as one of my top 3 marathons.'

BRISBANE MARATHON

QUEENSLAND

AUGUST

July 2015 saw Mo and I back in Australia. The holiday had a triple purpose: to catch up with old friends in Perth before moving on to spend some time with our son Ross in the Sydney beachside suburb of Manly and then, finally, to fly up to Brisbane for the marathon there on 2nd August. This was the actual date of my 70th birthday and I desperately wanted to celebrate by running a marathon. The only question was where. I'd looked for alternatives without success. San Francisco and Rio de Janeiro both hold marathons around this time and in the past they'd occasionally been on the first weekend in August. Not this time. A pity really as I've got them both on my 'must do' list. For my 70th, however, I was determined to find a big city marathon on the actual day. Brisbane was the only one. Besides, as I've documented in an earlier publication, I'd got unfinished business to settle with Brisbane – having travelled all the way there for the World Veterans Marathon Championship in 2001, only to have to pull out at the last moment due to my one and only serious running injury.

It's not that I needed an excuse to re-visit Brisbane. It's my favourite Australian capital in my favourite Australian state. Queensland was considered something of a 'no-go' area during my time living in Australia during the 1970s and 80s. Its reputation back then was that of a politically backward Cinderella state lacking the pace of modernisation found elsewhere in the country. Much of the blame for this was attributed to the reactionary attitudes of its long-serving Premier, Joh Bjelke-Petersen, one of the most controversial figures in Australian politics. Bjelke-Petersen was a fundamentalist, blinkered, rural politician whose right-wing Country (later National) Party misgoverned Queensland for almost twenty years. Just to give you a flavour of the type of guy he was, here's two of Joh's more interesting observations. On press criticisms, 'The greatest thing that could happen to the state and nation is when we get rid of all the media ….then we could live in peace and tranquillity and no one would know anything.' On condoms/birth control, 'We don't want any of that sort of thing.' A 1987 Royal Commission found his government to be institutionally corrupt, leading to the jailing of several ministers and Joh's political demise. After that Queensland began to prosper. Known, for obvious reasons, as 'The Sunshine State' its economy has enjoyed a significant boom in the tourism and mining industries over the past 20 years. A sizeable influx of interstate and overseas migrants, large amounts of federal government investment, increased mining of vast mineral deposits and an expanding aerospace sector have all contributed to the state's economic growth. In the years following Bjelke-Petersen's removal from office, the Gross State Product of Queensland regularly outperformed that of all the other Australian States and Territories. Queensland is no longer considered a backwater – it's the place to go to these days.

Its gateway is Brisbane, the exciting State capital. Mo and I together with son Ross and partner Hayley made our way there from Sydney on the Friday before the marathon courtesy of a ridiculously cheap Tiger Air airfare of $45. Last time I made the same trip it took me six days in a car, stopping at places like Port Macquarie, Byron Bay and the Gold Coast en route. Visitors arriving in Brisbane by air are hit with a hefty indirect tax imposed on transport into the city centre. The regular, every 30 minutes Air Train direct to the city has a monopoly on the route and costs a whopping $17 for the 25 minute journey to the Roma Street Transit Centre. This is the main terminus and booking office for most forms of road and rail transport in Brisbane. If there's more than two in your party it's cheaper and usually quicker to pay the approximately $50 for taxi share. That's what we did. We'd specifically chosen our hotel, the George Williams, for its location on inner city George Street, close to the river, city centre and, most importantly, the Start and Finish of the marathon in the nearby Botanic Gardens. Cost for 3 nights without meals, booked from the UK, was £144 per double. I've no complaints with what was provided.

With a population of 2.3 million in its metropolitan area, Brisbane is the third most populous city in Australia. It was founded in 1825 on the homelands of the Turrbal and Jagera Aboriginal People on a bend in the Brisbane River where the city's Central Business District now stands. It takes its name from the Scotsman Sir Thomas Brisbane, the Governor of New South Wales at the time. An earlier attempt at a penal settlement for 'difficult' convicts at Redcliffe on Moreton Bay had to be abandoned due to a combination of inadequate water supplies and hostile Aboriginal inhabitants. The Moreton Bay area was eventually opened up to free settlement in 1842, marking the beginning of Brisbane's rise to prominence. Today it is one of the major business hubs in Australia with most Australian as well as numerous international companies having offices there. It has enjoyed consistent economic growth in recent years on the back of the state-wide resources boom mentioned earlier. White-collar industries like IT, financial services, higher education and public sector administration generally congregate around the CBD while blue-collar industries like oil refining, paper milling and metalworking tend to be located nearer the mouth of the river.

Tourism also plays a major part in Brisbane's economy either as a destination in its own right or as a gateway to other parts of what is a most beautiful state. In fact, after the marathon Mo and I travelled up to the Sunshine Coast just north of Brisbane to spend a week relaxing on the gorgeous beaches there. Even though it was the winter seasonal temperatures rarely dropped below 23 degrees. As well as having a fantastic climate, Brisbane is also considered as the arts capital of Queensland with dozens of art galleries, museums and concert halls. These days, Brisbane has the justifiable reputation as one of the most desirable places to live in Australia because of its sophisticated and cosmopolitan atmosphere, impressive riverside setting, busy cultural scene and energetic nightlife. Certainly, if I'd had my time over again I think I would have made my way across to Brisbane instead of staying in Perth for 15 years. But, there again maybe not, I doubt if I could have survived long under Mr Bjelke-Petersen's governmental style.

Most of our time in Brisbane seemed to be spent on or around the banks of its river. Possibly the heat had something to do with this or perhaps it's just that I like being by water. The ideal way to familiarise yourself with what locals call 'The River City' is to cross the Victoria Bridge to the South Bank and then follow the riverside path along to and over the pedestrian Goodwill Bridge. This can then be followed through the city's Botanic Gardens and on to a section jutting out into the river to finish at the eastern riverside suburb of New Farm. We were to make extensive use of sections of this path and its connecting cycleways during the weekend's marathon. An even better way of seeing the city by water is to jump on one of the free hop-on-hop-off public transport ferries that ply their way between the Elizabeth Street and New Farm jetties. These cross and re-cross the river on their way downstream providing excellent snap-shots of important locations en route. These include the iconic South Bank Parklands, Kangaroo Point and the historic Story Bridge. Mo, Ross and I spent an enjoyable afternoon on one of these ferries, sitting in the sun for an hour and a half taking in the best that Brisbane has to offer. Next day, while Ross and Hayley explored the South Bank cultural scene, Mo and I went back on the river again. This time we paid the $5.60 for a 2 hour ticket on one of the sleek City Cat ferries that take commuters up and down the river between St Lucia to the west and Hamilton near the river's mouth. Although the full journey took longer than the 2 hour ticket limit, no one seemed to mind and we were encouraged to stay on board for as long as we liked by the friendly crew.

Once the ferry rides were over it was routine to disembark on the city's South Bank foreshore – an area that is the jewel in the crown on the city's tourist trail. This is Brisbane's premier lifestyle and cultural destination where the locals in their thousands go to relax in its 17 hectares of lush parklands. This beautiful green strip of preserved riverbank is home to outdoor theatres, al fresco dining, BBQ areas, oriental pergolas, pockets of rainforest and hidden lawns. The big attraction is Streets Beach, an artificial swimming pool and lagoon with sandy beaches refreshed regularly with sand from Moreton Bay. Nearby is the London Eye-styled Wheel of Brisbane offering 360-degree views of the city. Adjacent to the parklands is the Stanley Street Plaza, a renovated section of historic Stanley Street with trendy shops, restaurants and especially the Heritage listed, colonial Plough Inn. This is the almost-perfect Aussie pub with rooms heading off in all directions, magnificent staircases, live music, bars everywhere, good food and relaxing verandas with great views. We were to spend much of our free time enjoying the delights of the latter. I'd first been introduced to it in 2001 and am pleased to report that it's as good as ever.

We were even able to use the river foreshore to pick up my race number at the race's main sponsors In Training retail outlet in Milton. The suburb is less than a half hour's walk from the city centre along the foreshore bicycle path. Those not wanting to walk that distance in the heat can simply take one of the many ferries to Milton Pier. Close to Registration, on Milton Road, is the home of the famous Castlemaine-Perkins XXXX Brewery. If we'd been there earlier in the week when brewery visits took place it would have been good to go on one of these – the largesse at the end of which is legendary! Registration itself took place in what seemed to be the back room of the In Training shop. We'd got there early on the Friday but space was still at a premium. Clutching my number and 'free' singlet we were, of course, led out through the shop but there was no pressure to purchase any of the merchandise on offer. I mistakenly topped up on gels for the race – totally unnecessary as they were handed out freely on our way around the course.

We didn't spend a great deal of time on the north side of the river where the main shopping areas and office blocks are located. I wasn't too impressed by this side of the city. The Queen Street Mall looked tired and jaded from when I'd last been there and there were too many motorways and building projects on the northern foreshore. Those interested in architecture and politics might wish to confine their visits on this side of the river to the classical-style City Hall in King George Square, the nearby Old Treasury Building on George Street and the Old Government House and Parliament House further down the same street as it approaches the Botanic Gardens.

Race day saw us up and out early, making our way in darkness through deserted streets for a 6am start to beat the predicted heat of 27 degrees. Because it was my birthday, this was an event in which I was determined to do well. I'd researched the results for the winners and their times in the Vet 70 category for the last 3 years. The same guy, now obviously 3 years older than me, had won it each year in times of between 4 hour 17 and 4 hour 27 minutes. I figured that if, for just this once, I trained properly and focused on this event I was capable of beating each of these times and coming home with something I could be proud of to commemorate reaching the biblical three score and ten. With that in mind I upped my mileage following the St Petersburg Marathon at the end of June and, for the first time in years, introduced some interval sessions and tempo runs into my training. By the time I arrived in Australia I felt in pretty good nick. Unfortunately, as every runner knows, there's a fine line between being super fit and pushing your body too far. Five days before the race I finally succumbed to a pretty nasty strain of the flu virus that had been doing the rounds during the Australian winter. It ended up with sinuses totally blocked and having to breathe through the mouth. Try it for a day or two – it quickly wears you out. Disappointed that my ambitions had been trashed, I cut a sorry figure lining up, smothered in sun cream, in the half-light of the morning of my 70th birthday - at the back of the field with no expectation of performing as I'd hoped.

With the man on the loudspeaker trying to be as quiet as possible so as not to disturb nearby residents, we left Alice Street adjacent to the City Botanic Gardens just as first light started creeping into the sky. There were about 600 in the marathon and 1,832 in the half marathon event that started simultaneously. A 10k race with 1,224 runners left at 6.30am. The marathon was to be two non-identical laps of the half marathon course. A 5K Run/Walk with 431 starters and the usual Kids Mini Marathon with 216 kids left from a different start location at 10am and 10.15am respectively. As all events finished at the same venue, the Riverstage within the Gardens, 4-hour marathoners knew in advance that they'd be arriving at the Finish line at about the same time as hordes of energetic and excited youngsters. This wasn't a good idea!

The City Botanic Gardens provides a riverside refuge from the concrete and glass of the city centre. Unless you visit in the nesting season like we did. Though minding her own business, Mo was almost scalped by an aggressive small bird (species unknown) presumably protecting its young - unless it was just in a bad temper! I realised why so many cyclists passed through the Gardens with spikes sticking out of their helmets. The Gardens are home to many rare and unusual botanic species, including palms, figs, cycads and bamboos. The Queensland Heritage Register describes them as, 'the most significant, non-aboriginal cultural landscape in Queensland, having a continuous horticultural history since 1828, without any significant loss of land area or change in use over that time. It remains the premier public park and recreational facility for the capital of Queensland since the early 1840s.' A bit of a long-winded description, but it is a beautiful place to visit even if you're not horticulturally inclined. The Gardens were home for over 100 years to Harriet, a tortoise reportedly collected by Charles Darwin during his visit to the Galapagos Islands in 1835. There are no recorded attacks by Harriet on human beings! Due to its proximity to the river, the Botanic Gardens have been flooded nine times, the latest in 2011. There's a post you can stand next to that records the height of the major floods. The level for the disastrous 1974 flood went up past my waist.

After 3km of running backwards and forwards through city streets the course finally emerged out on to the historic Story Bridge. Here the views were spectacular, as the rising sun bounced of the steel and glass skyscrapers of the CBD and turned the river into a crimson sheen. The impressive heritage-listed bridge is the longest cantilever bridge in Australia. It carries about 100,000 vehicles a day on its three lanes in each direction. It also has a shared pedestrian and cycle path (that we ran over) on each side. A month before our arrival in Brisbane almost 75,000 visitors had celebrated its 75th anniversary on the bridge with food and drink supplied. Just like its famous Sydney counterpart, bridge climbs are a popular tourist attraction. Also, similar to many such iconic bridges, the Story Bridge has a history of attracting those seeking to commit suicide. Following two high-profile murder-suicides on the bridge in 2011 and 2012 telephones linked to suicide hotlines and three metre-high safety barriers have been installed. After only 3km into the marathon I didn't need either – yet.

Dropping under the bridge we then passed one of Brisbane's most famous colonial-era pubs, the Story Bridge Hotel. The hotel is a Brisbane icon, a local watering hotel that holds a special place in the hearts of generations of Brisbane residents. I'd spent quite a bit of time there in 2001 and was glad to see the old pub again – albeit without a beer in my hand on this occasion. Over the years the hotel has become home to some of Australia's quirkiest events: like the annual

Australia Day Cockroach Races and National Festival of Beers. It's one of those pubs you never forget.

From now until the finish we were to run virtually the rest of the route along closed cycleways on either side of the Brisbane River. I love running by water and its soothing influence had me forgetting the illness of the past few days and picking up my pace. Without advocating marathon running as a cure for sinus complaints, something definitely happened to unblock my nasal passages in the first few kilometres. For the first time in almost a week I could start to breathe through my nose again. To my amazement, I caught up with and passed the Over-70 winner of the last three years. I knew it was him because he had his name emblazoned on his chest. He had a determined look about him that led me to believe that I wouldn't be in front for long. We now had seven kilometres of the beautiful southern foreshore to run before the turn at 12km.

The first of these kilometres took us alongside the cliffs at Kangaroo Point. The Point is located on a peninsula formed of harder rhyolite rock which the river flows around to create a natural loop. The area has become a popular recreation spot, conveniently close to the city centre and the South Bank Parklands. Over the years the cliffs have become a popular picnic, rock climbing and abseiling site. It's a good place to visit – if only to watch some of the dare-devil climbers in action. It's easily reached by the free ferry that stops at the Kangaroo Point jetty.

At 7km we skirted around the Maritime Museum with its collection of classic ship models, marine engines, photographs, paintings and other historical maritime items. There's even a World War 2 frigate 'Diamantina' that visitors can clamber over for $16. Next up was the delightful South Bank Parklands that I've described earlier. Normally this area is a seething mass of humanity but, given that it was not yet 7am, we had the place virtually to ourselves. Even at this hour the artificial beach and lagoon looked particularly inviting. After passing the Brisbane Wheel and the Performing Arts Centre we arrived at the underpass of Victoria Bridge and its famous Abutment. The bridge is the historic link between the north and south banks of the city and is actually the fourth bridge on the site. One of the previous structures was washed away in the floods that seem to occur frequently on the river. A portion of the southern abutment of one of the former bridges remains adjacent to the new bridge. This heritage-listed abutment carries a pedestrian arch, a short remnant of tram track and a memorial to Hector Vasyli, a young boy who was killed in a traffic accident there when welcoming home servicemen from the First World War. There's a great practical joke story relating to the bridge. On Commemoration Day in the 1930s a group of students placed 'Bridge Closed' signs at both ends of the bridge. Apparently Police took these signs at face value without checking with the appropriate authorities and spent most of the day preventing vehicles from crossing.

Immediately north of the bridge we ran past the Cultural Centre with an Art Gallery, Museum and Science Centre and State Library on our left. At 9km we reached Riverside Drive before turning at 12km and making our way back along Montague Street to cross the Go Between Bridge over to the northern shore. This is a recently constructed (2010) toll bridge for vehicles, pedestrians and cyclists. Apparently it's named after a popular 'internationally influential' Brisbane-based indie rock band of the same name. (A bit like the John Lennon Airport then?) On crossing the bridge we turned sharp left to run along Coronation Drive to another turning point at 17.5km. I could see here that my main rival for the Vet 70 prize was still hot on my heels.

Running back towards the city I received a tremendous boost when Ross leapt out of the shadows just after 19km to wish me a Happy Birthday. The fact that he continued to run with me to the half-way mark chatting and taking photos, really made my day. It also increased my determination to do as well as I could for my family waiting at the finish. As the half marathoners peeled off into the Botanic Gardens to complete their event, the marathoners headed over the Goodwill Bridge and back onto the south bank of the river. Opened in 2001, purely for cyclists and pedestrians, the bridge takes its name from the most popular entry in a public naming competition. Halfway across there's a recess including a much-used coffee cart providing cushions, newspapers and excellent views of the city skyscrapers. Once across the river we did an out-and-back leg along the shores of Kangaroo Point, running in the opposite direction to that on the first lap. This time we were to pass under, rather than over, Story Bridge before returning to the Goodwill Bridge and following virtually the same route as on the previous lap. This time we missed out Montague Street entirely and simply ran back again along Riverside Drive.

We turned at 33km on the south side and again at close to 39km after crossing to the north side. On both occasions I could see that I was increasing the lead I had over the guy I thought was my rival in the Vet 70 category. At the second of these turns I was almost 20 minutes ahead. This was just as well as, by then, the heat was beginning to bite and my pace was slowing alarmingly. I reached the finish at the Botanic Garden's River stage outdoor entertainment venue in 4 hour 26 with sweat oozing from every pore. It was brilliant seeing Mo, Ross and Hayley waiting at the finish line. Also excellent was the dedicated area that the organisers had set aside for the exclusive use of marathon finishers. This cordoned-off, shaded area provided all manner of free food and drink to speed up recovery. We also picked up our medals there plus a finisher's T-shirt to go with the vest given out at registration. Ignoring for the moment the thousands of pounds it had cost to get there (there was a special reason for this – it's not every day you turn 70) I thought the marathon was full value for the $100 entry fee. It was a very well organised event on a beautiful riverside course. Drink stations were plentiful enough to cope with the 27 degree heat and there were more than sufficient gels and isotonic drinks to get you round.

After the race we retired temporarily to our hotel for cake and birthday presents. Then it was back over to the South Bank for an afternoon of celebration at the venue I'd chosen above everywhere else available – the lovely Plough Inn. Despite it being almost full to overcrowding with the Sunday swarm we found our perfect spot. We spent the whole of the afternoon in the sun and shade of the upstairs veranda overlooking the artificial lagoon and indulging in some serious food and drink. The Inn supplies the almost quintessential Aussie cuisine: giant barbequed steaks, pulled pork and chips and best of all, beer-battered barramundi - all for between $18 and $25. These were washed down by a fair few middies of the Matilda Bay Brewing Company's 'Fat Yak,' an American-style pale ale. Not the perfect dark beer I normally seek but .... When in Rome.... Later that evening Ross finally succeeded in bringing up the Race Results on his phone. I'd managed to come first in my age category by almost twenty minutes and would receive a trophy and a $200 pair of Adidas sunglasses as a birthday memento. It was to be the icing on the (birthday) cake – the perfect ending to a perfect day.

,

TOWNSVILLE MARATHON

QUEENSLAND

AUGUST

The Townsville Marathon was started in 1972 by a group of running enthusiasts who founded the 'Townsville Marathon Club'. This was subsequently changed to the 'Townsville Road Runners,' better reflecting the true nature of the club and perhaps less daunting for potential new members. From its enthusiastic beginnings in 1972 the club has held the Townsville Marathon every year since. This makes the marathon event the second longest-running annual Marathon on the Australian calendar. The event was changed to its current format in 1999 when Townsville Road Runners attempted to raise the profile of running in the region by hosting one of the country's first Running Festivals. From this the event has developed into what it is today. According to the organisers own description, 'It is a regional event, with its own vibe, feel and unique welcoming allure'....... 'We aren't just a run. We are an experience'. It offers runners a great way to see many of Townsville's beautiful attractions including the award winning Strand Beach, ANZAC Park, the recently revamped historic city centre and views across the Coral Sea to Magnetic Island. Having spent ten days enjoying glorious sunshine in Townsville and Magnetic Island while in Australia for the 2000 Olympics, I can vouch for the scenic nature of the event's location. My only regret is that the visit didn't coincide with the timing of that year's marathon.

For those who aren't familiar with the city, Townsville is located about 350 kilometres south of Cairns and 1350 kilometres north of Brisbane. Townsville Airport has links to major eastern seaboard cities, as well as Darwin, Bali and some Queensland regional inland towns. From the airport it's a 10 minute drive to the city centre. Townsville can also be reached by long-distance coach from most towns on the east coast of Australia as well as by the regular train service between Brisbane and Cairns. Both coach and train take around 22 to 24 hours from Brisbane. There's a wide choice of accommodation options available on arrival – from Backpackers' Hostels to luxurious hotels with the City Oasis Inn being the recommended accommodation partners to the event.

Considered the unofficial capital of North Queensland by locals, Townsville hosts a significant number of governmental, community and major business administrative offices for the northern half of the state. It's Australia's largest urban centre north of the Sunshine Coast with a 2015 population estimate of around 180,000 and is a major gateway to the Great Barrier Reef, the Wet Tropics and the Queensland outback. The city was named in honour of a Sydney-based sea captain and financier named Robert Towns who provided ongoing financial assistance during the city's early development in the 1860s. Townsville now acts as the city port for the vast inland mining and agricultural regions of Northern Queensland. As well as the port, Townsville is home to the James Cook University and is Australia's largest garrison town with Australian Defence Force bases and a fascinating military history to explore. It was a major staging point for battles in the South West Pacific during the Second World War. The

Ross River flows through the city and the historic waterfront on Ross Creek, site of the original wharves and port facilities, has some old buildings mixed with the later modern skyline. However, the central city is dominated by the mass of red granite called Castle Hill, 292 metres high and just 8 metres short of being a mountain. There is a lookout at the summit giving panoramic views of the city and its suburbs, including Cleveland Bay and Magnetic Island.

These days the city remains popular with backpackers and tourists drawn to Magnetic Island and the Great Barrier Reef. It has excellent diving and snorkelling facilities, with a variety of vessels using the port as a home base for their reef tourism activities. I found it an interesting and lively city sitting under the impressive backdrop of Castle Hill. You can enjoy alfresco dining on the Strand, admire the city's Federation-style architecture, go boutique shopping at the modern Flinders Street Mall and the colourful weekly Cotter's Market as well as take-in the cooling ocean breezes from the Coral Sea. Other attractions include the Town Common Conservation Park, the Townsville Military History Museum, The Museum of Tropical Queensland, the Reef HQ Aquarium and the opportunity to take both Great Barrier Reef and Magnetic Island Day Trips.

The Townsville Running Festival is usually held on the first weekend in August each year. Unfortunately, for reasons unknown, this is generally also the same day as the Brisbane Marathon. Wouldn't you think the respective organisers would get their heads together to avoid this clash? (Since this was written they have. The Brisbane event has now moved to June). Early Bird entry fees for the 2018 edition cost $110 until the end of May. After that the entry fee rises to $130. Early Bird registrants receive a race singlet/shirt when they collect their race packs. Normal registrants receive a singlet coupon from the Merchandise Stand. The full marathon can be run solo or as part of a 2 to 3 person team relay, with 50% of the entry fee going directly to Mates4Mates when entering the relay. Any competitor who has completed 10 Townsville Marathons is presented with his/her own personal permanent marathon number bib.

The event kicks-off on the Friday of the race weekend with the annual Welcome Dinner held at 6.30pm at the Fish Inn at the Rockpool. Tickets cost $30 per person. Next day runners must pick up their race number at 'The Live it, Love it, Run it' Expo held at Jezzine Barracks on the Strand between 11am and 4pm. Late entries are accepted on the Saturday but late fees will apply. The Jezzine Barracks area on the city's Kissing Point Headland at the northern end of the Strand is a significant site for both the Australian military and local Aboriginal People. The whole area was recently redeveloped in a $40 million partnership between Townsville City Council, the Queensland Government and the Australian Government. The 15-hectare heritage precinct commemorates the military and Aboriginal heritage of the Kissing Point headland through 32 specially commissioned public artworks, extensive interpretive signage and the restoration of significant elements of the Kissing Point Fort complex. Large-scale landscaping works have also opened up the area for public use.

2017 results show that there were 169 finishers in the Marathon as opposed to only 79 finishers in 2003, the first year that shows results since 2001 when the courses were measured and accredited. I have been unable to find results for the earlier years of the race. Altogether there were approximately 2,600 participants across all seven events included in the Festival in 2017. The majority of these took part in either the Half Marathon (508 finishers) or the 10K race (600 finishers) The fact that the various start times are staggered so that the majority of runners finish at close to the same time makes for a great carnival atmosphere at the finish. Course records for the Marathon are 2:22:49 (male) set in 2014 and 2:40:52 (female) set in 2012. Though roads reopen from 10.30am and runners are directed onto footpaths in order to finish, Marathon runners are given 6 hours 30 minutes in which to complete the course.

On race day it is recommended that competitors get to the Race Headquarters one hour before the race starts and to the start area at least 15 minutes before the start of their event. This makes it a very early morning affair for those heading to the 5.30am Marathon start. Half Marathoners don't have to get up quite so early for their 7.45am start. The 10K leaves at 8.40am with the start line for all races located on Jezzine Way and with all races heading in the direction of the Rock Pool. This is a tourist friendly swimming area at the northern end of the Strand which brings in sea water from the ocean into a man-made rock pool where you can enjoy a swim. There are lifeguards on duty and plenty of places to sit and relax on the grass in the shade with great views out to the sea and to nearby Magnetic Island. With the beach being a no-go area due to the jellyfish, I recall spending a disproportionate amount of my time there while in Townsville.

The Marathon is a fast, flat 3 loop course with AIMS certification. The early morning start means that runners leave with the sunrise and get to experience the stunning beach views of the Coral Sea across to Magnetic Island, and the pre-dawn glow of Townsville's winter months. It's an easy, uncomplicated course. The first two laps are each of 10.549 kilometres out-and-back along the Strand passing the Marina before turning at the resort's Casino (370 gaming machines and more than 20 gaming tables if you're interested)

As was made clear to me on several occasions during my visit, you can't over-emphasise the importance of The Strand to the city. It's the city's centrepiece and serves as a central hub for all sorts of entertainment and outdoor enjoyment. The Strand has been a part of Townsville's history since the city was founded in the mid-19th century. The current foreshore was opened in 1999 after the old foreshore was severely damaged and eroded after heavy rainfall and wind from Tropical Cyclone Sid in January 1998 and other monsoonal storms between 1997 and 1998. It was also moderately damaged by Cyclone Tessi in April 2000. Stretching for well over 2 kilometres, the Strand is home to a variety of facilities – from accommodation to barbecue areas to playgrounds to walking and biking tracks and more. It's a place that can be both relaxed and energetic at the same time. Food outlets of all sizes can be found along its length with fish and chip joints existing alongside higher-profile gourmet dining options, While the array of restaurants on offer is not staggering, they are almost all of a universally-high quality. The Strand has been described as a place that accurately reflects Townsville's balance between being a growing city while still retaining a strong sense of community and the family environment here persists even during crowded tourist periods. After taking in what The Strand has to offer the third and final loop of the race then heads North along the coast to the beachside suburb of Pallarenda for a single out and back loop of 21.098km. Drink stops are located at approximately 5km intervals along the course with Powerade electrolyte drink and water in that order. (Water-only stops are located at every 2.5km) Vaseline and sunscreen are also located on the course. At the end of the race all competitors are invited to the official After Party Celebration commencing at 1 pm in the nearby Wild Goose Brews & Chews.

Not having run this marathon as yet I looked for online comments from those who had. These were few and far between but posts on marathonguide.com were very complimentary about the event. A Brisbane athlete who had specifically made the trip up from Queensland's capital for this race felt that the journey couldn't have been more worthwhile. He found the race kit collection easy, the general organisation outstanding and, being concerned about the heat, was grateful for both the 5.30am start and the 'dead flat' course on closed roads – apart from an approximately 6km section along a pedestrian path on the waterfront with plenty of room for everyone. He felt that the spectators were great although there were parts of the course where they were few and far between. He seems to have particularly enjoyed the finish area, describing it as having a 'carnival atmosphere, with bongo drums beating, and fruit, ice cream and muffins given out - not only to competitors, but to anyone who was around at the finish line, which was great'. All in all, he described it as a great experience that he would recommend for anyone wanting to do a well-run, laid back, low-key marathon that is flat and fast. These comments are supported by a fellow finisher who summarises his experience of the event in the following terms, 'Well organized. Plenty of well-spaced aid stations. Course is marked with a blue line and aided by marshals - easy to follow. Small lower-key race with 60 or so participants. Very friendly atmosphere - stay for a beer after with the Townsville Roadrunners. Pancake-flat course of two 10km loops and a 20km loop. Scenic - runs along the road along the beach most of the way overlooking Magnetic Island. Not many spectators.' A friend who completed the event in 2016 had virtually the same comments to make about the race.

Townsville is one of my favourite places on the Queensland coast. It certainly deserves more than just a quick in-an-out overnight stay by those of us who enjoy our marathon tourism. Its glorious climate (300 days of sunshine) laid-back atmosphere and convenient coastal location make it a great choice for an all-around travel spot. It's best described as an underrated destination in Tropical North Queensland that serves as a great destination for those looking for an alternative, less touristy, less expensive spot than the likes of its nearby neighbours Cairns and Port Douglas – both of which host their own, more recent marathon events. I've got unforgettable memories of a great few days on nearby Magnetic Island and would recommended a visit there to anyone, even if it is only for a day trip. Adult return ferry prices in 2018 were $33 with SeaLink and, though just a 20 minute ferry ride from Townsville, it seems like a whole world away The island's settlements have got a nice, old- fashioned feel about them not found in the more glitzy resorts off the coast. We spent our time staying in a reasonably priced 2-bedroomed apartment in Arcadia, dividing the day between bush-walks to Horseshoe Bay and training runs then swims on one of the many glorious beaches. Evenings were generally spent in the local pub followed by fish n' chips from Bannisters, an island icon. While there we also took the opportunity of making an expensive day trip by glass-bottomed catamaran from Picnic Bay to Great Kelso Reef on the Outer Barrier Reef. The snorkelling was excellent. Back in Townsville, I'd also recommend not missing out on a hike up to the top of Castle Hill. It's a tough 2.8km trek up the length of the road to the top which can also be accessed via a range of individual walking tracks that differ in both length and difficulty, but anyone prepared to put in the effort will be well-rewarded. As the city of Townsville is relatively flat and expansive, views from Castle Hill are almost completely unobstructed and allow a great perspective on both Magnetic Island to the east and the various rugged mountain ranges to the west. Multiple viewing platforms are on offer all over the hill which can provide a clearer outlook to certain directions.

Among other attractions worth visiting by those seeking more relaxing activities before or after the race, both The Museum of Tropical Queensland and Reef HQ Aquarium are situated close together at the end of Flinders Street beside Ross Creek. The former combines typical historical exhibitions with its focus on all-things-tropical. As the name suggests, the Museum places a large emphasis on topics such as the natural history of rainforests, maritime exploration, modern and ancient animals that dwell in the tropics and the ecosystems of the Great Barrier Reef. Set out over 3 levels, it's an informative, interactive and hands-on museum with my favourite exhibit being the life-sized replica bow of the HMS Pandora, a British ship that sunk back in 1791. The Pandora's exhibition is thorough and details both the history of the ship, how its guns and weaponry functioned, and an in-depth look at life for both crew and prisoners during this period of maritime history. Directly across the street, Townsville's Reef HQ Aquarium enjoys the status of the world's largest living coral reef aquarium and the best available showcase of the beauty of the Great Barrier Reef. Its main attraction is its vast living coral reef which provides a home for hundreds of sharks, rays and other marine life to live in a shared environment that's about as close to how they would in the 'real world'. Make sure that your visit coincides with the predator dive shows featuring sharks, the turtle shows or shark feeding sessions.

Finally, even if museums aren't your thing it could be interesting to pop into the nearby Army Museum of North Queensland while picking up your race number. Townsville is closer to Papua New Guinea than it is to Melbourne or Sydney and geographically has always felt it necessary to maintain a military presence in the area. Given that Townsville's military has guarded Queensland's coast for over 100 years, it seems only right that they should have a museum dedicated to their efforts. In The Army Museum visitors learn of Japanese attacks and fear of Russian invasion, and also hear of Australia's involvement in the Korean and Vietnamese Wars. Collections include cannons, guns, and artillery that stood at Kissing Point Fort—some of which has only been discovered during recent, exceptionally low tides. You can take a walk through re-created tunnels that were used in World War I, and hear the tales of North Queensland soldiers who fought and died in battle. For visitors with an interest in military history, the museum offers gripping, first-hand accounts of Queensland's soldiers and battles. Admission is free.

While the Strand shouldn't be discounted as the place to eat and drink while in Townsville, I like the sound of what's available at the post-race party venue The Wild Goose Brews and Chews in Flinders Street. Described on the menu as 'Big Plates for the Hungry' are Flame Grilled Cheeseburger at $16, Chicken Schnitzel at $22, Pork Cutlet for $28, Porterhouse Steak for $32 and Atlantic Salmon for $26. It also advertises 2-for-1 pizzas every Sunday from $18. The Wild Goose also offers a good selection of wines and draft beers. Further down the same street is the premises of the Townsville Brewery Co. who have redeveloped the city's former Post Office into a brewery, restaurant and function centre. Among the beers brewed on the premises are the Company's Townsville Bitter, Bandito Loco - a strong Mexican lager,

Digger's Golden Ale, Ned's Red Ale and, best of all, Flanagan's Dry Irish Stout. If the latter gives you the taste for Irish beer just walk a little further in the same direction to find Flynn's Irish Bar and, virtually next door to it, Molly Malone's pub.

SUNSHINE COAST MARATHON

QUEENSLAND

AUGUST

Located on the scenic Sunshine Coast in Queensland close to the Great Barrier Reef and the late Steve Irwin's iconic Australia Zoo, this event has been timed to make the most of the ideal running conditions during the Queensland winter. A member of the Association of International Marathons & Road Races (AIMS), the Sunshine Coast Marathon and Community Running Festival is earning a reputation as one of the most-enjoyable running festivals in Australia. The event has been timed to make the most of the ideal Queensland winter running conditions. Blue skies, low humidity and mild temperatures combined with a flat course have usually produced fast times. The Sunshine Coast Marathon has helped raise more than $1,000,000 for charity and community groups since the event started in 2012. Money raised has been distributed to more than 70 charities including the event's two major beneficiaries Ronald McDonald House Charities and Westpac Foundation. A donation is also given to each of the volunteer groups who in total provide more than 500 volunteers to ensure that the event runs smoothly. It serves as a thank-you and a way to give back at a grassroots level. Since its inception the event has raised over $1.3 million for charity and community groups.

For its seventh edition in 2018, the Festival's organisers promised to again deliver a flat, fast and scenic course. The festival distances include the Marathon, Half Marathon, 10km, 5km and 2km. Each race follows the stunning coastline of Alexandra Headlands with white sandy beaches and spectacular vantage points alongside the ocean from which to view them. The Half Marathon is a one loop course with Marathon entrants additionally completing a multi loop course between the beach suburbs of Alexander Headland and Mooloolaba (1 x 21km plus 2 x 10.5km).This guarantees maximum exposure to the on-course entertainment and crowds of spectators before a red carpet finish. The event is promoted as 'A community event for every runner' with a distance to suit every ability and age group.' It caters to all those wanting to take part, including families and those with both physical and mental disabilities. The 2km, for example, event allows parents with prams and wheelchair entrants to take part and enjoy the festival atmosphere.

I have to say that for those who enjoy coastal scenery it's hard to imagine a much more beautiful location in which to hold a race. The area that stretches from Caloundra in the south to Noosa Heads in the north is not called the Sunshine Coast for nothing. I've been lucky enough to have holidayed in both of these resorts and visited Alexandra Headland on several occasions, always combining it with a walk along the esplanade to the nearby trendy resort of Mooloolaba – both part of the marathon route.

Located 100 km north of the state capital Brisbane, the Sunshine Coast is third most populated area in the state of Queensland with an urban area that spans approximately 60 km. The estimated urban population of the Sunshine Coast as at June 2015 was around 300,000 making it the 9th most populous in the country. The area was first settled by

Europeans in the 19th century with development progressing slowly until tourism became an important industry. Many of the region's towns began as simple ports and jetties for the timber industry during the 1860s and 1870s, as the area once had magnificent stands of forest and the region's road were used for hauling timber. After World War II, the Sunshine Coast grew into a favoured holiday and surfing destination. This tendency was further expanded in the development boom of the 1960s and 1970s to the extent that by 2016 it had become one of the fastest-growing regions in Australia. It's now a centre for tourism, attracting more than 3.2 million visitors a year. Among its attractions to have become internationally famous are: Steve Irwin's Australia Zoo, UnderWater World Marine Park, the Buderim Ginger Factory, the Big Pineapple and the Glass House Mountains. Sports tourism has also blossomed through such well-known events as the Mooloolaba Triathlon, the Noosa Triathlon and, of course, the Sunshine Coast Marathon.

The Sunshine Coast is served by its own airport located 10km north of Maroochydore. Jetstar, Virgin Australia. Tiger Airways and Qantas fly there from Sydney, Melbourne and Adelaide. The airport now also welcomes international flights, with Air New Zealand scheduling twice weekly seasonal services from July to October. The airport has excellent facilities for an airport of its size with ATMs, rental cars, transfer services, and food and shopping outlets. The race organisers have arranged a 10% discount with the locally owned and operated company, Airlink Transfers to help participants arrive at their destination. For those preferring public transport the Translink (Sunbus) 622 bus departs the airport terminal hourly between Maroochydore and Noosa Junction, but somewhat inconveniently stops before the last flights arrive from Sydney and Melbourne. You can also catch the train from Brisbane to various stations in the Sunshine Coast area. TransLink coordinates all rail services in South East Queensland, including suburban services in Brisbane and inter-urban services on the North Coast rail line from Brisbane to Gympie North and the intermediate destinations of Landsborough and Nambour. These stations have connecting buses to Caloundra, Maroochydore, Noosa, and Mooloolaba. The latter is the closest town to the marathon start and is also very easily accessed by car from Brisbane via a straight 1.5 hour drive on the Bruce Highway. Its Mantra Mooloolaba Beach resort featuring 178 fully furnished one, two and three-bedroom suites each with a private balcony and ocean or garden views has been chosen as the official race hotel. The four-star beachfront property is 200 metres from the race start and event precinct and is at the heart of Mooloolaba's vibrant Esplanade and cafe precinct.

Mooloolaba is a young, trendy part of the Sunshine Coast. In the past decade, the area has undergone massive tourism boosts with increased development and a higher skyline reflecting well the wealth that has come to the area. Commonly voted as one of the most beautiful and safest beaches on the Sunshine Coast with picture perfect sunrises and surf, Mooloolaba Beach is a crescent-shaped bay which includes The Spit, 500 metres to the south. Numerous up-market bars, cafes and restaurants occupy the Esplanade, the town's famous (or should that be infamous – it can get boisterous in season) main thoroughfare. Point Cartwright, also known as Point Atty on the southern edge of the bay, is a man-made rock wall offering boats safe entry to the canals and mooring docks of backwater Mooloolaba. A good way of seeing the place from the water is to take the Mooloolaba Canal Cruise on board the historic timber ferry MV Mudjimba which has been operating on the Sunshine Coast from the

Mooloolaba Wharf for 26 years. This still-water cruise with live commentary passes opulent waterfront mansions, yachts and historic landmarks. Wild pelicans are hand fed from the side of the boat and there's the opportunity to feed the fish at the end of the cruise. I found it a relaxing and enjoyable experience – particularly if combined with a visit to the nearby Wharf Tavern afterwards.

Alexandra Headland is a somewhat quieter destination. Located in the Maroochydore urban centre between Maroochydore CBD and Mooloolaba, the suburb consists of several restaurants, a bowling alley, resorts and the shortest beach in the Maroochy district. The Alexandra Headland Surf Life Saving Club has a building next to the beach. The headland was once known as Potts Point, named after overseer John Potts employed by William Pettigrew who lived on the land from the year 1880 to 1890, when it was used to transport timber between Cotton Tree and Mooloolah River by bullock. One of the things to look out for on race weekend is the HMAS Brisbane Memorial to ship and crew of the same name. The Memorial points to the ship's final resting place. Brisbane undertook two tours of duty with the United States Seventh Fleet off Vietnam, in 1969 and again in 1971, and was the last ship of the RAN to serve there. During the first Gulf War Brisbane was one of four Australian warships to serve a tour in Gulf waters.

The registration venue at Alexandra Headland is in one of the strongest clubs in the surf life-saving movement. Founded in 1924 and currently with over 11,000 members, the Surf Club is responsible for patrolling the beach between Mooloolaba and Maroochydore. The Club's headquarters have been designed to make the most of its prime, beachfront location with great views across the beach and the Pacific Ocean. It welcomes visitors and is a great place for a relaxing lunch or dinner or to just go and enjoy a quiet drink while enjoying the beach views. It also acts as the venue for the event's after-race party from 3pm until late on race day.

Entries for the Festival open on 1st December in the preceding year. Marathon entry fees rise in three stages from $110 to $130. There's also one of those unnecessary VIP-type entries that are creeping more and more into marathon events across the USA. In most instances their sole purpose centres around profit maximisation. Though I notice that this one includes a $100 charitable donation, I still question why marathon runners require such services as a personalised bag drop, access to VIP email and VIP registration and race pack collection. Those able to collect their own bags can do so in the Alexandra Headland Surf Club on the Friday (1pm to 7pm) and Saturday (11am to 4pm). Late entries are accepted until 3pm on Saturday. Brisbane based runners are able to collect their race pack at Intraining's premises in Milton (the same venue used by the Brisbane Marathon) between 11am and 4pm on the Saturday. In past years, each entrant has received a limited edition visor and every finisher has been rewarded with a finishers' medal and towel.

The Festival has grown considerably in numbers since inception. There were only 300 finishers in the Marathon in 2012 as opposed to 547 in 2017 when the Australian Half Marathon Championships were held on the course for the first time. 1712 athletes completed the Half Marathon and a further 1,306 finished the 10K race. Marathon runners are given 6 hours in which to complete their event. Pacers are provided at 15 minute intervals from 3 hours to 4 hours 30 minutes. The male course record currently stands at 2:18:30 set by Ethiopian, Samuel Woldemanuel in 2015. Elkie Belcher holds the female course record of 2:42:35 set in 2017. On the Sunday morning both the Full and Half Marathon runners start together in designated time zones at 6am. The 10K leaves at 9am with the 5K and 2K races leaving at 10.15am and 11am respectively. All races start and finish outside the Alexandra Headlands Surf Club.

The course is relatively flat and easy to follow with the Half Marathon course acting as the first of the Marathon's three loops. This takes runners south along the coastal road via The Esplanade towards the centre of Mooloolaba. Turning at Amarina Avenue just after 3.5 kilometres, runners retrace their steps back past the Surf Club at 6.5km before heading north along the coastline via Duporth and then Bradman Avenues. A second turn at 14km sees runners then heading back past the Maroochy Surf Club at 19km and on to the Half Marathon finish. After this Marathon competitors are on their own for a further two laps, each of 10.5km. These largely follow what was the second half of what they've already run. Both head up Alexander Parade, turning inland for a short stretch on Sixth Avenue before continuing again up Duporth Avenue to yet another turn at Picnic Point Road. It's then back to the finish for the medal and that well-earned beer or more in the Alexandra Heads Surf Club.

Provided you can get a table, the Surf Club is a great place to dine after the event. Its Lookout Restaurant serves a full range of pizzas from $18 as well as a whole variety of other dishes. Among these are: Seafood Chowder at $35, Lamb Rump for $30, Pork Cutlet for $30, Chicken Supreme $28, Rump and Porterhouse Steaks at $32 and $29. If the place is too crowded (which I suspect it might be on marathon day) you can always head along to the Esplanade where there's any number of decent places to eat. You might even fancy stopping off at O'Malley's Irish Bar on Venning Street at the Esplanade's northern end. This too serves a variety of dishes on its evening menu including: Stockman's Pie, Chicken

Breast, Beef Lasagne, Spaghetti Bolognaise, Roast of the Day and a number of strange sounding Irish dishes – all from around $20 to $25. The beer's not bad either.

KANGAROO ISLAND MARATHON

SOUTH AUSTRALIA

SEPTEMBER

The Kangaroo Island Marathon is a relative newcomer to the Australian Marathon Calendar. Held annually on the island of the same name off the coast of South Australia it rather grandly describes itself as, 'A boutique marathon through some of the world's most pristine and unspoilt wilderness,' and 'an adventure race that showcases one of Australia's best kept secrets.' This description gives the event a lot to live up to. The race is the brainchild of the 1908 Sports Management Company whose grandiose aim is to be a leader in the adventure tourism industry by raising the profile of the Marathon to one of the Top 10 Destination Marathons in the World. According to their promotional literature they intend doing this by aligning the Kangaroo Island Marathon with the island's 5 strategic values of: connecting with nature, sharing authentic Australian experiences, building relationships with like-minded people, and celebrating the seclusion and peace of being on an island disconnected from normal everyday lives.

First held in 2015, the marathon route is located in the remote south-west corner of Flinders Chase National Park. Runners are taken along undulating roads that cut through dense forest, an exposed coastal section with views of the Southern Ocean, a loop that travels by historic landmarks such as Cape de Couedic Lighthouse and Admirals Arch, a trail run into Snake Lagoon, and a zig-zag boardwalk leading to the iconic Remarkable Rocks. The undulating nature of the course means this race isn't about fast times, but it's about running amongst the natural beauty of what is considered one of Australia's best kept secrets. It's described as one of the only marathons in the world where you could literally be passed by a kangaroo – hence the race slogan of 'Run with the Roos.'

    I think it's fair to say that the event hasn't yet reached the profile intended by the organisers despite numbers having slowly improved each year. Though the island location and national park track limit the maximum number of runners to 500 across both the Half and Full Marathons there were only 42 finishers in 2015's Marathon race (35 in the Half), 41 finishers in the Full in 2016 (57 in the Half) and 60 Full Marathon finishers in 2017 (77 in the Half). What is increasing is the number of international entrants each year. In 2015 there was only one overseas finisher in the Marathon (a New Zealander). The 2017 Marathon results included runners from Italy, China, USA, UK, New Zealand, Singapore and Hong Kong. Runners' times for the event ranged between 2:51 and 6:27.

    I'm not sure about 'boutique.' I can't even imagine the term being used in the context of a marathon race, but the Kangaroo Island Marathon is certainly a unique event in a unique location. Kangaroo Island has an enviable reputation as one of Australia's great scenic treasures and a must-see for anyone interested in travel to wilderness destinations. Situated 110 km south-west of Adelaide and easily accessible by ferry or plane the Island is said to be the place to see the best of Australia if you don't have time to see the whole continent. Known as 'KI' to the locals, the Island is a microcosm of many Australian landscapes: pristine bushland; white sand dunes; and spectacular seascapes where rocky cliffs plunge into a wild ocean. Classified as one of Australia's National Landscapes (areas selected for their distinctively Australian natural and cultural significance) Kangaroo Island has long been regarded as a shining example of how tourism and conservation can work together. Over half the native bushland remains just as it was when British explorer Matthew Flinders named it in 1802, and more than one-third is protected as either a National or Conservation Park. Due to its separation from the Australian mainland some 9000 years ago, the Island has managed to remain unaffected by the introduction of pests such as foxes and rabbits, so its wildlife has continued to flourish without interference. Kangaroos and other marsupials far outnumber the Island's 4400 permanent residents consisting largely of farmers, artists, ecologists and fishermen. Though kangaroos are ubiquitous, the Island's wildlife is far more varied than its name suggests. Many of the species of plants and animals found on the Island are either threatened or exist nowhere else in Australia. Koalas, wallabies, goannas, echidnas, brush-tailed possums and even the rarely seen platypus lives in parts of Kangaroo Island. Not only are the land based animals in abundance, but marine life is also prolific and includes: dolphins, whales (in winter), seals, sea lions and Little Penguins. Bird-lovers will find some 270 species of bird among the diverse range of habitats, including the rare Glossy Black Cockatoo, an endangered species found only on KI.

The island also has an interesting human history. Evidence suggests that Aboriginal people inhabited the Island as early as 16,000 years ago and as recently as 2,000 years ago though the reasons why they left remain a mystery. The answer is hinted at in the Indigenous name for KI: 'Karta' (Land of the Dead). In 1800 the British Government commissioned Captain Matthew Flinders to explore and map the southern coastline of Terra Australis in HMS Investigator. Flinders made the first recorded European sighting of the island in March 1802. He came ashore on the north coast and named it Kangaroo Island. Among the early settlers were sealers, escaped convicts and runaway sailors, seeking refuge and leading a self-sufficient life trading salt and skins for spirits and tobacco. In the early 1800s an Indigenous presence (albeit a tragically displaced one) was re-established on KI when whalers and sealers abducted Aboriginal women from Tasmania and brought them there. Since then the island's economy has been principally agricultural, with a southern rock lobster fishery and with tourism growing in importance. Today, Kangaroo Island is one of South Australia's most popular tourist attractions, attracting over 140,000 visitors each year, with international visitors, primarily from Europe, accounting for more than 25% of these visits.

The island's largest town, and the administrative centre is Kingscote. Originally established at Reeves Point in 1836, it is South Australia's first colonial settlement. It was later suggested that Kingscote could serve as the capital of South Australia, but the island's resources were insufficient to support such a large community, so the settlement of Adelaide was chosen. There are also several smaller towns on the island. Penneshaw, the second largest town, has a population of around 300, and is located on the north eastern tip of the Dudley Peninsula, on the eastern end of the island. It contains the ferry terminal which brings most of the visitors to the island, along with all the necessary freight to sustain the local population. American River, on the north coast between Kingscote and Penneshaw, is home to about 220 residents. Parndana, in the centre of the island, has a population of around 150 while the historic area to the southeast of the township set up in the 1940s and 1950s to research the viability of agriculture in the area, is still home to a small settlement of about 20 people. Penneshaw and Parndana each have basic facilities, including a general store and fuel and are home to hotels. Facilities such as banking and large supermarkets are available in Kingscote and Penneshaw.

For those travelling to the Marathon, Kangaroo Island SeaLink operates two large, luxurious vehicle and passenger ferries, between Cape Jervis, around a 2 hour drive from Adelaide on the Fleurieu Peninsula, and Penneshaw. There are four departures daily, with additional services during peak times. Bookings are necessary and travelling time is about 45 minutes. Mainland coach connections are available between Adelaide and Cape Jervis while Inter-Island connections operate between Penneshaw to American River and Kingscote, a 20-minute drive from the ferry terminal. Regional Express Airlines also services Kangaroo Island daily and I believe Qantas has plans to fly to fly there soon. The current 30 minute flight operates between the main terminal at the Adelaide Airport and Kangaroo Island Airport, a short 10-minute drive to Kingscote. Flinders Chase National Park, home of the Kangaroo Island Marathon, is a further 60-minute drive from Kingscote. The National Park is a protected area located at the west end of Kangaroo Island. It's a sanctuary for endangered species, a reserve for a range of flora and fauna, and home to interesting geological phenomena. It consists of three sections; Cape Borda lightstation reserve in the northwest corner, the Gosse Lands and Snake Lagoon in the centre of the west end, and Cape de Couedic in the south-west corner which includes two significant monuments, the Remarkable Rocks and Admirals Arch.

The event's website recommends a number of accommodation options for would-be entrants. These include the Kangaroo Island Wilderness Retreat, located 5-minutes from Flinders Chase National Park and offering a range of accommodation to suit both the budget traveller and those seeking the comfort of a first class international hotel. Guests can choose from 20 courtyard suites or a lodge containing 4 self-catering apartments and 8 motel rooms. Another recommendation is The Mercure Hotel in American River, just a short 20-minute drive from the Penneshaw ferry terminal. Located over-looking the picturesque American River this 4.5 star hotel offers guests a range of accommodation options in close proximity to local amenities. A third option is the Southern Ocean Lodge regarded as the premier accommodation option on Kangaroo Island with 21 luxury suites in a dramatic wilderness setting and featuring excellent views of the Southern Ocean. Runners staying in accommodation across the island are offered a bus service to the start of the race as part of the entry package. As an example, arrangements in place for the 2018 event included pick-ups at 5:00am from the Mercure Hotel, Kingscote. 5:10am from Kangaroo Island Airport. 5:45am from Vivonne Bay, General Store and 6:15am from the KI Wilderness Retreat. The same buses departed on the return leg from 12:00 noon after the official race presentations had been completed.

Entry fee for the 2018 Kangaroo Island Marathon held on 1 September was $129 per person. For this runners received return bus transfers, pre-paid National Park entrance fee, a metal engraved drink bottle, electrolyte drinks at aid stations, post- race refreshments and a Finishers medal. Registration numbers can be collected the day before the event from 9:00am-1:00pm at the Mercure Hotel, American River and from 2:00pm-6:00pm at the Kangaroo Island Wilderness Retreat, Flinders Chase. Alternatively, runners can collect their numbers on the morning of the race from 6am. The full marathon start time is 7:00am and the half marathon starts at 8:00am. The bus that transports runners to the start of the half marathon departs the visitors centre at 7:45am sharp. A shuttle bus service also operates between Flinders Chase park entrance and the start/finish line from 6:30am to 7:45am. Runners can park their vehicles on the road verge of West End Highway and wait next to the park entrance sign for a bus. After 8:00am family and friends can access the park by vehicle and drive to the visitors centre car park and cafe where they can watch runners finish both events. The Marathon cut-off time is 7 hours and 4 aid stations are located at regular intervals accessible in both directions and providing runners with water, electrolytes, bananas and lollies. A selection of light refreshments is also available at the finish line.

The marathon, which starts at the Visitor's Centre, has a total elevation gain of 632m and a maximum elevation gain of 154m. The half marathon starts at Bunker Hill Lookout. The marathon route travels south along Cape de Couedic Road offering runners consistent elevation changes on primarily sealed roads and a flat 3km trail section that travels into Snake Lagoon. Diverting east via Boxer Drive, marathon runners are exposed to the elements on a cliff-top section that leads to the iconic Remarkable Rocks. The Rocks are a huge outcrop of weather sculptured granite boulders perched on a large granite dome that drops 75 metres to the sea. This unusual work of nature has been shaped by the erosive forces of wind, sea spray, and rain over more than 500 million years. The golden orange lichen covering some of the rocks offers visitors good photo opportunities at different times of the day. Runners then enjoy some respite as they travel downhill towards the coastal tip including a detour into Weirs Cove before passing by Cape de Couedic Lighthouse which has guarded the island since 1909. All runners loop around the car park at the entrance to Admirals Arch, before being tested by a short climb that peaks at 4% incline. Admirals Arch is a former cave, eroded away over thousands of years to become a distinctive rock bridge. Stalactites protrude from the rocky ceiling in contrast to the floor which is polished smooth. The boardwalk leading to Admirals Arch is almost as scenic as the landmark itself, and provides an ideal place to observe the fur seal colony that rest and breed in the rock pools. The finish line for both the half and full marathon is located directly in front of the Flinders Chase National Park Visitor Centre's cafe.

Finishers' comments about the event have generally been very appreciative and the following are typical of what I've read. 'What a truly amazing experience. The start of the race with the Didgeridoo was great and very uplifting. Even with the wind and rain, running down to the Remarkable Rocks will be something I will remember for a long time. You have something special here.' (D. Turnbull). 'This was my first marathon. I felt so free and inspired by the scenery that I had a truly spiritual experience. A great event, beautiful people participating and volunteering.' (K. Brown). Also, 'I've run 72 marathons and this is one of my favourites. Everything exceeded my expectations - the quality of the medals, the gift bags, the signage at the start finish line, using a drone to video runners, enthusiastic volunteers and very well stocked aid stations - it was all top notch. You put on a world-class race, so thank you.' (from B. Johnson). Finally, 'A must run marathon, unlike no other. It will test your mind as much as your muscles, but the feeling you get when you cross the finish line will be worth it.' (Z. Heath)

Kangaroo Island offers a number of excursions and attractions that might be of interest to fellow Marathon Tourists. For example, the Marine Dolphin Tour on board the Island Explorer provides a 3-hour marine adventure to discover remote beaches, ancient fossil beds, and a host of ocean creatures. If conditions allow guests have the opportunity to swim with the dolphins during the trip. The Island Beehive is one of the largest organic honey producers in Australia, extracting over 100 tonnes of honey per year which is exported nationally and internationally. An arranged visit includes insight into the role of the Ligurian Bee, a tour of the processing plant, and a tasting of a range of honey flavours all produced on Kangaroo Island. A visit can also be arranged to the Island Pure Dairy which opened in 1992 as South Australia's first sheep dairy and cheese factory. Located on 260 hectares of land in the Gum Creek region of Kangaroo Island, tours include a full tasting experience plus some background information on how to make natural homemade cheeses and yoghurts. Another option is to visit Kangaroo Island Spirits, South Australia's only boutique micro distillery, which specialises in handcrafted premium Australian spirits, gins and liqueurs. Visitors can enjoy a range of award winning 'pure spirits' made from local ingredients such as coastal daisy and native juniper berries. Kangaroo Island also has five protected marine parks that ensure water quality is high, helping to produce some of the best tasting oysters in the world. A visit to The Oyster Farm Shop provides the opportunity to taste a selection of freshly shucked oysters from local oyster farms located in Eastern Cove. Oysters grown in this region are said to be known for their distinctly sweet flavour. Finally for the more energetic, Little Sahara is a naturally occurring sand dune system that covers two square kilometres, and is designated a national heritage area. The dunes vary in size, with the largest peak 70 metres above sea level. Kangaroo Island Outdoor Action offer visitors the chance to sand board or toboggan down the dunes.

As you can imagine for such a small island, there aren't too many places to eat and drink that aren't tied into some sort of accommodation package. Sunset Food and Wine in Hog Bay Road, Kangaroo Head, a modern bistro which overlooks the beautiful American Beach, is an exception. It was the first restaurant on Kangaroo Island to win an award from the Australian Good Food Guide in 2017. Among the Main courses listed on the menu are: King George whiting milanese for $38 plus locally caught fish, sweetcorn and zucchini for $36 and Kangaroo Island lamb rump and eggplant for $37. A much less-expensive option is the Bella Café and Pizza Bar in Kingscote offering 12-inch pizzas, pasta, burgers and soups. I've read that probably the best place for a beer on the Island is in the 112-year old Penneshaw Hotel. Affectionately known as the 'Penny,' the hotel's bar area has commanding and uninterrupted views over Backstairs Passage with absolute water frontage from its cliff-top setting. Beers on offer include Cooper's Original Pale Ale, Carlton Draught, Hahn Premium Light and West End Draught among a range of others. It also serves a superior selection of your typical pub grub including Fish and Chips from $20, Burgers from $20, Chicken or Beef Schnitzel $23, chargrill Lamb Chops, Porterhouse Steak and Kangaroo Fillet all from around $27. Combine these treats with the magnificent views and cosy log fires when the temperature drops and there's really no need to go anywhere else on the island for your post-race meal.

DUNEDIN MARATHON

SOUTH ISLAND, NEW ZEALAND

SEPTEMBER

The annual Dunedin Marathon reaches its 40th anniversary in September 2018. As well as the full marathon distance, the programme also includes a half marathon, featuring the New Zealand Half Marathon Championships plus a 10km run and recreational walk. Established in 1979, this is one of the most scenic marathons in New Zealand, starting close to the Albatross Colony on the Otago Peninsula and running around the beautiful Otago Harbour before finishing inside Forsyth Barr Stadium Dunedin. The original event in 1979 consisting of a marathon and half marathon was initiated by the Otago Branch of the New Zealand Federation of Sports Medicine. In 1985 organisation of the event was taken over by the local Caversham Harrier and Athletic Club which has continued to organise the marathon to the present day. Initially the only officially recognised events were the Marathon and Half Marathon. However, in order to give more people the opportunity to participate and improve their fitness and to keep up with innovations, over time the Caversham organisers added further events and technology: The Half Marathon Recreational Walk was added in 1995 and in 2015 a Quarter Marathon Run and Walk events were also included.

Over the years the race has gone through a succession of name changes. It has been known, in order, as the: Dunedin

Round the Harbour Marathon (1979-1982), the Dunedin Harbour Marathon (1983), the City of Dunedin Round the Harbour Marathon (1984), Speight's City of Dunedin Marathon (1985-1987), the Cadbury Moro City of Dunedin Marathon (1988-1996), the Cadbury Moro Harbour Marathon (1997), the Moro Marathon (1998-2012), the Cadbury Dunedin Marathon (2013-2017) and finally the Dunedin Marathon (2018). The Half Marathon was scrapped for two years in 1980 and 1981 but was revived again in 1982 with changes in the start position. The specific finish position has also changed a number of times. Races finished initially on the street in Port Chalmers, but in most of the last two decades they have ended at Watson Park in Port Chalmers. There are major changes planned to the courses and finish in 2018 driven largely by safety concerns along the route expressed by competitors and the lack of atmosphere at the finish for late finishers. Also, as the Quarter Marathon is not an officially recognised event it was decided that this distance is to be replaced by 10 km run and walk events in 2018. As in all previous years the full marathon will start at Harington Point near the Royal Albatross Centre. However, the marathon along with the half marathon and 10 km events will finish inside Forsyth Barr Stadium rather than Port Chalmers. The Forsyth Barr Stadium is a futuristic rugby and soccer stadium, opened in 2011 for the Rugby World Cup and is fully enclosed with a grass surface—the only such stadium in the world. (Apparently the roof is transparent, allowing grass to grow.) This has led to some wags starting to call their new stadium the 'Greenhouse of Pain' —a play on 'House of Pain', the traditional nickname of the Carisbrook stadium it replaced.

Dunedin (from Dun Eideann, the Scottish Gaelic name for Edinburgh, the capital of Scotland) is the second-largest city in the South Island of New Zealand, the principal city of the

Otago region and one the country's largest ports. It has become known as the 'Edinburgh of the South' and appears to take great pride in its Scottish heritage. The city centre features a large statue of the poet Robbie Burns and many of its streets carry the same name as streets in Edinburgh. Dunedin is built in a natural harbour on a relatively small area of flat land surrounded by steep hillsides. The city skyline is dominated by a ring of seven hills which form the remnants of a volcanic crater. Notable among them are Mount Cargill (700m), Flagstaff (680 m)), Saddle Hill (480 m), Signal Hill (390 m), and Harbour Cone (320 m). With so many hills it's no surprise that some of its streets are steep and hilly. Baldwin Street is recorded as the steepest street in the world by the Guinness Book of World Records, (a claim which is celebrated during the annual Cadbury chocolate festival by rolling 75,000 chocolate, orange-coated sweets called Jaffas from the top of it). The city suburbs extend out into the surrounding valleys and hills and onto the isthmus of the Otago Peninsula. I'm told that the best views available of Dunedin and surrounds can be had from the lookout point of Signal Hill overlooking the head of Otago Harbour. It's the most prominent viewpoint accessible to the public and provides a wonderful birds-eye view of the city and its surrounds that makes for a good first port of call on a visit to the city to get a sense of the lay of the land and where everything is.

Dunedin's history of European settlement started in 1848 when the Lay Association of the Free Church of Scotland established a Scottish settlement was in the area. Many thousands of Scots then emigrated to the new settlement between 1855 and 1900. The city became wealthy during the Central Otago Gold Rush, beginning in the 1860s. In the mid-1860s, and between 1878 and 1881, it was New Zealand's largest urban area. Today, Dunedin has something of a reputation as a university town with its population of more than 120,000 swollen during term time by its large number of students. Founded in 1869, the University of Otago, home to some 18,000 students, is New Zealand's oldest university. It's said to be well worth a visit, with many magnificent bluestone buildings to admire. Dunedin's centre is described as having a genuine old-world feel, rich in some of the most beautiful architecture examples of Victorian and Edwardian construction south of the equator. Hiking and cycling trails crisscross the dramatic landscape of the adjoining Otago Peninsula, home to colonies of albatross, sea lions and rare yellow-eyed penguins. Taken together, the city's architecture and coastal location provide Dunedin with a wonderful balance of natural and the man-made attractions.

Dunedin airport is 30km out of town on the nearest piece of flat land that was big enough for the runway. It is primarily used for domestic flights, with regular flights to and from Auckland, Christchurch and Wellington but it also has international flights arriving from and departing to Brisbane all year round. In recent years, a decline in International passengers can be attributed to fewer international flights operating direct to the airport. Taxis and shuttle buses operate from just outside the terminal and are usually there when flights arrive. The fare into the city for a shared shuttle is around $18-25 and around $50-80 for a taxi. Though trains no longer run to the city getting to Dunedin by bus is an affordable way to travel, with the added bonus of seeing some decent scenery en route. There are several daily services from Christchurch, Invercargill, Wanaka and Queenstown. The major operators are InterCity, Atomic Shuttles, Wanaka-Connection and Knightrider. The journey from (or to) Christchurch takes about 6.5 hours. If arriving by car, State Highway 1 passes through Dunedin reducing the journey time to around 4 hours 30 minutes from Christchurch and 2 hours 30 minutes from Invercargill. While Dunedin is a very accessible city it is also hilly, so if you arrive in the city and do not have a vehicle getting around the city by public transport is relatively easy, as distances are not great. Booking.com showed 97 available properties in the Dunedin area for 3 nights, Friday to Monday, over the 2018 marathon weekend. When booked online from the UK these ranged from £81 for a double room in the Stafford Gables Hostel to £125 in the 2-star Leviathan Hotel and £162 in the 3-star Law Courts Hotel. 4-star hotels like The Victoria Hotel started from around £200 a double over the same 3 nights.

The Dunedin Marathon isn't a big event in world terms. In 2017, only 133 runners (88 males and 45 females) completed the Marathon while 648 runners finished in the Half Marathon with a relatively even split of males (319) and females (329.) There were a further 121 in the accompanying Half Marathon Walk. The now defunct Quarter Marathon had 274 participants that year plus another 169 in the walk. Early bird entry fees for the Marathon start at $75 and rise in increments to $105 for last-minute, in-person entry up to 4pm on the day before the race. Race Pack pick-ups and Late Entries can be made at the Sargood Centre Logan Park Drive. The Race Pack contains Race Number, timing chip, Gear Bag and T-Shirt (if ordered as part of the online entry process). Free transport is provided from outside the Sargood Centre between 6.00.am and 6.30am on race day to take Full Marathon runners to the start at Harington Point. Marathon start time is at 8:00am, 1km south of the Royal Albatross Colony, Taiaroa Heads on the Otago Peninsula. Runners are given 6 hours in which to complete the race. The other main events start and finish at the Forsyth Barr Stadium with the Half Marathon leaving at 9:00am and the 10K at 9:30am.

Marathon runners start their race close to the world's only mainland Royal Albatross Breeding Colony. A visit to the nearby Royal Albatross Centre offers the opportunity to access the nature reserve to see giant albatross court, mate, raise their chicks and show off their three metre wingspans. The 2012 Lonely Planet publication '1000 Ultimate Sights' features the Centre alongside the Taj Mahal and Grand Canyon, describing it as 'one of New Zealand's hottest attractions.' The Royal Albatross Centre is located on the tip of the Otago Peninsula, about a 45 minute drive from Dunedin. The Peninsula is a long, hilly indented finger of land that forms the easternmost part of Dunedin and boasts a wide diversity of flora and fauna. The Peninsula's coasts are prominent habitats for marine mammals. Seal and sea lion colonies have regenerated during the 20th century after massive exploitation in the 19th century which almost wiped out both them and whales. A number of New Zealand fur seals and Hooker's sea lions currently breed around Taiaroa Head while several species of dolphins and small whales also occur constantly around the peninsula. Dunedin's suburbs encroach onto the peninsula's western end and runners pass through the seven townships and communities that lie along the harbourside shoreline. Largest of these are Macandrew Bay (the peninsula's largest settlement, with a population of 1,100), Portobello, and Otakou. The latter is the site of the first permanent European settlement on the Harbour, and the site of an early whaling station, commemorated at nearby Weller's Rock.

The course follows the peninsula for over 25km all the way towards Dunedin and joins the half marathon and 10 km courses at the Harbour Mouth Molars. The three courses then share a path past Toitu Otago Settlers Museum followed by Dunedin's Railway Station. The station was built in Victorian times, is Dunedin's most celebrated building and is regarded as the most photographed in the country. After another kilometre the course heads into the Otago University campus, passing the Univerity's gothic style clocktower on the other side of the Leith River. At edge of the campus on Dundas Street the full and half marathon course then heads to the Dunedin Botanic Gardens while the 10K course deviates to the edge of Logan Park to finish at Forsyth Barr Stadium. After doing a loop of the lower sections of the Botanic Gardens, the full and half marathon course heads along State Highway 88 to the suburb of Ravensbourne and turns back via The West Harbour Cycleway to the finish at Forsyth Barr Stadium. Eight drinks stations at 5km intervals serve water and drinks from Pure Sports Nutrition at each station as well as at the Finish Line. Everyone who finishes receives a medal.

After their race Marathon Tourists might want to take a closer look at some of the stunning heritage buildings and Edwardian architecture from the early Scottish settlers. An easy walk around downtown Dunedin following one of the two Heritage Trails will take you past those that have been categorised by the New Zealand Historic Places Trust. A good place to start would be at the beautiful Dunedin Railway Station in ANZAC Square. Described as 'the outstanding monument of Edwardian architecture in New Zealand,' the station was constructed in 1906, during the New Zealand rail system's period of growth that occurred between the late 1890s to the early 1900s. Notable features of the station are the large dome at the SW corner of the building and the stained glass windows depicting locomotives and tiled arches that surround the ticket boxes. The Law Courts building in Stuart Street is also worth a visit. Built in 1902 on the site of the city's old jail, this is reputedly one of the finest examples of Gothic civic architecture in the country. For anyone with

Scottish connections, Larnach Castle is a must-see while in Dunedin. The castle is set high above the harbour in Company Bay where William Larnach commission the construction of what is New Zealand's only castle in 1871. The view from the castle over the city, harbour and peninsula is said to be magnificent. The Victorian castle is also well known for its 14 hectare garden and grounds which has been recognised as a Garden of International Significance. The connections to Scotland are reinforced by the Robert Burns statue. Over 100 years old, the recently restored statue of the famous Scottish poet Robbie Burns sits in The Octagon at the heart of the city. (Dunedin's centre is shaped like an octagon instead of the standard square). The statue is one of four nearly identical statues cast by the same Edinburgh sculptor, one of which rests in Central Park, New York. Finally, you couldn't (I couldn't) pass-up on a visit to Speights Brewery in Rattray Street. The brewery is one of the fixtures of Dunedin's city centre and an icon of South Island beverages. The name Speight's is synonymous for beer in the region as its brewery has been churning out bottles of quality amber since way back in 1876 on the same site that it can be found today. It's more than just a factory granting visitors an insight to the brewing techniques of the past, the building itself is ripe with history and has been listed as a local heritage centre for many years.

    For those who want to get out of the city a trip on the Taieri Gorge Railway is recommended. Travelling directly into the heart of the Central Otago Hinterland, this scenic train trip is said to provide one of the most interesting sightseeing adventures the coastal Otago region has to offer. The train heads out from Dunedin's historic train station and passes through the city before making its way towards the spectacular gorge itself. Carved out over the course of thousands of years by the waters of the Taieri River, the Taieri

Gorge brings to mind how much of an alpine landscape there is in New Zealand. The journey also shows just how much the marvels of engineering are able to achieve. The train spends much of its time actually within the gorge and the viewing platforms at the ends of carriages are ideal for taking pictures. There's also several stops along the way for the chance to stretch your legs, walk across a suspension bridge, and take some photos of the Gorge and its surrounds from different vantage points. The journey takes roughly 2 hours each way.

Lovers of the outdoors are spoilt for choice when visiting Dunedin. The city has easy access to some remarkable landscapes and there are many organised tours that explore its outdoor attractions; walking tours, cycling tours, kayaking tours, fishing tours, bird watching tours, nature tours, golfing, horse treks and more. Those who prefer to go it alone can explore numerous scenic walks around Dunedin. Short tracks criss-cross Otago Peninsula, the Town Belt and Ross Creek; and there's the attraction (or otherwise) of tackling Baldwin Street, the world's steepest street. Further afield, there are tracks near the Taieri River and Silverstream, half-day hikes along Dunedin's dramatic skyline (the Pineapple, Leith Saddle and Mt Cargill Tracks), walks to unusual places like Tunnel Beach, and serious hikes in the nearby Silverpeaks. Dunedin is also a biker's playground. A compact layout and a flat run all the way from the top of North East Valley through to South Dunedin and St Clair beach, or around the Harbour, make Dunedin easy to get around by bike. The West Harbour Cycleway encountered in the latter stages of the Marathon provides flat riding and beautiful scenery for commuters and recreational riders alike, while the hills and bays around the city and on the Peninsula provide ample opportunity for riding, at all levels of difficulty. There's also the opportunity to ride along the historical Otago Central Rail Trail. This is a 150-

kilometre walking, cycling and horse riding track that runs in an arc between Middlemarch and Clyde, along the route of the former Otago Central Railway.

After all that fresh air and exercise it's important to find somewhere reasonable to eat and drink. Fortunately, with Dunedin being a student town, there are a few interesting restaurants on Albany Street south of the University Of Otago and cheap take-away food can be found near the university campus. A visit to Zucchini Bros on Highgate Street, Roslyn is well recommended for good-value pizza & pasta. They also serve Emerson's and Green Man beer. Those who enjoy their drink could also try the Craic Irish Tavern in the Octogon. As well as Irish favourites like Guinness and Kilkenny the pub offers a good selection of international and New Zealand beers, wines, spirits and whiskeys as well as an extensive seafood menu for lunch and dinner. I liked the sound of the draught Emerson's BookBinder and they even stock one of my particular favourites, Leffe Brune a full-bodied Belgian beer at $10.00 a bottle. It seems a pretty good way to round off the marathon weekend.

SYDNEY MARATHON

NEW SOUTH WALES

SEPTEMBER

My main focus in 2014, apart from attempting to run in as many different countries as possible had been to combine a visit to my son Ross, now living in Sydney, with an attempt on what the Australian 100 Club call 'The Australian Sweep.' This involves completing a marathon in each of the country's 6 States and its 2 Territories, (Northern Territory and ACT). I'd worked out an itinerary that would allow me to run in each of the eight regions during what constitutes the Aussie winter/spring period between July and October. As usual when you make plans, fate intervened and, at the last moment, Ross decided to come to Europe in August for a friend's wedding in Sweden. This meant us delaying our visit by several weeks and by the time we arrived in Australia there were only three marathons on the calendar that my itinerary allowed me to run: Sydney, Western Sydney and Melbourne. I entered all three. Completion of 'The Sweep' will have to be put on hold until another year.

Mo and I eventually headed Down Under at the beginning of September, having arranged a two-day stopover in Dubai en route. The city plays host to an increasingly popular marathon in mid-January and, always on the look-out for new countries in which to run, I wanted to check it out. The idea of combining it with a beach holiday, when temperatures settle into the mid-20s as we suffer the UK winter seemed appealing initially. That was until I visited the place. Dubai in the summer is not for me. We arrived to 42 degree heat to find ourselves the only ones seemingly prepared to venture outdoors. Everyone else was living in an air-conditioned bubble; moving only from air-conditioned homes to air-conditioned cars, to air-conditioned offices and in the evening to air-conditioned shopping malls. The whole place seemed like a nightmare vision of a futuristic hell on earth: of cities judged on how tall they can erect their skyscrapers and how fast, straight and congested they build their motorways. I found out that the marathon course simply runs down the straightest of Dubai's motorways, turns around at half-way and then comes back down the other side – like running up and down the M1, but with buildings. My initial reaction was, 'I think I'll give it a miss.' (As things turned out I ended up returning to Dubai in 2017 and thoroughly enjoyed completing that year's Dubai Marathon.)

It was a relief to arrive in the relative sanity of Sydney. No one can accuse this city of lacking character. I've been visiting it on and off now for over forty years and on each occasion have never failed to be taken-in by the splendour of its location. Its spectacular waterside setting ensures that it has few rivals for the title of one of the 'World's Most Beautiful Cities.' Sydney is fortunate to be built on one of the world's greatest harbours, where its twin icons of the Bridge and the Opera House are complemented by a myriad of vessels from great ocean liners, to historic ferries and colourful sailing boats all vying for space on its clear, blue waters. At times, standing by the harbour at Circular Quay, hemmed in on three sides by the city's skyscrapers, you have to pinch yourself to believe that it was just over 200 years ago that the First Fleet of 1,000 people (736 of them convicted felons) arrived at that very spot to kick-start the European colonization of the Continent as a penal colony - all in conditions of great brutality and despair. These days Sydney is a dynamic, international city; the epitome of sophistication and cosmopolitan charm. Its citizens now enjoy an enviable lifestyle in one of the most multicultural cities in the world with Australia having long ago abandoned its 'White Australia' policy and accepted its true geographical position and the proximity of its Asian neighbours. Almost one-third of Sydney's 4.5 million citizens were born overseas; many from China, India and Vietnam and these newer migrants have contributed significantly to Sydney's current position as a global, cultural and economic centre.

For most of the six weeks of our stay Mo and I were based in a rented apartment in Manly, just around the corner from our son. For those of you who've never heard of the place, Manly is a rival to Bondi as Australia's most famous surf beach. Situated on an isthmus, surrounded on three sides by water, a half hour's ferry ride from the centre of Sydney, Manly is an affluent suburb within an affluent city, within an affluent country. You need deep pockets to meet both its rent and restaurant costs - even the beer prices are inflated compared to elsewhere in the city. With the Aussie dollar strong against the pound, I wasn't sure how I'd cope. It's mainly inhabited by young professionals working in the city on six-figure salaries or by those flaunting their inherited wealth. Nowhere I've visited has the old Jewish expression along the lines of, 'It's fortunate that his father was born before him,' appeared more appropriate. Rightly or wrongly I got the distinct impression that some people I met were so full of themselves that it never crossed their minds to appreciate how lucky they were to be living in such a beautiful place. A recently retired friend, looking for voluntary work tells the story of how he approached the local library offering to assist migrants with their reading of English, only to be informed that, 'We don't have migrants in Manly.'

Most mornings during my stay I ran along the beautiful mile-long surf beach. When the tide was in I was left with no option but to run along the adjacent promenade. There I came into contact with the beautiful people and their perfect bodies: a tribe of narcissists that congregated there each day. I found it interesting to observe the strange protocols that appeared to be part of their daily ritual. Even before 7am the place was like Piccadilly Circus during the rush hour. Hordes of swimmers from the Manly Surf Club would disappear into the waves for their morning safari around the bay to Shelly Beach and back. Meanwhile, the really serious athletes would be pounding the pavement before heading off on the ferries to work. Next came what Mo and I called the, 'Pink and Blacks' – a large contingent of fashionistas; female runners all clad head to toe in a uniform of boutique running gear as if by prior arrangement. It wasn't a club, most of them didn't seem to know each other, yet each somehow had managed to equip themselves in the same designer outfits expressing the same fashion statement, like something out of Aldous Huxley's 'Brave New World.' Headgear was a black peaked cap, preferably with a blond ponytail trailing through the hole at the back. Then came the chic, pink lycra vest, the state-of-the-art, black, knee-length compression tights finished off with the latest-in-pink Nike trainers. Virtually every one of them came complete with wires dripping out of their ears leading to mobile phones strapped on to one arm and heart-rate monitor on the other. Some of them could run, some seemed more content to be part of an unofficial fashion carnival.

After 9 am, having got their husbands off to work and their older children to school, the buggy brigade appeared: a collection of pram-pushing mothers determined to keep in shape regardless. Woe-betide anyone who got in their way as, heads down, they careered their streamlined chariots along the prom; sometimes three-abreast. The majority of these adhered to the same uniform as the Pink and Blacks. The final group was to be found standing in circles on the nearby grass in front of what was usually a male figure barking out instructions. These were those with so many disposable dollars they preferred to pay others to show them how to exercise. The personal trainer usually sported an expression that can only be described as 'laughing all the way to the bank.'

The activities I've described up to now usually took place during the week. The weekends were an entirely different kettle of fish and, if the tide was in, it was better to avoid the prom at all costs. While the above groups were all still in action they were joined by a whole phalanx of out-of-schoolers and their dangerous toys. The younger ones rode scooters into your Achilles with reckless abandon while their teenage counterparts crashed skateboards into your calves as you tried to run. Surfers of all ages attempted to weave their twelve-foot surfboards through the throng while those on bikes simply refused to adhere to the rule of giving way to pedestrians. There was even a guy who insisted on riding his penny farthing among the crowds. While I loved Manly as a place, the problem was that nearly everyone else in Sydney loved it too and made a bee-line there when free at weekends. At such times I longed to be back running along the deserted beaches of my Northumberland coast. Relief of sorts could be had later in the day after the crowds had all gone home. At these times it was a pleasure to stroll unmolested along the prom. Each day I'd pass a succession of plaques either commemorating those who'd died tragically in the surf, or that simply celebrated the lives of those who'd spent time there. One such plaque always caught my attention. It was in memory of a young Manly triathlete named Saxon Bird who'd been tragically killed while competing in an Ironman contest in 2010. It read, 'Only those who will risk going too far, can possibly find out how far they can go.' This simple epitaph resonated so much with my own philosophy on life that I found it difficult to pass without stopping to reflect.

After two weeks of attempting to train in these congested conditions I was glad when the day of the Sydney's Marathon finally arrived. With approximately 5,000 entrants I expected there to be a degree of congestion but was confident that scooters, skateboards, surfboards, buggies and cycles would be banned. Registration for the marathon was open from the Wednesday prior to the event. As it was being held in the basement of Sydney Town Hall on George Street; the building in which Ross works, I was looking forward to attending the Expo there. Other than the fact that it allowed us to meet him for lunch afterwards, the whole registration process turned out to be a huge disappointment; the least said about which the better. I've already made my views clear elsewhere on the marketing aspects versus the captive runners' theme. This was the worst of the lot. I felt sorry for those out-of-town entrants who'd been dragged into the city to what was basically an Asics' shop and then simply handed a bib with a chip attached. There was little there except highly-priced Asics' merchandise and a stall for some obscure Japanese marathon. Melbourne, an equally prestigious but less costly marathon, had already posted out the same number/chip combination meaning that we could travel there at our own convenience and not that of the race organizer. Given its $135 entry fee I'm sure Sydney could have afforded to absorb the cost of the postage too. The only positive feature about the Registration was the facility to leave baggage there for collection after the race.

Sunday's race day started cool and showery: a welcome change from what had been a very hot week in Sydney. Our race numbers were meant to give us free public transport to the Start under the northern end of the famous Harbour Bridge. What the organizers had neglected to mention was that, given the 7 am start, public transport for such an early hour on a Sunday was virtually non-existent from some of the outer suburbs. So, after a very expensive taxi ride we lined up under the Bridge itself, a short stroll away from Luna Park, Sydney's version of Blackpool Pleasure Beach. A Half Marathon had already set off from there an hour earlier and, later that morning, a well-attended 9km Bridge Run plus a Family Fun Run were to leave from the same spot. Altogether there were over 35,000 runners entered in the four events with everyone wanting to make the most of the once-a-year closure of the Bridge.

Almost as much as Paris, Sydney is a Marathon Tourist's dream in that the course takes you on a tour of most of the city's iconic and historic sights. Before setting off I took the opportunity to reacquaint myself with Luna Park, the city's longstanding amusement centre at the harbour's edge. I recall that during the time I'd been living in Australia in the late 70s, there'd been a major fire on the Ghost Train ride, which killed six children and one adult. After this, most of the park was demolished and a new amusement park constructed. When I last visited it a dozen or so years ago this new park had fallen into disrepair and appeared in urgent need of refurbishment. After another redevelopment in 2004, Luna Park reopened in its current format. It contains popular rides such as the Hair Raiser, the Wild Mouse Rollercoaster and the FerrisWheel that continue to attract thousands of Sydneysiders each week. The Park is also one of only two amusement parks in the world that are protected by government legislation with several of its buildings listed on the NSW State Heritage Register.

Leaving the street adjacent to Luna Park at 7am the route took us uphill initially before levelling out on the northern approach to the charismatic Harbour Bridge. Standing proudly above the harbour and instantly recognizable as an iconic symbol of the nation, the Bridge is the world's tallest steel arch bridge. Since 1932 it has connected the northern suburbs of Sydney with the city centre, making it a vital link in the city's transport infrastructure: more than 20,000 cars travel across the bridge each day on its 8 road lanes. It also carries 2 rail tracks as well as pedestrian and cycle ways. There's an interesting story about the Bridge's opening. Just as Jack Lang, the Labour Premier of New South Wales was about to cut the ribbon to officially open the Bridge, a man in a military uniform rode up on horseback, slashing the ribbon with a sword and declaring the Bridge open in the name of the people of New South Wales. The intruder was Francis de Groot, a member of a right-wing paramilitary group, the New Guard, opposed to Lang's leftist policies and angry that a member of the Royal Family had not been asked to the opening ceremony. De Groot successfully appealed against his £5 fine for offensive behaviour and was subsequently awarded an undisclosed out of court settlement for unlawful arrest.

Running across the Bridge reminded me very much of crossing my local Tyne Bridge during the Great North Run but on a much bigger scale. The views too were much more spectacular. Behind us sat Admiralty and Kirribilli Houses; the official residences of the Governor General and the Prime Minister respectively. Ahead of us across the water the world-famous Opera House, our final destination, awaited us some 40 kilometres later. The only obstacles were those caused by fellow runners stopping mid-stride to take the inevitable selfies of themselves in such a famous setting. They would have got better views by forking out the $260 or so to take part in the organized Bridge Climb where every ten minutes, groups of 12, tied together with safety ropes, are taken to the very top of the bridge. Apparently celebrities such as Matt Damon, Sarah Ferguson and Kylie Minogue have all done the climb. Imagine following behind Kylie all the way to the top! Personally, I prefer the view from below, aboard one of the harbour ferries, (costs less too).

After about 4km we left the Bridge behind and headed along the Cahill Expressway, parallel to busy Circular Quay. This is the home of the gold and green city ferries: the workhorses that take both tourists and commuters to all points on the harbour's compass. A train station and nearby bus terminus complete the set to make this area one of the city's major transport hubs. On the eastern side of the Quay lies the controversial Opera Quays development of mega-expensive high rise apartments that somehow managed to get built fifteen years ago despite protestations that they obscure the views of both the Opera House and Botanic Gardens. The locals have dubbed them 'The Toaster' due to their resemblance to the kitchen accessory of that name. The Aussies have an amusing tendency to give nicknames to buildings: the Bridge is 'The Coathanger,' an ungainly apartment block in Manly has been dubbed 'The Toilet Bowl' and, best of all, a shipping facility that regulates the docking of vessels in the harbour, is known as 'The Pill' (because it controls the berths).

Leaving Circular Quay we turned right into historic Macquarie Street where in 2000 I'd stood and watched cyclists in the first Olympic Triathlon flashing past. The street is named after Governor Lachlan Macquarie who was instrumental in setting the course of development in the colony's early years. It was designed as a ceremonial thoroughfare leading from the harbour to the vast expanse of Hyde Park through which we were later to run. Among the buildings commissioned by Maquarie that we were to pass en route were the original Sydney Hospital, Hyde Park Barracks, the State Library, Parliament House, the Mint and St Mary's Cathedral. Some of these buildings including the Barracks have been preserved largely unchanged. Today, the street is the location of the main governmental institutions of New South Wales and the term 'Macquarie Street' is often used as a metonym for the State's government in the same way that 'Whitehall' is used for its British counterpart.

At 5km we were taken into the beautiful Botanic Gardens, a haven of peace and tranquility for office workers and tourists alike in the midst of a busy city. The Gardens occupy 30 hectares of land between the Opera House and Farm Cove where the early settlers struggled to grow vegetables for the hungry colony. As well as providing examples of trees and plants from all over the world, the Gardens also present some of the most stunning views of the harbour. As we made our way around the perimeter of the Gardens a giant, white cruise liner chose that moment to berth alongside our route. The views past the ship back to the Opera House and the Bridge were simply breath-taking. While running we passed Mrs Macquarie's Chair, a well-known local landmark carved out of a rock ledge, where legend has it, the wife of the Governor used to sit forlornly looking out to sea, waiting for ships to arrive.

At 8km we passed the Domain, once the Governor's private park, but now a popular picnic spot with the Art Gallery of NSW and a well-used outdoor swimming pool. 10km brought us out of park and alongside the huge Gothic-style St Mary's Cathedral. A short out-and-back section then took us into Hyde Park, named after its London equivalent. This is the oldest public parkland in Australia and was used in the early days mainly as a venue for sporting contests: particularly cricket, rugby, boxing and even horse racing. These have long since moved elsewhere and today the park is best known for its spectacular Archibald Fountain, designed in honour of Australia's contribution to World War 1. There's also an Anzac War Memorial, a Pool of Remembrance and even a giant chess set on leaving the park.

We then entered on an unremarkable long, straight section taking us out of the city along Oxford Street, (home to Sydney's gay community), Flinders Street and into Moore Park Road. At this point I was running and chatting with Bob Fickel, Chairman of Australia's 100 Marathon Club. On his 229th marathon that day, Bob was four ahead of me. Recognising kindred spirits we managed to keep in touch. Bob was subsequently kind enough to invite me to his club's post-race celebration after the following month's Melbourne Marathon. Moore Park at 14km is the home to some of Sydney's premier sporting and entertainment arenas. The first stadium we passed, the Allianz Stadium, is home to the Sydney Roosters Rugby League team, the Waratahs Rugby Union team and Sydney FC Soccer club. The previous evening I'd watched on TV one of the season's rugby preliminary finals being played there in front of a sell-out crowd. We also passed the Horden Pavillion, an important entertainment venue, next door to the

Royal Hall of Industries, (fondly remembered in my time in Oz as the Showbag Pavillion in the days of the annual Royal Easter Show). Most impressive of all though, was to run past the famous Sydney Cricket Ground: the ground where Bradman scored his record 452 not out and where England caused controversy with their bodyline bowling tactics in the 1930s. The ground is also home to the notorious Hill where, fuelled by alcohol, the rivalry between Australian and English supporters often reaches boiling point.

Next came a giant loop around yet another park; this time Centennial Park, where the half-way point was reached. Emerging from the park at 23km there followed a slightly uphill drag back along Anzac Parade, Flinders and Oxford Streets, back again through Hyde Park and on through the near deserted Central Business District to arrive again at Circular Quay. At this stage I was running quite well and had managed to maintain an even 6km per minute pace up to 32km. The final 10km were, as usual, the hardest part of the race. Passing the liner-shaped International Passenger Terminal we made our way under the southern side of the Bridge. The area around here is known as the Rocks and was where Captain Phillip of the First Fleet proclaimed the establishment of Sydney Town in 1788. It's the historic heart of convict era Sydney and home at one time to the notorious 'pushes' – gangs of louts who brawled continuously and mugged passers-by. It still retains something of its original character and, for those who like their pubs with atmosphere, it's a great place to visit. We headed there immediately after the race, to the upstairs bar of the Glenmore Hotel with its sweeping views across to the Opera House and the back-markers arriving at the finish line. The food there was pretty basic pub fare but, with lashings of carbohydrate, just what I needed after finishing a marathon.

The final 8km out and back to Darling Harbour along Hickson and Sussex streets were the least scenic on the course; the views being obstructed by the multi-million dollar Barangaroo development of high-rise apartments and casinos designed to attract future, mainly Chinese, high-rollers. Darling Harbour itself was once a grimy, industrial docks area until the State Government decided on its regeneration as part of the 1988 Bi-centenary project. Today, its numerous attractions make it a favourite place for Sydneysiders to spend their leisure time. Returning back under the Bridge at 40km we enjoyed a pleasant run-in along the harbour to the finish at the Opera House steps. I was delighted to see Mo, Ross and his partner Hayley among the huge crowds cheering us on as we turned the final corner at Circular Quay. The World Heritage listed Opera House, such an icon of the nation, was an excellent place to end the race, with its white roofs evocative of full sails complemented by the sparkling blue water of the harbour. I'd first visited this in 1973 shortly after completion and recall being spellbound by its appearance on that occasion, never thinking that 41 years later I'd be finishing a marathon on its forecourt. I'd even got to see inside this time too as Ross had managed to secure tickets for my favourite musician, the legendary Bob Dylan, as a surprise Father's Day treat two weeks earlier.

I was satisfied with my run and pleased to finish well under my targeted 4 hour 30 minutes. Under the steps there was a dedicated marathon recovery area where we were handed our medal and T-shirt. There were also the usual freebies to be had. Nearby in the Botanic Gardens, a whole tented village had been erected incorporating all sorts of stalls selling food and drink, (including Manly's local Four Pines Brewery stall), allowing runners to sit out in the sun with their families and celebrate. We headed off to the Glenmore and the Rocks.

As you can imagine, travelling and socializing for six weeks in Australia involved an awful lot of eating (and drinking!) out. Australia has come a long way from the days when it appeared to survive on a combination of meat pies smothered in sauce and giant steaks sizzling on a BBQ; all washed down by copious quantities of cold lager. Sydney has become one of the great restaurant capitals in the world, offering a wide range of sophisticated restaurants catering for every imaginable cuisine. Many ethnic areas reflecting the city's diverse immigrant communities have become noted for that community's particular food speciality. For example, Sydney has a large, central Chinatown district near Haymarket for those who enjoy Chinese cooking. East Sydney is known for its Italian cuisine, Anzac Parade for Indonesian food, Surry Hills for Turkish and Lebanese cooking while, rather surprisingly, the famous beach area of Bondi contains a number of Jewish restaurants. I'd like to say that I sampled the food in each of these places. I didn't; there was no need to when each of these cuisines could be found within walking distance of our Manly apartment. I did make a point though of taking the ferry across to the world famous Doyle's restaurant in Watson's Bay, a place I'd last visited some 40 years earlier when, even then, it had a reputation as the haunt of the rich and famous. With the likes of Russell Crowe having been spotted there recently, I wasn't surprised to find that my plate of fish and chips (except they didn't call it that) was over two and a half times more expensive than what I was paying in Manly.

Before leaving for Australia we'd received many warnings from both friends and family who'd recently returned about the excessive cost of eating out. We found most main courses in mid-range restaurants to come within the $20 to $25 mark; not a great deal different from what you'd pay in the UK.

What we did find expensive was the cost of a half-decent bottle of wine to go with our meal; this was often more than the cost of the meal itself – ridiculous really when you consider that the wine is produced right on the doorstep. It had us nostalgic for the golden days we spent in Perth when a 5-litre flagon of good Australian wine could be purchased for the princely sum of $2. Times certainly have changed and not necessarily for the better. We soon learned to avoid any restaurant that didn't offer BYO (bring your own wine) and to nip into Coles Liquorland for a bottle of the on-special $6 Cabernet Sauvignon to go with our meal.

Of course, with the country's booming economy and the rise of the A$ against the £GB, Sydney certainly is an expensive city for UK citizens to visit these days. However, a lot of the expense can be avoided by anyone sensible and frugal with their money. We were able to save on food costs by shopping in the big supermarkets and cooking at home in our apartment. Likewise, though the price of a schooner, (425 ml) of beer was in the $6 to $7 range in local hotels, a 30 can case of 'Hammer and Tongs' lager could be bought for $30 in Coles supermarket. (We did a lot of our shopping in Coles!) Even eating out needn't to be that expensive. Many of the restaurants we frequented offered mid-week specials of which to take advantage. Monday evening's goulash in an Eastern European restaurant could be bought for $11, Tuesday and Wednesday's Thai menu in Manly's 'Pat Ploy' was priced at $10.95, (it was hard to get our friend Ross James out of there). On Wednesday the local Four Pines microbrewery had an excellent offer of a huge rack of ribs and a pint for $25, (the pint alone would have cost $10). Other nights had other 'specials' to enjoy without any deterioration in the quality of the food served.

As with food, Australia has made giant strides in its attitude to the consumption of alcohol in the 40+ years I've been visiting. The Barry Humphries inspired, Private Eye comic-strip image of the puking and chundering Australian beer-swiller is now almost a thing of the past. Australians drink a moderate 9.89 litres of (pure) alcohol each year putting them behind the UK, but ahead of the US. While beer is still the average Aussie's favourite tipple, per capita consumption is declining annually with the growing popularity of wine and ready-to-drink mixed spirits. What has also changed considerably is the rising popularity of micro-breweries filling the market-place with high-end beers to the disadvantage of many of the traditional suppliers. When I moved to Australia in 1972 virtually every state had its own monopoly brewery. In West Australia it was almost impossible to purchase any draught lager other than Swan, produced by the brewery of the same name. Queensland had Castlemaine, South Australia was Coopers, Victoria was Tooheys and so on. Today many traditional suppliers have been forced by competition to invest heavily in boutique operators, especially with a number of the latter (like Manly's Four Pines) combining their brewery operations with catering ventures on the same premises. From past experience, I had no expectations of finding the perfect dark beer in the Sydney area so wasn't disappointed when I didn't. What did surprise me though, was the number of darker beers now available in what is often considered Foster's Lager Land. It isn't, Foster's is not a particularly popular drink in its own country. Most of these darker ales are produced by some of the aforementioned microbreweries: like the Four Pines 'Dark Bitter,' 'Endeavour' brewed in Sydney by Endeavour Vintage Co. and 'White Rabbit' from a Victorian micro-brewery. Even the big breweries are getting in on the act and recognizing that not everyone enjoys weak, pale lager. Tooheys, for example brews a 'Tooheys Old' while Carlton has chipped in with a 'Carlton Dark.' All of these are between 4.5% and 5.5% so aren't strong enough to meet the Manford criteria for the perfect dark beer but are nonetheless worthwhile purchases. I certainly miss my daily 'Endeavour' in the perfect setting of Manly's Wharf Bar watching the ferries come and go as the sun set in Manly Cove. All that remains, as I mentioned earlier, is to return as soon as possible to complete the Australian Sweep.

MELBOURNE MARATHON

VICTORIA

OCTOBER

This was the third of the three marathons I'd booked to run during a six week holiday in Australia while visiting my son Ross in Sydney. The other two: the Sydney Marathon and the Western Sydney Marathon are described elsewhere in this book. I'd last been to Melbourne many moons ago in 1973 and was interested to see how things had changed since then. One of the major changes was that there were now a number of low-cost airlines operating within Australia, making the long journey between Sydney and Melbourne so much easier these days. My wife Mo and I found a cheap return flight with Tigerair (a subsidiary of Singapore Airlines) costing a mere $45 each way for a Friday to Tuesday trip, that fitted the bill perfectly. The $30 return bus journey to the City Centre with Skybus cost almost as much as the flight itself. The service operates 24/7 at 10 minute intervals between the airport and Melbourne's Southern Cross station. Knowing this we'd booked ourselves into the Great Southern Hotel virtually opposite the station and within reasonable walking distance from Registration and the early morning start of the marathon. Unfortunately, the hotel was still in the process of major renovation works that we were informed would have been completed well before our arrival. The moral is; always check these things out for yourself before making any payment. It could have ruined our stay if we'd allowed it to. We complained, of course, but got nowhere. Particularly disappointing was the fact that we'd recommended the hotel to our friends Barry and Kerry Atkinson (Bazz and Kezz) from West Australia, whom we'd last seen almost twenty years ago and who were flying over to Melbourne to spend time with us. Bazz had been my regular squash partner during our university days and the man largely responsible for getting me involved in running in the first place. It was his invitation to join him in the annual City-to-Surf race in Perth, WA in 1981 that kick-started my running career. I've a lot to thank him for.

Hotel apart, our first impression of Melbourne was that unlike Sydney it reminded us of a large English city. Perhaps the weather had a lot to do with this; on arrival it was wet, windy and at least 10 degrees cooler than what we'd been used to in Sydney. Mind you, all that was to change on the day of the marathon when, for one day only, temperatures soared into the 30s.

Melbourne is, of course, the capital and most populous city in the state of Victoria with 4.3 million inhabitants. It is also the second most populous city in Australia and for a brief period following Federation had served as the nation's seat of government. Bitter rivalry between Melbourne and Sydney eventually led to the artificial creation of Canberra, equidistant between the two, as capital of Australia. Founded in 1835, in what was then the colony of New South Wales, by settlers dissatisfied with their opportunities in Tasmania, it was incorporated as a Crown settlement two years later. It was subsequently named Melbourne in honour of the British Prime Minister at that time. The boom years brought about by Victorian Gold Rush era of 1850s soon transformed it into one of the world's fastest growing and wealthiest cities. Today it's the leading financial and some would say, cultural, centre in Australia as well as the Asian Pacific region. It has been ranked amongst the top three liveable cities in the world since 2002 while, in 2013, it was also named as the joint fourth expensive. The city centre is located on the banks of the Yarra River at the northern end of the huge, natural Port Phillip Bay.

By far the easiest way for any new arrival to become acquainted with the city centre is to take advantage of the free City Circle Tram that circumnavigates the city in both directions. This original hop-on, hop-off, Melbourne heritage tram provides free audio commentary on the city's history and landmarks en route and is a great introduction to the city. As a magnet for visitors, it can be crowded and uncomfortable at times but it's not to be missed. Melbourne's residents seem to have a thing about trams and can be justly proud of their tram network. The trams are an iconic symbol of the city. With almost 50 trams on 250 kilometres of track, Melbourne has the largest urban tramway network in the world ahead of St Petersburg, Berlin, Moscow and Vienna – other cities noted for their tram systems. Since first operating in 1884, they have become an instantly recognisable part of the city's scenery and feature prominently in tourism and travel brochures. We used the tram extensively during our visit to take us to many of the city's outer suburbs. In the process we tried, but never quite managed, to get to grips with Melbourne's complicated ticketing system that required the one-off purchase of a $6 'Myki card before travelling. This seemed to penalise short-stay visitors at the expense of locals. We were informed that the card was ours in perpetuity but what's the point of that if you're leaving after a couple of days? No one manning the ticket booths could explain this to any degree of satisfaction. Even more confusing was when exactly to touch the card on and off when boarding. We were given several different versions of this process ending up so confused we almost gave up and walked everywhere instead.

Not quite though, we couldn't resist the convenience of the free, hop-on-hop-off Circle Tram and rode it extensively whenever we needed to sightsee. The city centre is contained within its circle of a north/south, east/west grid system, consisting of no more than a dozen streets between La Trobe to the north/Flinders to the south and Harbour Esplanade to the west and Spring Street to the east. From our base near Flinders Street we were able to take the free tram clockwise to view all the main attractions. Around the corner was the new Etihad Stadium; nothing to do with Manchester City but, instead, a multi-purpose venue with several name changes and the subject of much controversy since construction in 1997. On the night we arrived we could hear the noise of a 30,000 plus sell-out crowd as local soccer club Melbourne Victory played host to one of their Sydney rivals.

The next hop-off stop on the tram is the new development of Victoria Harbour in the docklands area of the city. This is an ongoing urban renewal project designed to extend the area of Melbourne CBD by over one third into what was previously swamp land along the Yarra River. We visited it on the morning of our final day in Melbourne and came away impressed by the mixture of exclusive residential apartments, retail outlets and public open spaces. We didn't know quite what to make of the statues of Australian 'legends' Barry Humphries, Johnny Farnham, Kylie Minogue plus a series of lesser lights. The Wall of Fame still contained a tribute to Rolf Harris, but surely not for much longer.

Leaving here the tram turns eastwards along La Trobe Street, past the former Royal Mint and the State Library of Australia to a stop close to the Old Melbourne Gaol. When it was built in the mid-1800s it dominated the Melbourne skyline as a symbol of authority. Between 1842 and its closure in 1929, the gaol was the scene of 133 hangings including that of Australia's most famous bushranger Ned Kelly. The three-storey museum now displays information and memorabilia of former prisoners and staff, including the death masks of those executed. I guess it's worth a visit to anyone with a taste for the macabre.

On turning south into Spring Street, the tram passes in front of the Parliament building and the Old Treasury Building Museum. The former is one of Melbourne's best known landmarks and has been the seat of Victorian government since 1855. It was also the home of the Commonwealth Parliament prior to the construction of Canberra. A little further down the street, the Old Treasury Building, considered one of Australia's finest examples of Renaissance architecture, was built from the wealth accumulated during the Victorian Gold Rush era to house the state's gold vaults. Directly opposite is the Hotel Windsor, Australia's only surviving grand 19th century city hotel, famous not only for its clientele, but as the place where Australia's constitution was drafted in 1898.

The next stop on the tram, at the end of Spring Street, gives access to the famous MCG; about which more, later. The tram then completes its loop with a journey along historic Flinders Street, passing en route, Federation Square, Flinders Street Station and the Immigration Museum. Before you reach either of these you'll come across the former Corporation Lane, now known as AC/DC lane in honour of Australia's most famous rock band. Further down is Hosker Lane, full of tourists taking pictures of the ever-changing graffiti art. The world's most famous street artist, Banksy, once painted the walls, only to have his two 'works of art' painted over by the local council. Continuing along Flinders

Street, the tram passes St Paul's Cathedral with its gothic spires and arches. Diagonally across from this is the iconic entrance to the Flinders Street Station; an architectural gem whose entrance is covered in clocks showing the times in cities all over the world. Apparently it's a popular meeting spot for locals with 'I'll meet you under the clocks' being a common reference point. The only photo I had from my last visit there in 1973 is of a young Mo standing in front of the clocks. We attempted to recreate the pose on this occasion. My, how we've changed!

Opposite the station is the recent Federation Square, a stark example of modern architecture that is loved and hated in equal measures. I hated it. Built on a concrete deck above busy railway lines it is paved with almost half a million coloured sandstone blocks meant to invoke images of the Australian outback. The common consensus of those I spoke to considered it to be a design failure. A pity really; Melbourne deserves better. Though, since its official opening in 2002 it seems to have replaced the nearby station as a regular meeting place. The final stop worth visiting on the tram's circle is the Immigration Museum on Flinders Street. The exhibition showcases the stories surrounding immigration to Victoria, exploring why people came, where they settled and how they started a new life. It also looks at the Victorian identity: what it is, what others think it is and what it means to belong or not to belong to Australia. As someone who went through the process over forty years ago, I found the whole experience fascinating.

Plumb in the middle of the tram's circle is the city's main shopping district centred around Bourke and Collins Streets. The latter's Precinct is a boulevard of chic designer-label shops, expensive jewellers and exclusive hotels that has come to be known as 'Little Paris.' This area is crowded during shopping hours but escape can easily be had by heading down to the scenic walkways on the south side of the River Yarra. Having undergone extensive development in recent years, Southbank's promenade epitomizes the revival of the river as Melbourne's major tourist and leisure attraction. It's a great place to sit with a drink and watch the world go by. Be warned though, it's glitzy and up-market and the price of the drink reflects the cost of the building you're sitting in.

    I strolled along there en route to visit the marathon Expo. Melbourne is almost unique in Big City marathons in that it actually still posts out your number and bib so that going to Registration is unnecessary unless you specifically want to visit the Expo or pick up your T-shirt, (this can be done post-race if required). I specifically wanted to visit the Expo. How could I resist given that it meant making a pilgrimage to the mighty MCG (Melbourne Cricket Ground) home to both Australian Cricket and Australian Rules Football and one of the world's most famous sporting arenas. I've early memories of watching televised events from the 'G' since I was a child; including my earliest memory of the Olympics held there in 1956. Only two weeks previously I'd enjoyed this year's Aussie Rules Final between Sydney and Hawthorn, played at the 'G' in front of a crowd of 99,000. The ground has also held attendances of over 95,000 for a pre-season soccer friendly between Melbourne Victory and Liverpool in 2013 as well as an Australia v Greece soccer match in 2005. Melburnians are passionate about their sport. Where else would you find a crowd of that magnitude? I couldn't wait to visit in person. Of course, as luck would have it, this year's marathon wasn't allowed to finish inside the stadium due to renovations, (I'm beginning to think everything must be being renovated in Melbourne at the moment). Never mind, I was determined to fulfil a lifetime ambition and succeeded in sneaking inside the ground despite the security.

The stadium, which in the past has held record crowds of up to 130,000 for a Billy Graham Crusade (over 120,000 attended the 1970 Aussie Rules Final) is now included on the Australian National Heritage List and is often referred to, with good reason, as 'The Spiritual Home of Australian Sport.' An interesting feature outside the ground are the statues of famous Australian athletes, known as the Parade of Champions. I was familiar with those of cricketers Dennis Lillee, Don Bradman and Keith Miller as well as Aussie Rules footballers Leigh Matthews, Ron Barassi and Hayden Bunton from my years of living in Australia.

The 37th edition of the marathon started at sunrise outside the Rod Laver Arena where the annual Australian Open Tennis Championships take place. A special section of the Start is reserved for the Melbourne Marathon Spartans: runners who have completed the majority of the city's marathons. Different coloured running vests are awarded for those who've done 15, 20, 25, 30, 35 and 37 races. Among these were a number of members of the Australian 100 Marathon Club whom I'd encountered during my time in Australia and in different countries around the world. With only 45 members, the Club is the epitome of Aussie sociability and while they take their running (but not themselves) seriously, their emphasis is heavily on the social side of marathon-running. I felt at home in their company and, holding Aussie citizenship, have joined their Club as an International Member. I'm determined to complete their Australian Sweep – a marathon in each of the 6 States and 2 Territories.

The Marathon with 7,400 entrants was the first of 5 events incorporating 32,000 runners to take place that morning. (10,000 in the Half and 7,000 in the 10k). A few words of encouragement from local marathon personality Steve Moneghetti preceded a rousing version of the National Anthem before we set off into the Australian dawn for a tour of the city and its beach suburbs. Australia is synonymous with hot weather and the day's forecast was for 30 degrees. Knowing that, it was important to make the most of the first couple of hours before the sun began to bite. I started this one at a slightly faster pace than normal, acknowledging that I had little hope of keeping it up.

The first kilometre or so was slightly uphill before things evened out on historic Flinders Street. The next 4km took us arrow-straight south along the broad St Kilda Road. Originally a dirt track linking the fledgling city with the beachside suburb of St Kilda, the road was the scene of many bushranger robberies in its early days. Today it's the major arterial road into the city, lined by a mixture of office and residential towers. The road is known for its width and surrounding greenery particularly its elm and London plane trees. Running along its length took us past several of Melbourne's famous parks, landmarks and institutions including: Alexander Gardens, the National Gallery of Victoria, the Arts Centre, Victoria Barracks, the Shrine of Remembrance and Melbourne Grammar School. The latter counts Barry Humphries (Dame Edna) among its many distinguished former pupils. Before turning towards the coast the route took us into the city's huge Albert Park – home to Australia's Formula One Motor Race since 1996. For the next 10km we lapped the giant lake within the park: turning back on ourselves on more than one occasion to see those ahead and behind us in the race. Nico Rosberg had lapped the park at 195 mph earlier in the year. I was going much slower than that. A short section down the trendy Fitzroy Street brought us to the St Kilda seafront at 16km.

This turned out to be a lovely suburb fronting Port Philip Bay, with a safe, sandy beach and a long palm-lined promenade. It's very much Melbourne's premier seaside playground and former red-light district. During the 1960s it became known for its bohemian style and attracted artists and musicians taking advantage of the cheap housing on offer. I liked the look of the place so much as I was running along that the four of us returned the next day to see more. We were especially taken in by the historic St Kilda Pier and its iconic Pavilion, dating back to 1904. When it was destroyed in an arson attack in 2002, massive public support ensured that it was rebuilt exactly in keeping with the original plans, utilizing some of the salvaged components

We followed a 14km, flat out and back section along the Esplanade, with excellent ocean views of Port Phillip Bay and just the hint of a breeze. This didn't last long, however, and at 30km we turned inland into the heat of the sun as we returned towards the city skyline, back along St Kilda Road. The 35km mark brought another loop through an underpass to emerge into Melbourne's beautiful Royal Botanical Gardens. These are 38 hectares of internationally renowned gardens on the south bank of the Yarra, containing a mix of native and exotic vegetation including over 10,000 individual species. Of most interest to runners is The Tan Track, a former horse riding track, now extended to form a well-used running circuit of tan-coloured stone aggregate. In recent years it has gained something of an international reputation and is used by both professional athletes and joggers alike. Running legends such as Steve Ovett, Cathy Freeman, Hicham El Guerrouj and Sonia O'Sullivan have all been seen running there. I was surprised to find Mo handing out encouragement at 36km – it certainly spurred me on at a time when I was seriously flagging. The course followed an undulating route through the Gardens with some welcome tree-shade until finally we were back among the cheering crowds on Flinders Street with less than 2km to go. A sharp turn soon had us staring uphill at the magnificent MCG and the finish gantry on the main concourse. What an iconic place to finish a marathon – though at this stage it was sheer pandemonium with runners from various events appearing to be finishing at the same time, encouraged by hordes of screaming supporters. Bazz and Kerry had managed to position themselves at the finish line as I arrived. I was delighted to see them after all the years and quite satisfied with a 4hr 18 minute finish in the heat. The large medal more than compensated for the ugly T-Shirt.

There's loads of great places to eat and drink while in Melbourne. The phrase 'Spoilt for choice' doesn't do it justice. We tried to go somewhere different on each of the four nights we were there starting off with an Italian meal in the trendy suburb of Carlton. This is a lively neighbourhood frequented by University of Melbourne students and known for its 'Little Italy' precinct on Lygon Street, lined with old-school trattorias and casual pizzerias. While in Carlton we came across The Lincoln, a historic Carlton pub dating back to 1854 with a great atmosphere and an even better range of beers. The next night we made our way to Melbourne's Chinatown centred at the eastern end of Little Bourke Street and extending between the corners of Swanston and Spring Streets. Established during the Victorian gold rush in 1851 when Chinese prospectors came to Australia for in search of gold, the district is notable for being the longest continuous Chinese settlement in the Western World and the oldest Chinatown in the Southern Hemisphere. With almost 100 places to eat and drink in the area you really can't go wrong. After that we moved a little further out of the centre to the suburb of Richmond to try a Hungarian restaurant that had been recommended by Aussie friends. The restaurant turned out to be a bit of a disappointment (none of the dishes were what I considered authentic Hungarian food) – not so the nearby Spread Eagle Hotel with its cosy fireplace on a very wet night. Finally, as a special treat after the marathon we splurged on one of the upmarket eateries overlooking the Yarra River on Southbank Promenade. While the food was excellent the bill for the night left a huge hole in our budget.

The Melbourne Marathon was not as scenic as Sydney had been three weeks earlier, nor did it take us past as many historic or internationally famous parts of the city. There were also too many out-and-back sections watching runners in the opposite direction to make it as interesting a marathon as that of its big city rival. Nonetheless, it was a brilliantly organised, thoroughly enjoyable event providing another excellent day out in the sun. I'd happily travel back to Australia to do it again.

ROTTNEST ISLAND MARATHON

WEST AUSTRALIA

OCTOBER

Rottnest Island, colloquially and affectionately known as 'Rotto' is a beautiful small island off the coast of Western Australia, located 18 kilometres west of Fremantle. I've got fond memories of enjoying idyllic weekend escapes on the island while living and working in Perth during the 1970s and 80s. In those days it was a much quieter and much cheaper place to visit than it has become in recent years. As it is now, the main attraction was its traffic-free environment and the chance to simply hire a bike and cycle to one of its magnificent turquoise bays for a spot of swimming or snorkelling in the sun.

Rottnest is a popular holiday destination with daily ferry services operated by Rottnest Express and Rottnest Fast Ferries. These sail from Perth, WA's capital as well as from Fremantle and the northern resort of Hillarys. Ferries take approximately 25 minutes from Fremantle, 45 minutes from Hillarys, or 90 minutes from Perth. The island covers 19 square kilometres and is administered by the Rottnest Island

Authority under a separate act of parliament. It has a permanent population of around 300 people, with around 500,000 annual visitors and up to 15,000 visitors at a time during peak periods. 70% of all visitors come for the day only with the majority of these arriving during the in summer months. Rottnest is perhaps best known for its population of quokkas, a small native marsupial found in very few other locations. The island was given the name 'Rotte nest' (meaning 'rat's nest' in the 17th century Dutch language) by Dutch captain Willem de Vlamingh who spent six days exploring the island in 1696, mistaking the quokkas for giant rats. The island is also home to colonies of Australian sea lions and southern fur seals while a number of native and introduced bird species nest near the shallow salt lakes in the island's interior.

It is believed that Rottnest Island was separated from the mainland 7,000 years ago when the sea level rose, cutting the Island off from the land mass. It is now the largest in a chain of islands (which includes Garden and Carnac Islands) on the continental shelf opposite Perth. These islands all are formed of limestone rocks with a thin covering of sand – though only Rottnest has been turned into a major tourist destination. Artefacts reveal that before the rise in sea level Rottnest Island was inhabited by Aboriginal people. It features in Noongar Aboriginal mythology as Wadjemup, meaning 'place across the water where the spirits are'. The local Aboriginal people were not sea-faring and did not have vessels capable of making the crossing from the mainland and therefore did not traditionally inhabit the Island following the rise in sea level (though there are currently 17 sites on Rottnest Island listed under the Aboriginal Heritage Act 1972-1980).

The earliest discovery of Rottnest Island by Europeans is credited to Dutch navigators during the 17th century in their search for a shorter route from the Cape of Good Hope to Batavia. The first Europeans to actually land on the Island are believed to have been Samuel Volkerson and his crew of the Dutch ship Waeckende Boey while searching for survivors of another Dutch ship the Vergulde Draek in 1658. The first Europeans took up residence on Rottnest Island shortly after the first settlement of the Swan River Colony was established in 1829. At the time, the Island was considered to be of interest as a place with potential for salt harvesting, farming and fishing. The major settlement of Thomson Bay was named after Robert Thomson, who became a major landholder on Rottnest Island during the 1830s.

For almost a century the Island served as a prison for Aboriginal people (except for a short period of closure between 1849 and 1855) during which some 3,700 Aboriginal men and boys were imprisoned. Over the prison period, the Aboriginal prisoners constructed a large number of buildings and other structures including the seawall, lighthouses and other heritage buildings. Most of the development took place in Thomson Bay, and of particular significance is the Quod (meaning 'prison') that was the prison accommodation for the Aboriginal men. The Quod is now part of the Lodge, which is operated under a private lease as holiday accommodation. Closure of the prison in 1904 meant that the Island became largely devoted to recreational use from the 1900s, aside from a brief period of exclusive military use. Rottnest was the site of internment camps in both World War I and World War II. In World War I it was mostly used for German and Austrian suspected enemy aliens, and was closed towards the end of the war due to poor living conditions.

One of the Island's main attractions is that the only motor vehicles permitted are emergency and service vehicles, although there is also a tourist bus service. Cycling is the transport of choice for most visitors, with many either bringing a bicycle with them or hiring one on arrival. Apart from the main settlement of Thomson Bay, other settlements are located at Geordie Bay and Longreach Bay on the northern side of the island. All are sheltered bays and well suited for boating and swimming. The Island has accommodation for up to 5,500 visitors and Rottnest Island Authority accommodation options include 291 self-catering villas, units and cottages. While this style of accommodation is reasonably basic, demand is generally very high during the summer months or when popular events (like the Marathon) are being held. Other accommodation options include group accommodation at Kingstown Barracks, the Hotel Rottnest (once the Governor's residence and better known by its former name of the 'Quokka Arms Hotel'), the Rottnest Lodge (Karma Group). A landscaped 40 site camping ground has just been reopened complete with ablution block and camp kitchen facilities while Cabins at Caroline Thomson provide an alternative to camping and are popular with families.

I looked to find some idea of what it would cost to travel to and spend the weekend (Friday and Saturday night) on the Island during Marathon weekend in October 2018. Rottnest Express ferries quoted $105 for an adult extended return fare sailing from Perth including the Island 'admission fee' tax. (The Rottnest Island Admission Fee is the entrance fee to an A-Class nature reserve and contributes to the conservation of the island. This is a government tax payable by all visitors to the island and is collected by the ferry companies on behalf of the Rottnest Island Authority). The same fare was given as $71 from Fremantle while Rottnest Fast Ferries service sailing from Hillarys charged $92.50 for an extended stay return. Return fares are a few dollars cheaper for those simply crossing to the Island on the day of the event. Early morning ferry services (approx. 5.15-5.30am) have been arranged by race organisers through both ferry companies and tickets are released well in advance of race day. I also researched Budget Accommodation options for the weekend on the Rottnest Island Authority website. Unfortunately the event comes right in the middle of the Peak Season (September 24th to December 13th) for booking purposes. All prices are on a per night basis. 2-bedroomed self-contained accommodation at the Couples Island Resort cost $372 per night while a 4-bed bungalow at the Caroline Thompson complex cost $158 per night. Cheapest rates were to be had at the Kingston Barracks at $69 for a 2-bed dormitory room. Single beds at the Rottnest Hostel were priced at $53 per night. Most of the Premium Accommodation at places like the Hotel Rottnest and the Rottnest Lodge had already been taken well in advance of the date. (£1 converts to 1.74 Australian dollars at the time of writing).

October 21st 2018 saw the 25th edition of the Rottnest Marathon which was first run in October 1994. In that year 72 runners completed the marathon with Ray Brown winning the men's race in a time of 2:35:50 and visiting New Zealand runner Nyla Carroll taking the women's title in 2:52:20 – this remains the course record for women. The current course record for men is 2:29:24, set in 1998 by Todd Ingraham. The current Goodlife Rottnest Marathon and accompanying 21.1km, 10km and 5km fun run is organised by the West Australian Marathon Club with the event proceeds being donated to Royal Flying Doctor Service. Entry fees for the Marathon are $110.00 (WAMC Members Price is $95.00) The Marathon event has a cut off time of 6.5 hours while Half Marathon runners are given 3 hours in which to finish. All Marathon Only entrants are sent their bibs in the first week of October. Anyone who registers after this date will need to collect their bib from Heritage Common on either Saturday afternoon or Sunday morning before the race starts. Bib collection for the Half Marathon, 10km & 5km will occur on Saturday afternoon or from 7.00am, Sunday on Heritage Common. All entrants receive an Essential Guide in September outlining what will happen on race day and any special discounts that will be available whilst visiting the island.

All races start and finish at Heritage Common on Rottnest Island with the Marathon starting first at 6.30am followed by the Half Marathon at 7.10am. The 5km race leaves at 10.25am with the 10km event leaving five minutes later. The Marathon start is heralded by the wail of bagpipes at dawn on the Sunday morning. These have become a traditional part of the marathon and can be heard throughout the race at Armstrong Hill. It is anticipated that over 200 runners will tackle the Marathon course that circumnavigates the salt lakes in the centre of the Island via the sealed roads. The Rottnest Marathon consists of four laps. The first lap is 12.2km and includes a loop out towards Kingstown Barracks with the following three laps, excluding the Kingstown loop, being approx. 10km each, with the finish on Heritage Common. For the Half Marathon around 400 runners will cover the same route as the marathon course but only twice! It is anticipated around 600 runners and walkers will participate in either the 5km out-and-back course or the 10km fun run that covers the same route as the marathon course. There are five drink stations on the course manned by volunteer army cadets, who will issue runners with water at approximately 2km intervals. Electrolyte drink will be available at approximately 5k intervals for those running the full marathon distance. Post-race Presentations are held at 12 noon on the Heritage Common. All Marathon finishers receive a medal, finishers' shirt, and Goodlife Health Club goodie bag. All Half Marathon finishers get a medal, Goodlife Health Club goodie bag, and 3 pairs of Mizuno socks!

If you're planning to stay on the Island after the race there's a whole range of interesting things to do and see. The Island offers diverse experiences from walking trails and fishing to wildlife encounters and bike tours. Many choose to simply spend time rehydrating in the beer garden of the Rottnest Hotel taking in the wonderful views over the bay while enjoying a well-earned drink. Not that there's anything wrong with that. I've done it myself on numerous occasions over the years without needing the excuse of just having completed a marathon. Those with energy to spare may wish to head the short distance to The Basin – my favourite place on the Island. This is a popular spot for locals and tourists and with its crystal clear turquoise waters, it's not hard to see why. With a shallow reef platform home to an array of small marine life, a large hole in the reef acts as a natural swimming pool. If snorkelling, you'll be able to see schools of buffalo bream as they swim between your feet on top of the soft, white sand. If you want to experience more marine life and are a confident swimmer you can venture out into deeper water off The Basin in the direction of the neighbouring Longreach Bay. Another great snorkelling option, Parker Point offers visitors with a more structured snorkelling adventure. With underwater plaques guiding you on an exciting snorkelling trail, you can learn about the flora and marine life in the area while also exploring it for yourself.

For those keen to explore on foot, the Wadjemup Walk Trail covers most of the island's stunning landscape. Stretching over 50 km around the island, you can chose to complete the entire trail, or instead stick to one of its three designated sub-sections. For example, the island's Bickley Bay

Walk explores the Coastal Defence systems that were installed during World War Two, The Lakes Walk takes you through the lake system on the island and the Salmon Bay Walk offers panoramic views of the Indian Ocean from the Wadjemup lighthouse. If you don't fancy either cycling or walking you could always take the Island Discovery Bus, a 90 minutes bus tour that circumnavigates the whole island with an informative commentary. The tour gives you a great overview of all areas, so that you know what you want to explore later by yourself. There's also a range of other activities on offer from private helicopter flights to Segway tours and tandem skydiving experiences but these tend to be more expensive options aimed at the well-heeled tourist. I've always viewed my visits to Rottnest as an escape from the commercial aspects of modern living and have been happy to give them a miss.

GREAT BARRIER REEF MARATHON

QUEENSLAND

OCTOBER

The Great Barrier Reef Marathon Festival takes place in Port Douglas, a seaside town nestled between the Daintree Rainforest and the Great Barrier Reef – two World Heritage sites that David Attenborough once described as his perfect holiday destination. The first ever Marathon Festival was hosted in Port Douglas on 12 November 2011. Aptly named after the region's most famous icon, the first edition featured 4 individual running events: a 74 km Ultra Marathon, a Half Marathon, a 10K race and what is described as a Fundy 5000 (Don't ask. I assume it was a 5K race) Note, there was no marathon distance event in the Festival's inaugural year. The 2011 event was organised by locally owned Port Douglas Event Management, as the precursor to the following year's much anticipated Solar Eclipse Marathon being arranged in association with event owners Travelling Fit, NSW and Albatros Travel from Denmark. This was to ensure the actual Marathon event and its course in 2012 was as unique to the region as that year's Solar Eclipse itself. Marathon legend Steve Moneghetti, the race ambassador also ran in the first race, eager to help consolidate the Marathon Festival as an annual event on the worldwide running circuit. The idea was that from 2013 onwards the Great Barrier Reef Marathon Festival would include the Marathon event each year. It has, though the Solar Eclipse race was by no means the first marathon held in Port Douglas. I've read that the town's original marathon was run 3 times around a 14km looped track on the peninsula back in the early 1990s.

The Tropical Journeys Great Barrier Reef Marathon Festival (as it's now branded) is rapidly becoming one of the 'must do' events on the Australian Running Calendar. Dubbed 'the world's best adventure course' by Steve Moneghetti, the diverse landscape of Port Douglas offers a combination of beach, road and trail running for all distances, enabling runners to see this lovely area at close hand. The Marathon has also been described as one of the most beautiful events on the calendar with Port Douglas providing the perfect backdrop for runners to test their fitness and endurance in a tropical environment. With the race being held in the tropical oasis of Port Douglas in Tropical North Queensland, the Festival advertises under the banner, 'The icing on the cake ... you get to recover right here in paradise.' With temperatures fluctuating between 19 and 24 °C in 'tropical beach season', this reef and rainforest destination boasts lots of clear blue skies during the day and comfortable, balmy temperatures in the evening. Competitive events include: 42.195km Steve Moneghetti Adventure Marathon, 21.1km Sheraton Grand Mirage Resort Half Marathon, a 10km Newsport 10000, a 5km Calypso 5000 Fun Run and a 2.3km Star FM Junior Challenge. The 74km Ultra Marathon is no longer held.

Port Douglas is situated in Far North Queensland, Australia, approximately 70 km north of Cairns. The town's population of approximately 3,500 inhabitants can often double with the influx of tourists during the peak tourism season from May to September. The township was established in 1877 after the discovery of gold at Hodgkinson River by James Venture Mulligan. It grew quickly based on the mining industry, and at its peak Port Douglas had a population of 12,000 and 27 hotels. When the Kuranda Railway from Cairns to Kuranda was completed in 1891, the importance of Port Douglas dwindled along with its population. A cyclone in 1911 which demolished all but two buildings in the town also had a significant impact. At its nadir in 1960 the town, by then little more than a fishing village, had a population of 100. It was certainly an unknown quantity during my years in Australia in the 1970s and 80s. Cairns, to the south, was about as far north as holidaymakers ventured in those days and I've been as surprised as anyone to see how the town has prospered in more recent years. It wasn't until the late-1980s, that tourism boomed in the region after investor Christopher Skase financed the construction of the Sheraton Mirage Port Douglas Resort. Since then Port Douglas has developed into an upmarket tourist resort with an ideal location from which you can explore the Great Barrier Reef and Daintree Rainforest. With its multi-million dollar holiday homes, five-star resorts, sophisticated eateries and bars, award-winning restaurants, stylish boutiques and a busy marina, Port Douglas has a reputation as the upmarket glamour town of Tropical North Queensland. The once sleepy seaside village now attracts hundreds of thousands of tourists every year; from both Australia and across the globe and is a well-known haunt for celebrity spotting and the place where the rich and famous mingle with the locals. Let me give you two examples of this. In November 1996 United States President Bill Clinton and First Lady Hillary Clinton chose the town as their only holiday stop on their historic visit to Australia. When dining at a local restaurant they witnessed a couple's wedding certificate. On a return visit on 11 September 2001, Clinton was again dining at a local restaurant, when he was advised of the September 11 attacks. He returned to the United States the following day. In September 2006, television personality and conservationist Steve Irwin died at Batt Reef, off Port Douglas, after a stingray barb pierced his heart during the filming of a documentary called 'The Ocean's Deadliest.' Irwin was filmed snorkelling directly above the stingray when it lashed him with its tail, killing him almost immediately. The event was widely reported in Australia and overseas.

For those travelling to the marathon, there are no major airports located in Port Douglas and it's a rather long drive if you are coming to Port Douglas from pretty much any major centre in Australia. Cairns is approximately 1700km or 21 hours of driving north from Brisbane, Queensland's capital so most travellers generally opt for a flight into Cairns, and then either get an airport transfer to Port Douglas or hire a car for the 1-hour drive. Cairns Airport boasts international, domestic and general aviation terminals. Flights are available from a small number of international locations and from most major cities in Australia. There are a number of limousine and shuttle companies to choose from that operate to and from the Cairns Airport from about $25 each way. If you are driving the distance yourself, Port Douglas is a short 70 km drive north along a sealed highway. There is a range of accommodation in Port Douglas from Backpacker Hostels, to swanky apartments and high-end hotels. A perusal of the UK's booking.com website for a basic 2-night stay for the marathon weekend five months prior to race day revealed that 71% of these were already booked. What remained varied in price from £97 for a hostel bed to a whopping £1,398 in the Reflections of Port Douglas apartment complex.

The standard entry fee for The Great Barrier Reef Marathon is an expensive $210 but those who get in early can see this reduced to $152 in March climbing to $170 in August. Race Kit collection of bib and race singlet, included in the entry fee for the Marathon and Half Marathon only, takes place both on the Esplanade in Cairns on the Monday beforehand or on the Saturday on Port Douglas Esplanade from 9:00am - 5:00pm. Race day emergencies and last-minute registrations are available up to a minimum of one hour before the race briefing. Organisers advise that participants arrive a minimum of 45mins prior to race start to ensure adequate time is allowed to walk from the parking location and pre-race toilet stops. The Marathon starts in the darkness at the northern end of Four Mile beach at 5:30am after a very early race briefing at 5:00am. This is followed by the 10K at 6:00am, the Half Marathon at 6:30am, the 5K at 8:00am and the 2.3K race at 9:00am. Marathon runners have 7 hours in which to complete a difficult course over a variety of surfaces. In 2017 104 runners managed to do this in the Marathon (67 males, 37 females) with a total of 382 finishers in the Half Marathon.

All distances start on the flat, compact sands of Four Mile Beach with marathon runners being treated to the colours of the sun rising over the Coral Sea. Depending on the distance chosen, the runners will face courses in mixed environments covering asphalt, sand, grass and gravel terrain. All courses are on flat ground, except for a 2km incline over 380m up the infamous 'Bump Track.' The first 4.5km are spent running on compact beach sand. At the end of the beach runners turn inland and weave through the resort town's streets before heading out into the Mowbray Valley. The course then goes along Mowbray River Road, past the sugar cane fields and towards Black Mountain, crossing over the historic Diggers Bridge before heading down Connolly Road to confront the Bump Track. The Bump Track itself is a historic trail where gold & tin miners used to transport their finds from the Atherton Tablelands all the way down to the Port Douglas sugar wharf with carts and bullocks. It's described as the point everyone should train for. The combination of trails, changing elevation and the heat of the tropics means that a decent level of fitness is required to complete the course.

The first part of the Bump Track ascends 360m in just 2.2km, it is very steep and most people will walk it. Runners are rewarded by remarkable views along the way, with the Mowbray River Waterfalls to the right and the best view in the region at the top, taking in the Mowbray Valley and across the Coral Sea to Low Isles. There's even a bench for a rest at a place known as The Landing, if needed. From The Landing it's a further 4km to the top of the Bump Track but this part is shaded, undulating and not nearly as difficult. Once runners have reached the top, they turn left onto Black Mountain Road and head towards East Black Mountain Road for approximately 3km. Runners turn around and it's all downhill from there. The course continues back down the Bump Track before heading back in towards Port Douglas with the final 5.5km weaving through the streets of town with a final straight past The Sheraton Mirage Resort. The last 1500m brings runners back to the start/finish area with a glory lap of the Port Douglas Esplanade in front of the gathered crowd. A distinctive medal awaits everyone as they cross the finish line. There are plenty of great cafes along the beach and a short walk to the main street for re-fuelling after the event. Following the race all participants together with their friends and family are invited to the post 2018 marathon After Party at the Central Hotel on the Sunday evening. Entertainment is provided, with food and drink available for purchase.

I'm sure that most Marathon Tourists would wish to stay longer than the basic 2-night marathon weekend mentioned earlier to take advantage of the fact that Port Douglas is perfectly positioned for day trips to the World Heritage-listed twin attractions of the Great Barrier Reef and the Daintree Rainforest. As everyone knows, the Great Barrier Reef is the largest coral reef system in the world. This reef system in the Coral Sea, off the coast of Queensland in northeast Australia is composed of over 2,900 individual reefs and 900 islands. There are number of boat tours leaving from Port Douglas to The Great Barrier Reef each day, on either a day trip or an extended overnight trip. These tours cater for diving, snorkelling, fishing, jet skiing or just sitting back on a yacht and sailing the Coral Sea. For example, Calypso Reef Cruises provides a full day reef experience with Reef tours and dive trips suitable for all ages from $246.5pp adult. All participants competing in the 2018 Marathon Festival are offered to the chance to enjoy one of these cruises at a hugely discounted rate (savings of $80 per adult are mentioned on the website) For those who prefer to fly, GBR Helicopters, Port Douglas even offers helicopter tours over the Great Barrier Reef, landing on your very own private sand quay from $159pp.

Visitors can also explore the world's oldest rainforest, meet unique wildlife, go croc spotting and experience the local Indigenous culture on a tour of the World Heritage Daintree Rainforest. As the world's oldest Rainforest the Daintree provides the ultimate in unique fauna and flora. Waterfalls and waterholes line the drive through the forest, supporting some of the world's most famous animals such as the rare and endangered flightless bird, the Cassowary. Mossman Gorge, the southernmost part of the Daintree, is only a 20-minute drive from Port Douglas. After exploring the walking trails, visitors can take a dip in the pristine, clear waters, surrounded by dense rainforest and gigantic granite boulders. Locally owned and operated Discovery Tours offer full and half day tours that include a Daintree River Cruise, exclusive access to Cassowary Falls and a visit to Mossman

Gorge with option to swim from $95pp. These tours might sound expensive but some might consider it well worth the cost for a once-in-a-lifetime opportunity to see two of the most amazing natural features on the planet. Port Douglas is a long way away from most places and who knows if they'll ever be back.

In keeping with its status as a high-end, upmarket resort town, Port Douglas can be an expensive place to eat and drink. That's not to say that there aren't a number of reasonably priced food outlets among its estimated 75 eateries that would satisfy the needs of the hungry Marathon Tourist. Dominos has always been one of my go-to pizza places while in Australia – you can't go wrong for only $5 for a basic pizza. Fortunately, they have premises in the Port Village Centre, Port Douglas. The Pizza Shop in the Portico Centre on Macrossan Street is also reasonably priced. Other cheap options available are Dave's Takeaway serving fish and chips and burgers, also on Macrossan Street. You can dine in or take out. On the same street, Under Wraps offers $10 meal deals (2 for 1 on Tuesdays) while N17 Burger Co. serves Beer and Burger for $15. The latter also has a BYO wine option. Those who like a beer or two with their food need simply to walk a little farther down the street to Paddy's Irish Pub and Grill. This offers all your traditional favourite Irish dishes mixed with some Aussie classics. Beef and Guinness Pie can be had for $19, Irish Stew for $18 and Lamb Shank for $20 with Fish and Chips, Steamed Mussels and Roast Pumpkin also on the menu. The pub also serves all-day Sunday roasts for $15 and advertises 'the best tasting Guinness in FNQ!' That'll do for me.

AUCKLAND MARATHON

NORTH ISLAND, NEW ZEALAND

OCTOBER

Some would say that this is a heck of a long way to go travel from the UK just to run a marathon. They're right, of course, but I wouldn't be going all that way solely for a single race. I've a long-standing ambition to hire a motor home and take a leisurely drive around the two islands that make up New Zealand. My two sons drove around some years ago as part of a World Trip and the photographs they brought home together with descriptions of their experiences have had me wanting to follow suit. I particularly want to go hiking in the Southern Alps and visit the beautiful town of Queenstown - though will probably give bungee-jumping a miss. As luck will have it Queenstown hosts its own marathon three weeks after Auckland so I'm sure I can arrange an itinerary to combine the two. There are a number of other marathons in New Zealand that I've described in this book that I'd also like to shoe-horn into the itinerary. Anyway, it's an awful long time since I was last in the country – 1974 to be exact and all I can recall of my two days spent in Auckland during the trip is the hasty visit Mo and I made to Eden Park, the legendary home of New Zealand's cricket and rugby (I was a big cricket fan in those days).

Auckland has a long and varied history of marathons, often with two or three marathons being held within or in the vicinity of Auckland in any given year during the 1970s and early 1980s. Marathons in Auckland date back to 1936, when J. W. Savidan organised, and then won, a marathon along the waterfront. That event attracted just 16 runners. It was only in 1962 that the annual series of Marathons began. There has only been one year since then (1988) in which a Marathon has not been held in Auckland. By the late 1980s, these several competing marathons had passed away. It was not until October 1992 that the Auckland Harbour Bridge crossing was first used in the race - becoming the first ever sports event to cross the iconic Bridge. The 1992 event constitutes the present series of Auckland Marathons and by changing the course to include the Harbour Bridge and the city centre the organisers finally achieved the international profile that they'd been seeking for their event. Just out of interest these are some of the other, now defunct, marathons that have been held in Auckland over the years: the Great Northern Marathon (3 editions from 1989 to1991), the Winstone People's Marathon (9 editions from 1979 to 87), the Auckland Marathon (28 editions between 1956 to 86), the Pasta/Auckland Marathon (2 editions 1982 and 83) the Reidbuilt-Calliope Marathon (16 editions 1965 to 80) and the Owairaka Lovelock Track Marathon (13 editions 1961 to 73) I wonder how many other cities around the world can match this record. I can't think of any.

These days the Auckland Marathon is a big, well-established event with over 16,500 runners participating in the various races on offer: Marathon, Half Marathon, 12K and 5K races plus a Kids Run. The half marathon is the most popular race distance, with over 7000 competitors, and usually sells out within days of being advertised. The marathon takes approximately half as many entrants with a growing number of international competitors each year. In

2012 visitors from more than 50 different countries took part in the race, all interested in seeing what New Zealand has to offer.

The Maori people's Polynesian ancestors are thought to have discovered and settled in New Zealand as early as 950AD it wasn't until after the Treaty of Waitangi was signed with the Maori in 1840 that significant numbers of Europeans arrived in what is now modern day Auckland. In September of that year Captain Hobson and a government party of 12 planted the British flag and celebrated the founding of the new town that Hobson named Auckland. By the 1890s, the city had a cosmopolitan flavour, with dozens of languages heard in the bustling streets and new inhabitants from Europe, China and India. This theme continued throughout the 20th century, particularly in the 1950s when the population was boosted by the post-World War II baby boom. Many rural people relocated to seek work in the new city, and large numbers of rural Maori migrated to Auckland. They were followed by migrant workers from the Pacific Islands, peaking in the 1960s. Misunderstandings between Maori and the settlers continued, and it was not until the 1970s that they were revisited and the reconciliation process began. Today, Auckland is the world's largest Polynesian city and one of the great cities of the Pacific. Aucklanders come from all corners of the world – around 56% of its residents are of European descent, 11% are Maori, 13% are of Pacific Island descent and there is a growing Asian population of around 12%.

These days Auckland is a world-class international destination renowned for its stunning natural beauty and vibrant city culture. It is New Zealand's largest city, with approximately 1.5 million people, about one third of New Zealand's population, living in the greater Auckland area. Set on three beautiful harbours: Waitemata (an arm of the

Hauraki Gulf), Manukau and Kaipara, Auckland is home to more than 50 islands. The Pacific Ocean on the east coast and the Tasman Sea on the west coast, less than an hour's drive apart at their furthest, form the coastline around the Auckland region. The mainland coastline is over 1,600 kilometres long and Auckland is home to hundreds of beaches – sheltered white sand on the Pacific east coast and spectacular black sand beaches on the Tasman west coast. The central part of the urban area occupies a narrow isthmus between the Manukau Harbour on the Tasman Sea and the Waitemata Harbour on the Pacific Ocean. It is one of the few cities in the world to have harbours on separate major bodies of water. Bridges span parts of both harbours, notably the Auckland Harbour Bridge crossing the Waitemata Harbour west of the Auckland Central Business District. The Mangere Bridge and the Upper Harbour Bridge span the upper reaches of the Manukau and Waitemata Harbours, respectively. Auckland's landscape is also dotted with 48 volcanic cones. The largest and most iconic is Rangitoto Island, Auckland's youngest volcano and New Zealand's youngest landform, which emerged from the water approximately 600 years ago.

One of Auckland's nicknames, the 'City of Sails' is derived from the popularity of sailing in the region. Thousands of yachts and launches are registered in Auckland with about one in three households owning a boat. Between 1842 and 1865, Auckland was the capital city of New Zealand when Parliament met in what is now Old Government House on the University of Auckland's City campus. The capital was moved to the more centrally located Wellington in 1865. Most major international corporations have an Auckland office, as the city is the economic capital of the nation. The city's sparkling waters, varied landscapes and cosmopolitan city life combine to make it one of the most desirable places in the world to live or visit. Auckland was ranked the 3rd most live-able city in the world in the 2011, 2012 and 2013 Mercer Quality of Living scale.

Entries to the 2016 marathon ranged from $155 before mid-September 15th to $175 up until mid-October and then $200 after that date if places were still available. Number, chip and T-shirts are given out on the two days prior to the race at the Registration & Expo, Viaduct Events Centre. Race packs also include any pre-ordered ferry and bus tickets to get runners to the start on race day. One of the more interesting features of the event is that those staying within the city centre have the opportunity to take an early morning ferry across the harbor to the start on the North Shore. Due to traffic congestion on the North Shore from participants accessing the start line in Devonport, the organisers strongly recommend that runners consider using the pre-race services of the Ferry or Bus to get to the Marathon and Half Marathon start. In association with Fullers Ferries, the event provides a Chartered Ferry Service to both starts. They recommend that you park on the Auckland City side where the race finishes, purchase a $9.00 one-way ferry ticket and catch the ferry to the start line. Ferry tickets must be purchased when completing your online entry form. Return Supporters Tickets are also available and can be purchased for $19.00. Due also to the expected congestion in down-town Auckland a finish cut-off time of 1:00pm is imposed for the marathon. Finish times and results are not recorded after 1:00pm. That shouldn't bother too many runners given that the race's start is 6am. Nor should they worry too much about the cut-off time for reaching the Harbour Bridge at the 13km mark. Apparently it is a requirement that the Auckland Harbour Bridge be fully open for traffic from 10:30am. This means that participants reaching the 9k mark at Smales Farm Bus Station after 8:15am will not be permitted to continue along the Busway. Transport will be available at this point for those not making this cut-off time to transport them at 8:20am to Akoranga Bus Station or 8:35am to the Onewa Rd on-ramp by 8:40am where they will disembark to continue the event across the Harbour Bridge. (It doesn't say whether they'll be allowed to count this as having 'run' a marathon).

On race day the marathon and half marathon runners start from the same venue at 6am and 6:50am respectively. Other races start from other places with the 12K leaving at 9am, the 5K at 10am and the Kids Run an hour later. The first half of the Auckland Marathon course runs from Devonport on Auckland's North Shore with the second half of the course run on the opposite shore. The start is on King Edward Parade overlooking the Waitemata Harbour. Runners make their way through Takapuna to the Smales Farm Bus Station where it joins the Busway southbound to the Auckland Harbour Bridge. Going over the harbour bridge is a new experience for many participants – a completely different feeling to whizzing over it in their cars every morning. The crossing affords a dazzling view of New Zealand's biggest city at its finest. After crossing the Bridge, the course takes in Westhaven Marina, the Viaduct Harbour (the halfway mark), before heading out along Auckland City's waterfront. This section of the course is an out and back, with the turn point being in St Helier's Bay. The return leg follows the same course back to the Viaduct Harbour for a finish at Victoria Park. The first half of the course is best described as 'rolling' while the second half, other than two small road bridges, is flat. The course is scenic throughout with the Party in the Park welcoming finishers to Victoria Park with bands, entertainment and a variety of hospitality tents.

The event website offers some suggestions as to what Auckland has to offer but here's some of my own that might be of interest. Attractions and landmarks in the Auckland metropolitan area include: Auckland Civic Theatre – an internationally significant heritage atmospheric theatre built in 1929. It was renovated in 2000 to its original condition. Auckland Town Hall – with its concert hall is considered to have some of the finest acoustics in the world. This 1911 building serves both council and entertainment functions. Aotea Square – the hub of downtown Auckland beside Queen Street is the site of rallies and arts festivals. St Patrick's Cathedral – the Catholic Cathedral of Auckland is a 19th century Gothic building which was renovated from 2003 to 2007 for refurbishment and structural support. I'd also want to re-visit Eden Park – the city's primary stadium and a frequent home for All Blacks rugby union and international cricket matches. It was the location of the 2011 Rugby World Cup final. Also of interest is the New Zealand Maritime Museum which features exhibitions and collections relating to New Zealand maritime history at Hobson Wharf, adjacent to Viaduct Basin. Queen Street is the main street of the city, running from Karangahape Road down to the harbour. The Sky Tower – the tallest free-standing structure in the Southern Hemisphere at 328 metres tall is said to have excellent panoramic views. Viaduct Basin, a marina and residential development in downtown Auckland, and the venue for the America's Cup regattas in 2000 and 2003 is also worth a visit.

Also among Auckland's must-see landmarks is Mount Eden, a volcanic cone with a grassy crater. The highest natural point in Auckland City, it offers 360-degree views of Auckland and has a reputation as a favourite tourist outlook. Mount Victoria is another volcanic cone on the North Shore offering a spectacular view of downtown Auckland. A brisk walk from the Devonport ferry terminal, the cone is steeped in history, as is nearby North Head. Also worth looking at is One Tree Hill – a volcanic cone that dominates the skyline in the southern inner suburbs. It no longer has a tree on the summit after a politically motivated attack on the tree but is crowned by an obelisk.

Without recent personal experience of the city I've looked at the results of Metro Magazine's 2013 poll on 'The best food and drink in Auckland.' Though now a bit dated these places still exist and prices quoted are from 2018. New Zealand is, of course, famous for the quality of its fish and chips and the Mount Eden Village Fish Shop came top of the poll for these in the Auckland area. Beer battered Fish of the Day and chips there will cost you $12. If it's pizza and pasta you're after Toto' Pizza in Harding Street serve a range of 10-inch pizzas from $16 (you can even order by the metre from $45) For those looking for burgers, BurgerFuel came out top in the survey for its range of Gourmet Burgers with fancy names like 'Steak of the Nation' and 'The Bastard' – both starting from $16.90. You can find these at its stores in Queen's Street and Custom's Street. Sadly, The Golden Dawn Tavern voted 'Best Bar' in the poll has recently closed its doors for good. Runner-up The Roxy on Fort Street still exists and is described as 'an ideal spot for after work drinks or to while away the evening enjoying top local and international DJs.' The pub takes its name from the century old theatre that once occupied the site and features a rooftop deck offering excellent views of the midtown city skyline. Finally, for lovers of craft beer the Hallertau Brewery in Riverhead, Auckland was voted number one in the 'Craft Beer' category. Hallertau has a reputation as one of the leaders in the craft beer boom in New Zealand for its wide-ranging choice of beers branded in four distinct categories: The Numbers Range, the Heroic Range, Sour Beer (described as 'Beer that any monk worth his salt would be proud of') and a Seasonal Range. A Brewery Tour and tasting includes sampling of what's currently being brewed at a cost of $25 per head.

QUEENSTOWN MARATHON

SOUTH ISLAND, NEW ZEALAND

NOVEMBER

Queenstown, located among spectacular scenery on the South Island of New Zealand, enjoys a well-deserved reputation as the 'Adventure Capital of the World'. For decades it's offered a huge variety of activities for adrenaline junkies and outdoor enthusiasts: river rafting, jet boating, bungee jumping, skiing, hiking, trail running, climbing, mountain biking, kayaking - there is a never-ending supply of activities to satisfy the two million visitors the town receives every year. My two sons were there recently to enjoy a spot of bungee jumping and to walk on some of its hiking trails. The photos they sent home were amazing. With such a strong tradition of outdoor activities, I guess it was only a matter of time before someone added marathon running to the list. This happened in November 2014 when an event company with experience of organising major triathlon events joined forces with sponsor Air New Zealand to arrange the first edition of the Air New Zealand Queenstown International Marathon. The organisers had an ambitious 5-year plan aimed at attracting around 10,000 runners to the original events on their programme: Marathon, Half Marathon and 10K race, Their chosen course for the Marathon was set between the backdrop of the world renowned Crown and Remarkable mountain ranges and incorporated the best highlights of the

Queenstown Lakes region including Millbrook resort, Arrowtown, Lake Hayes, Shotover River, Lake Wakatipu and Queenstown Gardens with the finish in the heart of Queenstown itself. Air New Zealand head of sponsorship James Gibson felt at the time that, 'The course does a fantastic job of taking in so many of the scenic highlights of the region. It has the potential to be a destination marathon that sits alongside some of the world's great marathons. People both here and abroad will be adding it to their bucket list.' He wasn't wrong.

Entries for the inaugural Queenstown Marathon sold out five months before race day and the event has continued to expand in terms of numbers of international participants in every year since 2014. Shortly prior to last year's race (2017) the New Zealand Herald provided an interesting breakdown of figures relating to the event as a whole (i.e. not just the Marathon race) With online entries still open there were already 41 countries represented on the start list of 9,588 spread among the five events on offer that year: the Air New Zealand Marathon, NZ Sothebys International Realty Half Marathon and First Half Marathon (a new event starting and finishing at Millbrook Reserve), the 10km event and the Kids Run. Event Director Nicole Fairweather was thrilled at another strong turnout that had already exceeded the previous year, and the benefit it brought to the region She is reported as saying, 'The numbers have again been amazing and a testament to just how attractive the Air New Zealand Queenstown International Marathon is to New Zealanders and our many international visitors …. Queenstown's reputation as a world class holiday destination combined with the rolling hard packed off-road trails that make up the bulk of our courses combine to make this hugely attractive to overseas runners.' She added, 'With each of those entrants often comes family or supporters, boosting the economic impact to the Queenstown Lakes District and beyond, as people take in the sights, an adventure or two and sample the wonderful wine and food on offer in this stunning part of the world.' Of the international visitors, Australia led the way with 1,183 entries, with strong numbers from America (150), China (100), Japan (48) and the United Kingdom (44). Runners also featured from Afghanistan, Ethiopia, Macau, Tonga, Mexico and a host of European countries. The economic impact to the Queenstown area was estimated as an $8.5-million boost to the local economy based on a 5 nights average stay for international visitors, a 3 nights average stay for domestic visitors and 3000 extra seats into Queenstown with race sponsor Air New Zealand. Significantly, the women outnumber the men on this event, with 63% of the entire entry list being women. 1,555 runners completed the full marathon distance in 2017 in times ranging from 2 hours 27 minutes to 8 hours 35 minutes. 3,982 athletes finished the NZ Sotheby's RE Half Marathon race with a further 403 running the first half of the Marathon course to complete the NZ Sotheby's RE First Half Marathon. (Yes, there are two separate Half Marathons on the programme.)

I was alerted to this event in 2015 when a friend, who knew that I was returning to Australia for a series of marathons that year, sent me a copy of an article that appeared in the UK's Daily Telegraph in February 2015. He thought that I might be able to fit this one into my itinerary. (I'm afraid that some of us in the UK have difficulty in comprehending the enormous distance between the two countries). Lack of geographical knowledge aside, I was intrigued by what the article had to say. Entitled 'An Epic Marathon in Lord of the Rings Country,' Adventure athlete Tobias Mews described the Queenstown International

Marathon as 'a race worth journeying to Middle Earth for.' Mews wrote about how his initial doubts about entering the inaugural race of a marathon taking place in late November on the other side of the world were overcome by the sheer beauty of its course. This, he felt, was a perfect blend of 70 per cent trail and 30 per cent road that took the 1,890 marathon competitors past all the local tourist hot spots adding, 'As we ran through the 19th century gold rush village of Arrowtown, I cursed that I hadn't brought a camera. Charming cottages, cafes, hotels and a rather fabulous sweet shop set along a tree-lined avenue tempted us to stop and stay.' He described the incredible mountain scenery around the course as having a keenly familiar look, reminiscent of the Lord of the Rings sagas while, 'Every single hill we ran up offered another heart-wrenchingly beautiful view of the Remarkables' (supposedly named because they're one of two mountain ranges in the world that run directly north to south). The event has been on my bucket list since first reading the article.

Queenstown is a resort town in Otago in the south-west of New Zealand's South Island with an urban population of 15,300. The town is built around an inlet called Queenstown Bay on Lake Wakatipu, a long thin Z-shaped lake formed by glacial processes, and has views of nearby mountains such as The Remarkables, Cecil Peak, Walter Peak and, just above the town, Ben Lomond and Queenstown Hill. 84km long and 5km wide at its widest point, Lake Wakatipu was formed by a huge glacier that pushed through the land from the north-west. The jagged mountains that surround it run straight into its depths, forming a canyon that is 399 metres at its deepest point. There's a lovely Maori legend about its origins. It tells of two star-crossed lovers: the young warrior Matakauri and Manata, the beautiful daughter of a Maori chief who forbade them to marry. One night, the cruel giant Matau stole Manata and hid her away in his mountain lair. Completely distraught, her father declared that the warrior who was brave enough to rescue her could marry her. Matakauri accepted this challenge, because he knew that the next time the warm wind blew from the north-west it would put the giant to sleep. Soon enough the wind blew, and as the sleeping giant lay curled on his side, Matakauri tried to rescue Manata. But a magical rope, made from a two-headed dog, tied Manata to the giant and Matakauri could not cut through it. In despair, Manata began to weep, but when her tears fell on the rope it melted and she was able to break free. As the couple escaped, Matakauri set fire to Matau to ensure he would never steal Manata again. The giant's body melted, creating a massive hole that filled with melted ice and snow. The large 'S' shaped lake left in his place is now called Wakatipu, which translates as the 'hollow of the sleeping giant'. People say Matua's heart still beats in the lake, creating the mysterious, rhythmic rise and fall of its waters. Listen out for it on your way round the marathon course.

European explorers William Gilbert Rees and Nicholas von Tunzelmann were the first non-Maoris to settle the area. Rees established a high country farm in the location of Queenstown's current town centre in 1860, but the discovery of gold in the Arrow River in 1862 encouraged Rees to convert his wool shed into a hotel named the Queen's Arms, now known as Eichardt's. Many Queenstown streets bear names from the gold mining era (such as Camp Street) and some historic buildings remain. William's Cottage, the Lake Lodge of Ophir, Queenstown Police Station, and St Peter's Anglican Church lie close together in a designated historic precinct. Tourism is now the mainstay of Queenstown's economy with most jobs in the city being tourism or accommodation related.

Many visitors come to the city inspired by the beauty of the locations used in the filming of The Lord of the Rings film trilogy and attracted by the 220 adventure tourism activities on offer. In particular, Queenstown has become a major centre for snow sports in New Zealand, with people from all over the country and many parts of the world travelling to ski at the four main mountain ski fields (Cardrona Alpine Resort, Coronet Peak, The Remarkables and Treble Cone). It is also a base for exploring the region's vineyards and historic mining towns. The city lies close to the centre of a small wine producing region, reputed to be the world's southernmost. The Two Paddocks vineyard is owned by local actor Sam Neill. Neighbouring, historic Arrowtown features restaurants and bars. Largely due to its popularity as a tourist destination, Queenstown is now one of the fastest growing cities in the country with residential property now the most expensive - overtaking Auckland at the start of 2017 when average house prices in the Queenstown area became $1 million.

For those flying in for the Marathon, Queenstown Airport is located in Frankton, Otago, 8 km or a 10-minute drive from the Queenstown CBD. The airport receives flights from Australia by Air New Zealand, Qantas, Virgin Australia and Jetstar and in particular, to Brisbane, Gold Coast, Melbourne, and Sydney (the frequency is much increased over the ski season and during summer). Domestic flights operate to Auckland, Christchurch, Dunedin, Hamilton, Nelson and Wellington. Buses, airport shuttles, taxis and limos are all lined up outside the terminal waiting for arrivals. Taxis and Airport Shuttles offer door-to-door service and the public bus comes through every 15 minutes. Orbus is the easiest, most convenient and most affordable way to get around Queenstown with flat-rate fares for just $2. The $2 fare is only available to GoCard holders. There is a one-off cost of $5 to buy a GoCard but once you have it you'll have ongoing access to the $2 fare. You can purchase a GoCard for $5 from Queenstown Airport (at the Tourism desk next to the baggage claim area), O'Connell's Mall kiosk in the city centre, or on every bus that's part of the $2 bus network. Without the GoCard, cash fares will be $4 for a child and $5 for an adult. If travelling to Queenstown Airport, the fare will be $2 with a GoCard or cash fare $10 for an adult. Queenstown is accessible by road and air but not by rail and there are many bus services that operate into the city, with daily services to and from Invercargill, Dunedin and Christchurch, which are the main cities closest to Queenstown. On arrival there are plenty of accommodation choices to suit everyone's budget, from backpacker hostels to five star hotels with 3-star hotels booked from the UK averaging £104 and 5-star averaging £159 per night.

Entries for the 5th edition of the Marathon in 2018 started at $145, rising in stages to $175 close to race day. These prices do not include an 8% booking fee. A portion of the entry fee is allocated towards a $30,000 donation to the Queenstown Trails Trust for the maintenance and further development of trails throughout the Wakatipu Basin. The fee gets entrants a personalised race bib, an official gear bag, finisher's medal, medical support/assistance and aid stations on the course with water, Powerade sports drink, toilets and first aid. A post-race recovery area is also provided at the finish with food and drink available. Number pick-up takes place on the Thursday and Friday before Saturday's race at the Queenstown Memorial Centre, Memorial Street for overseas competitors. New Zealand based entrants have their race numbers mailed to them. With limited parking available at all start areas, athletes are encouraged to use the shuttle service provided to take them from Queenstown direct to the start line of the Marathon, Half Marathon or 10km race. This operates as a continuous direct service from the Event Hub at Queenstown Recreation Ground on race day between 6:45am and 7:25am for marathon runners. The service costs an extra $15 for Marathon and Half Marathon entrants.

While all events finish at the Queenstown Memorial Centre Recreational Ground each has a different starting point. The 10K runners begin at Lake Ave, Frankton at 7:45am followed 10 minutes later by the 10K Walk from the same venue. 8:00am sees the start of the NZ Sotheby's RE Half Marathon Run at Speargrass Flat Rd with the NZ Sotheby's RE Half Marathon Walk leaving 15 minutes later. The Full Marathon starts at 8:20am at Millbrook Resort with the walkers departing at 8:30am. The final event of the day, the Kids Run starts at 1:00pm in Queenstown Gardens, Park Street. Prize Giving is at Queenstown Recreation Ground at 3:30pm. Due to course management and road closure restrictions, the course officially closes at 4:00pm and cut-off points are in place along the way. For example: Marathon runners must reach the start of the Lake Hayes Trail (distance 11.65km) by 11.00am, the start of Domain Rd Track (distance 25km) by 1:10pm and the SH6 crossing (distance 32.2km) by 2:25pm.

The start of the Marathon is at the exclusive Millbrook Resort, voted in the top 5 hotels in New Zealand for the past four consecutive years by TripAdvisor Travellers' Choice Awards. Millbrook is a five-star accommodation resort on the outskirts of Queenstown set in 500 acres of lush green fairways, rolling hills and babbling streams. Its 27-hole golf course plays co-host to the BMW ISPS Handa New Zealand Open Golf Tournament. It sounds nice but with accommodation costing between $219 and $1,600 per night, it's out of my price range I'm afraid. The course is said to offer a mix of running terrain including smooth hard packed trails and road running. It features easy running on a mainly flat course, with some undulations to keep it interesting. From the start runners make their way down The Avenue at Millbrook Resort, heading towards the settlement of Arrowtown. The settlement is a historic former gold mining town, rich in heritage and one of the South Island's iconic visitor destinations. Arrowtown is built on the banks of the Arrow River, once a rich source of gold, which attracted miners from around the world in pursuit of their fortune. In 1862 thousands of miners flocked to the Arrow River when gold was discovered there and, at the height of the gold rush, the population reached 7,000. While the miners have now gone, the legacy of those early settlers has been retained through careful preservation and Arrowtown has become a treasure in its own right. The Lakes District Museum, located on the main street, is the focal point for the history of the settlement and the surrounding areas and is also the town's major Information Centre. Located only 20 minutes' drive from Queenstown, the spectacular scenery, distinct four seasons and charming character of the place make it a must-visit destination while in the area.

The Arrow River track leads runners onto the Arrowtown-Lake Hayes Road and across onto Lake Hayes lakeside trail at the northern entrance and around Lake Hayes in a clockwise direction. Lake Hayes is at the very heart of Queenstown's 120 km of trails. Described as Arrowtown's 'jewel in the crown,' mountains and poplars are reflected into its clear waters. The Lake is said to be the most photographed lake in New Zealand, a highlight for artists and nature-lovers, a magnet for anglers, swimmable, and great for mountain-biking thanks to the Lake Hayes Circuit shore-side loop. Just a stone's throw from the lake shores on Lake Hayes Road is the award-winning Amisfield Winery and Bistro – a great place to enjoy the magnificent views.

Runners exit the lake on to Rutherford Road heading eventually onto the Domain Road trail, down and along the trail beside the river passing under Old Shotover Bridge before turning left up to meet Spence Rd and left over the Old Shotover Bridge. The Shotover River is a favourite among thrill-seekers. Incredibly fast currents make this one of the best places to go jet boating and white water rafting. The 75 kilometre long river flows south of the Southern Alps through to the Kawarau River. The course continues left onto the trail under the Frankton-Ladies Mile Highway, left onto Shotover Delta Road until the trail veers left from the road and onto the Twin Rivers trail alongside the Kawarau River. Finally, the Frankton Arm Walkway trail leads towards Queenstown. Describing this section in a Runner's World article in March 2016 finisher Lisa Nolan declares, 'There was nothing quite like seeing the start of Lake Wakatipu as we were on the home straight. Hitting the lake I was so excited, but we still had another 10km to go … the scenery took my breath away and the dirt trails were fantastic – wide enough for you to comfortably run two abreast sometimes three. Some were covered with was wooden boardwalks too and little bridges. The aid stations were fantastic, with plenty of water, Powerade and sports jelly beans.' Runners finish by turning left around Queenstown Gardens on to Marine Parade, into Rees Street, up Duke Street and to the finish area in Queenstown Recreation Ground.

Having crossed the finish line and received their medal runners are offered water, Powerade and bananas. The Event Hub gives everyone the opportunity to soak up the post-race atmosphere listening to music while MCs keep everyone up to date with snippets of event information. There's said to be food vendors galore and massage stations where a 10-minute walk-in massage can be had for $10.

After the race competitors can fill their boots by indulging in whatever takes their fancy from the myriad of outdoor activities Queenstown has to offer. If booked online from the UK before arrival, here's some idea of the cost of the most popular of these: Queenstown Nevis Highwire Bungy Jump £146, Queenstown Zipline Tour from £50.49, Skydive Queenstown from £158.92, Snowboarding at Cardrona First Timer Package £79.73, Helicopter and Snowmobile Tour £496, Dart River Jet Boat Ride and Wilderness Jet from Queenstown £132, Queenstown Quad Bike Adventure £142 and Kawarau River White Water Sledging £12. I think that just about covers it all! The less energetic or just the plain already worn-out might prefer taking things a little bit easier by cruising across Lake Wakatipu on a restored steamship - a great way to appreciate the magnificent alpine scenery. The old steamer TSS Earnslaw has earned the affectionate nickname of the 'Lady of the Lake' and is a favourite amongst the people of Queenstown. Since 1912, the vessel has been sending goods to inaccessible settlements and carrying passengers on Lake Wakatipu. The cruises depart at 12pm, 2pm, 4pm (& 10am in summer from the Steamer Wharf on Queenstown's lakefront from $70 for the 1.5 hour trip. You can also take in the stunning views by riding the Skyline Queenstown Gondola - the steepest cable car lift in the Southern Hemisphere and one of the must-do activities in Queenstown. Cost per adult is $39 (child $24) The Gondola carries passengers 450 metres above Queenstown and Lake Wakatipu to the top of Bob's Peak, where they'll enjoy the best views in the region. En route there's a spectacular 220 degree panorama with breath-taking views of Coronet Peak, The Remarkables, Walter and Cecil Peak and, of course, Queenstown. When you get to the top, you can make your own choice from the host of activities on offer. Those who prefer to walk could save money by following the Tiki Trail from the centre of town to the same spot. The really energetic can then continue on from there to the top of Ben Lomond, the highest peak in Queenstown. The track is well signed from the Skyline Gondola. This has been described as the closest experience to a backcountry hike you will get this close to Queenstown. The view looking down on the town from the top is the one that features on most Queenstown postcards.

Queenstown has a reputation as the resort that never sleeps with streets alive during the evenings. There's more than 100 places to dine, with live music and street entertainment, and plenty of places to have a drink. Thirsty Marathon Tourists in search of a decent beer might wish to try a pint-sized lakefront bar called the Atlas Beer Café. A relative who revisited Queenstown last year tells me that there are usually around 20 beers on tap headlined by brews from Dunedin's Emerson's Brewery and Queenstown's Altitude. He mentions eating at Fergburger, a hamburger restaurant located in Shotover Street next to the new addition of Ferg Baker. Fergburger specialises in gourmet hamburgers, and is quite well known internationally despite not being a chain and only having one location. Their burgers include those prepared with lamb, cod, falafel, a pork-and-chicken mix and venison. The restaurant started in 2001, operating out of a garage off Cow Lane, its obscure location making it hard to find but conversely giving it something of a novelty status, relying on word of mouth to attract customers. Lonely Planet guide has named Fergburger among the world's 'best and bizarre' burger experiences that serves 'protein-heavy fodder to fuel you up for any number of bungee jumps, jet-boat rides and zorbing forays.' It doesn't mention fuelling you up for marathon running but I'm sure it does that too.

Printed in Great Britain
by Amazon